My Aunt Edith

by Pheobe Hesketh

Lancashire County Books,
1992

My Aunt Edith
by Phoebe Hesketh

First published in 1966 by Peter Davies Ltd., London

This illustrated edition published by Lancashire County Books, 143 Corporation Street, Preston, 1992
Typeset by Carnegie Publishing Ltd., Preston
Printed by Cambridge University Press, Cambridge

British Library Cataloguing-in-Publication Data
A CIP record for this book is available from the British Library

ISBN 1-871236-12-6

To my sister Elaine
and my cousin Herbert
who share these memories

Acknowledgements

The publishers would like to thank all those who kindly gave permission for the reproduction of photographs in this book. The photographs on pages 91, 92 and 98 (bottom) are from the author's own collection. The following photographs are from the Selina Cooper collection deposited at the Lancashire Record Office by Ms J. Liddington, co-author with Mrs J. norris of *One Hand Tied Behind Us – The Rise of the Women's Suffrage Movement* (Virago, 1978): page 94 (top), L.R.O. DDX 1137/5/14; page 94 (bottom), L.R.O. DDX 1137/5/16; page 96 (top), L.R.O. DDX 1137/5/18; page 96 (bottom), L.R.O. DDX 1137/5/20. The photographs on pages 93, 95 and 97 (top) are from the collections of the Lancashire County Library. The photograph of 28 Winckley Square on page 98 is reproduced by kind permission of Marion Roberts.

I

Family background. Preston in the 1880s
Brothers and sisters. School days. Encounter with Ruskin.
Marriage

ONE of my earliest memories is of being taken for a walk in Miller Park, Preston, by my mother shortly before the First World War. We stopped in front of the statue of Lord Derby, whose august figure had lost all dignity, for it was woefully sprinkled with tar. After gazing at it in a silence heavy with disapproval, my mother said quietly: 'Your Aunt Edith did that.' Few words, but what a weight of criticism!

I knew my aunt was a suffragette, which word (exchanged in hushed voices between my mother and her friends) conveyed something shameful. There were also references to her regrettable friendship with two sisters who, nevertheless, supplied my dolls with lovely names: Christabel and Sylvia.

More explicit kitchen gossip related how 'she' had started 'them' in Preston, how she had damaged property and even burned down Lord Leverhulme's bungalow on Rivington Pike. One day I heard my nurse whispering to Cook that 'she' had been sent to gaol. I enquired what the word meant and received a terrifying account of prison life. Determined to spare me nothing, Nurse went on to describe how my aunt had refused to eat in prison and had been fed through tubes which were forced down her throat. 'Serve 'er right, after putting a bomb in the Liverpool Cotton Exchange!' she exclaimed hotly.

I couldn't reconcile these stories with the real Aunt Edith who lived in Winckley Square and wore extraordinary dresses like blue sacking, with heavy amber-coloured beads on chains, the Aunt Edith who never raised her voice and was utterly different from everyone else. Yet my first impression was not of rough home-spun clothes and eccentric behaviour, but of gentleness. She was the most gentle person I have ever met. I was fascinated by her low voice and speedwell-blue eyes which, though they twinkled at you when she spoke, seemed to gaze into distances – as though she were looking out to sea.

I couldn't have been more than four years old when one afternoon my nurse took me for a walk round Winckley Square. Portentously she stopped in front of No. 28 and took my hand – as though I were in need of protection. 'Look!' she commanded, pointing with her right hand at daubs of tar on the stonework around the front door. 'That's what they did because of the way she messed up the statue and burned the bungalow.'

[1]

Nurse sniffed and stiffened in condemnation. Even at that age, knowing only my aunt and nothing of the troublous times, I felt hot and helpless with anger – how *beastly* of them! I thought. 'How that nice husband of hers puts up with it, I can't imagine,' Nurse went on above my voiceless protest.

In those days I was conscious of sharp division between 'Mother's side' and 'Father's side'; it needed not one of Mother's sisters to inform me: 'We never thought your father was good enough for your mother!' Sometimes this aunt would elaborate: 'We were a very well-connected Blackburn family. Every Sunday morning we four girls would walk out with our two borzois – we were a good-looking lot! And your mother was a real beauty. She could have had anyone.'

My mother, in fact, came of a wealthy family of cotton manufacturers (no doubt occasionally infused with bluer blood) while my father and Aunt Edith and their three surviving brothers and sisters were the children of a doctor – Alexander Clement Rayner – and his wife, Mary Pilkington Sharples, commonly known as Polly.

Aunt Edith, who was unlike the rest of the family, showed her 'oddness' from the earliest days. Indeed, the unexpected flowering of her personality is best understood by contrast with its sturdy roots. That is why, in this first chapter, I give an account of her background.

Neither she nor my father were the sort of people to be concerned with family connections. Only quite recently I learned from Sir Harry Pilkington that Polly's mother, Eleanor Pilkington, was his (and my) great-grandmother. This same Eleanor was directly descended from James Pilkington who, in 1562, was appointed the first Protestant Bishop of Durham.

Alexander Clement Rayner, on the other hand, was the son of a Wesleyan minister, Thomas Alexander Rayner, named after his uncle, the chief constable of Sheffield. They were all Wesleyans; my grandfather's family were brought up strictly 'chapel' and Victorian, whereas my grandmother belonged to the Church of England.

Edith, the second of seven children, was born in Preston on St Luke's Day, 1872, at No. 1 Pole Street. This was, and still is, a drab street of red-brick houses leading off the lower end of Church Street in Preston's 'East End'.

As children we only drove past the entrance to Pole Street on our way to East Lancashire. While my father pointed it out with a certain pride, I early noticed Mother's unresponsiveness. No. 1 looked across Church Street to the Blue Bell Inn. This building I thought doubly romantic because of the meaningful layers of dirt on its painted sign, the Bell itself being hardly discernible and only dimly blue. Not far distant were remote, sooty regions with narrow, cobbled streets where children ran barefoot, and women, arms akimbo, stood gossiping or shouting at each other over the railings outside their stone steps. Sometimes my father would take me on his visits through Silver Street, Back Silver Street and – dingiest of all – Gold Street leading off Manchester Road. For me, those dark and twisting lean-cat lanes were fraught with the mystery and wonder of life on another planet.

Within ten minutes' walk of this area the young Edith (a year younger than her sister Lucy) lived to see the entrance into the world of her sister Alice two years later, and her brother Arthur (my father) three years after that. The following year they moved 'up' to No. 58, and here arrived, in quick succession, Herbert, Henrietta, and the young Harold, who also turned out to be a rebel.

Preston, in those days, was said to be a model example of prosperity under the Industrial Revolution. But when Dickens visited it in 1854 he found it a place so drab and disagreeable that he set his heart upon lifting the workpeople from such dreary conditions in dreary streets. There was a lock-out strike on at the time – the strike which he described in *Hard Times*, for Coketown is said to represent Preston. I remember objecting to my father that there are no moors, as mentioned by Dickens, surrounding the town. 'Nonsense!' he replied in springy tones, 'What about the Moor, as it used to be called? It was only enclosed into Moor Park shortly before Dickens' visit here.'

He told me that they used to run horse-races across the Moor. 'And there was an opposition meeting on Fulwood Moor – where we went to live after leaving Pole Street.' The Fulwood meeting was arranged by the political supporters of Lord Derby. 'We were never of their camp,' he said proudly, 'we were all strong Liberals!' As he spoke his cold blue eyes flashed with a frosty Viking fire.

Though angered by Dickens' disparagement of Preston, my father more than once reminded me: 'It was entirely owing to the efforts of your grandmother that Dickens came here a second time – to give a recital at the Theatre Royal in Fishergate.' And then, after a pause: 'I never much cared for his novels myself.'

Edith might well have been a Dickens heroine. Not only was she strikingly beautiful – tall, with wheat-gold hair and blue eyes, but she shared his views on humanity. Even as a young child she questioned the sharp division between the clogs-and-shawl brigade and the ladies of the town who were to be seen parading in Miller Park, all silks and satins and fringed parasols, on Sunday mornings. Many of these 'elect' would have attended matins at the parish church which stood nicely placed between the pastures of the 'sheep' and the rough place of the 'goats'. Indeed, black and solid at the top end of Church Street, one foot, almost, in Fishergate, it looked down towards the east end and westward to where the 'land was brighter', if not exactly bright.

Fishergate boasted the best shops; and the red-brick Georgian houses which composed Winckley Square and Ribblesdale Place glowed with prosperity. The houses with odd numbers on the 'fashionable' side of Ribblesdale Place (I was to be born in No. 1) overlooked their own pleasant gardens and the green park which sloped gently down to the Ribble.

All this was in sharp contrast to the street where the young Rayners first saw the light. Here they were awoken every morning by the knocker-up hammering on neighbouring doors: 'Ha'f past five! Ha'f past five!' Fifteen minutes later, sure enough, came the faithful, punctual rattle of clogs hurrying, hurrying to the mills.

Sometimes on a Saturday night Edith would escape from the house to watch the nearest butcher's auction mart. By the light of an oil flame he prepared to clear his stock in small portions: 'Prime piece o' scrag-end fer tuppence!' Often a heart (to be stuffed and roasted next morning) would be thrown in – if the butcher wanted to 'get shut'. Women and girls in clogs and shawls (for they worked on Saturdays) were grateful for tit-bits. A weaver's wages required careful spending.

When she was about eleven years old Edith began to be curious about the lives of the neighbouring children of her own age. She would get into conversation with them and ask them questions. It must have surprised her to learn that while she was at school they were already working – some as beginners at threepence a week while the eleven-year-old 'half-timers' earned two and ninepence.

At this time she herself, with her sister Alice, attended Preston High School in Winckley Square, secluded among gardens and green trees. Judging by her future actions, she must have thought deeply and disturbingly about the lives of the people among whom she lived, comparing their lot with her own.

Yet my grandfather, a hard-working doctor, much beloved by the workpeople whom he chiefly attended, had little enough money to keep and educate his own family of seven children. Even so, Edith felt – dimly at the time – that the social and economic divisions were unjust. Unconsciously she was already putting down tender roots into Socialist soil.

For all that Lord Derby and Mr Bright described such places as Preston as 'centres of manufacturing industry' she would have followed Dickens,[1] 'with Cobbett and Carlyle, in calling them "hell-holes" where capitalist fortunes were made.'

Soon after her twelfth birthday an incident occurred to show just how

---

1 *A Life of Charles Dickens*, by Una Pope-Hennessy.

'different' she was destined to be. It was a cold, dark Christmas morning, and her father and mother, for once, had remained in bed until after eight o'clock. The other children, laughing, shouting and undoing their stockings, were not unduly disturbed to find that Edith was missing. 'Ede not here!' the five-year-old Bert announced as he ran into his parents' bedroom. 'What on earth's she up to now?' exclaimed her father. They both dressed hastily and, with some apprehension, went downstairs. However, before her father had reached for his overcoat, Edith appeared, flushed and sparkling. She was carrying an empty basket.

'Where *have* you been?' Her father was curious rather than angry. After much persuasion she confessed her secret – for she was never a girl to talk about herself. Though so strongly individual, eccentric even, she was not self-centred. 'Causes' were to be her centre; and if hers was a much-criticized life, she came to believe that an uncriticized life is not worth living.

Meanwhile, she explained her absence from home this particular Christmas morning. It appeared that for weeks past she had been collecting small presents such as candied fruit, chocolate, soap, and odds and ends of jewellery. These she had stored in a large basket, or stuffed into the pockets of her coat. This very day she had got up soon after six o'clock in order to give her presents to the workpeople in the streets as they went to church – mostly to Mass because Preston was (and still is) the most strongly Roman Catholic town in England. She had walked up Church Street and up and down the many streets leading off it, wishing everyone she met 'A happy Christmas!'

'I'm later than I meant to be,' she explained on arriving home, 'because there weren't many people about at first, and I wanted to empty the basket.'

How much her outlook was coloured by her journeys to the High School in Preston's 'respectable' neighbourhood from the environs of Pole Street, no one can tell. But Dr Rayner intended to open his children's eyes to worlds a great deal more distant from Pole Street than Winckley Square. His passion for Wordsworth had living roots; and he longed for his family to experience with him that 'diurnal course/Of rocks and stones and trees'.

Every summer he took them, those who were old enough, to the Lake District. Together they tramped the green valleys, climbed the hills, and learned to know every lake by name. Though Baedeker was respected and followed, my grandfather's true *Guide to the Lakes* was his pocket Wordsworth. Through these pages his children came to know, not merely woods and hills, but also 'the light that never was on sea or land'.

He made up his mind to send the two girls, who were the eldest of the family, to school near the mountains. After much thought he settled on Penrhos College in north Wales. This was a move which profoundly influenced them both, and led them, in later life, to remove to the Conway valley, where they spent their last years.

And it led Edith to her lifelong friendship with Annie Taylor. On her first day at school, searching among fellow new girls, she remarked one with lively hazel eyes, who wore good, solid, country shoes, and seemed to be her kind. Without further hesitation Edith walked up to Annie in the dormitory. 'You and I are going to be friends!' she announced, and so it turned out.

These two, the same age, feminists from the start, and wary of authority, eventually made school 'headlines'. To begin with, however, Annie, who refused to work, was consistently bottom of the form – until Edith took her in hand. 'It's very wrong,' Edith pointed out, 'to waste your parents' good money and your own good brains!'

She challenged Annie to compete with her and thereafter they moved up the school together to the Sixth Form. Annie was the quicker, Edith the deeper thinker. If one of them was top of the form, the other was almost certain to be second.

For two years running Nancy (as Edith now called her) won the maths prize. But before the exam in the third year she had such bad toothache that Edith consoled her: 'It must have been sent by Providence – to give someone else a chance!' That year she won the prize herself.

An incident revealing Edith's youthful principles (which she never lowered) concerned Nancy and a boy-friend encountered while waiting for a music exam. At Penrhos boy-friends were taboo, so that when one Sunday morning in church Nancy spotted her recent 'find' and actually smiled broadly at him across the ranks, she was in deep disgrace with Miss Pope, the headmistress, who forbade the others to go out with her.

Edith, divided between affection for her friend and loyalty to the school, was won over by what she believed to be right. She refused to accompany Nancy on the excursion planned for the following Saturday afternoon. In spite of this, Nancy's flair for attracting too many boy-friends continued, and was to cause several jolts to Edith's serious mind. 'What's wrong is to *encourage* more than one at a time,' she would say reproachfully.

Even at school these two discussed the inferior position of women in society, and the unfairness of class and wealth divisions. Edith, who vowed to do something about it when she left, might almost have echoed Disraeli's words: 'The rights of labour are as sacred as the rights of property.' In fact, events in Parliament were blowing strongly in her direction. The third Reform Bill (under Gladstone) had recently become law alongside other measures of enlightenment. Had Edith been a little older, she might have smiled to learn that nowadays even nonconformists were allowed burial in churchyards.

During her late teens she felt herself drawn away from the family allegiance to the Liberal party which – untrue to its ideals – was set against giving women the vote. Not that she felt any sympathy with the Tories and the big houses outside town which they stood for. No, the fat red country villas and mansions of the Bounderbys were nowhere up her street. When I first knew her, the wife of a doctor in Winckley Square, cold-shouldered by her neighbours, I had no idea of the immense courage and determination it must have required to be 'different'. In those conventional days, stiff as the starched collars of our nurses, she must have had a will beyond the common metal.

'Yes, I believe Edith is a Socialist!' I once overheard my mother say in shocked tones to a kindly friend who could only shake her head in silent sympathy. The railings around Winckley Square were upright iron, indeed!

Sometimes I wondered if she would have been a different person had she been born and brought up within the protection of those railings. Pole Street had given her an open view of the dismal conditions endured by the working people, and she must have been influenced by her father's devotion to his patients – nearly all of whom worked in the mills.

An incident of another Christmas Day comes to mind: the family were sitting expectantly round the table while her father stood at the head of it, behind a steaming goose. After sharpening the carving-knife – with a joke about his skill as a surgeon – he was about to plunge it into the succulent flesh when a heavy knock on the door arrested him. One of the children ran to answer it and returned with the message: 'It's Mrs Margerison in labour – will you please come at once?' The family sighed, but he merely handed the carving-knife to his wife: 'Your turn today!' he said, and went out.

Soon afterwards came a severer test of his character. Lucy, his eldest and much-loved daughter, was invited into the house of a patient who took her on his knee, for she was a great favourite. The daughter of this man was at the time in bed with scarlet fever – a serious illness in those days. Less than a fortnight later Lucy contracted the disease, and within a month she was dead. The death of this child (who was named after Lucy Gray) came as a great blow. But my grandfather said no words of reproach. He was one of those rare people who are able not merely to accept suffering, but to turn it to good account. Well might it have been said of him, as was written on the gravestone of a country doctor: *And he went about doing good*.

A doctor in a working-class area could never hope for a big income; and it must have been difficult to pay boarding-school fees for Edith and Alice. In this connection I often think my grandparents must themselves have had advanced ideas. Few people would have sent the girls away while the boys had to make the best of the grammar school. Fortunately my father was happy enough with this arrangement. School work was no trouble to him; and when he was sixteen he passed his university entrance. Because he was eighteen months too young he spent the intervening time at home, reading – not medicine towards his career, but romantic novels and poetry which was probably more to his advantage.

Reminiscing about his schooldays, he told me how he had once been set upon by a gang of boys because he was wearing the red-and-green rosette of the Liberal Party. 'At that time,' he said, 'Preston was red-hot Tory. I remember being punched about and the boys shouting "Down with the dirty Liberals! Down with the red-an'-green!" They were all from working-class homes, far poorer than ours, but they wore the blue and orange – the Tory colours – and heaven help those who didn't!'

When Edith was about sixteen she somehow acquired the first lady's bicycle to be seen in Preston. It was solid-tyred and single-geared, a real devil to ride for any distance. At that time no one had ever seen a woman or a young girl riding a bicycle. Such a performance, conducted in bloomers, was regarded as highly improper, almost indecent. She certainly had a rough time of it; the boys pelted her with vegetables and eggs and the girls booed and hooted as she went by.

Not only boys and girls disapproved of these expeditions. My grandparents' friends looked at her askance, and the vicar, the Reverend J.W. Larke, unfaithful to his name, professed himself deeply shocked that a member of his Bible class, a potential Sunday-school teacher, should so immodestly display herself. In spite of this, when she was eighteen Edith set her mind on visiting, on the same old bicycle, her friend Nancy Taylor, who lived in Leicester. One morning at breakfast she announced her intention of cycling there that very day, staying overnight, and returning within the next day or so. I can imagine my gentle grandmother's protest, and my most kindly grandfather laying down his newspaper to remonstrate with her: 'My dear child, do you realize it's more than a hundred and fifty miles to Leicester? Quite a journey by train; and I wouldn't dream of doing it in the phaeton – even in two days.' No doubt he was disturbed also by the thought of the comments – and the missiles – she would certainly receive on such an adventure. Besides, the journey would be impossible in a day on *that* machine.

Nevertheless, by saying very little, Edith had her way. In later years I grew to appreciate the strength of her few words, always spoken slowly, with infinite gentleness and decision. 'Edith had a way of getting people to do what they wouldn't dream of doing!' This is how one of her 'victims' described her powers of persuasion. On this particular occasion, in the face of her parents' disapproval – distress, even – and her brothers' derision, she set forth, attired in the usual bloomers, upon that bumpy and intimidating journey. Whether she allowed herself one or two nights' respite I don't know. But two or three days later she returned home, having triumphed over cat-calls, vegetables, and discouraging roads – mostly laid with setts.

In August this same year she and Nancy went by train to the Lakes for a walking and fell-climbing holiday. An elderly friend seeing them off at the station criticized the shortness of their skirts – '*seven* inches off the ground!' she reported to her husband, 'I wouldn't allow a daughter of mine to appear in public like that!'

Edith thought differently; and in the railway carriage she produced a large bunch of safety pins – 'to pin our skirts well above our knees,' as she explained. 'We can't climb Scafell with these things flapping about our legs!'

And so, in comparative freedom, they attacked Scafell and the Pike, Great Gable, the Langdales, and Bowfell. One particularly hot and dusty day, descending towards Styhead, Edith was inspired by the glittering darkness of Sprinkling Tarn. 'We must bathe!' she exclaimed joyously. She loved water, and being an expert swimmer she couldn't resist this invitation. Nancy's objections that they had no swimming costumes were easily overcome. Like a pair of naiads transformed by the deep, enchanted water, they dipped and splashed keeping watch on the four tracks to the tarn.

Nancy got out first and was drying herself in the sun when suddenly there appeared, scrambling down the nearest fell regardless of tracks, the figure of a man. Edith, from the water, saw him first. 'A man, Nancy, a man!' she cried. 'Throw me my hat, and come in with yours!'

At the sight of two women wearing wide-brimmed hats as they swam naked around Sprinkling Tarn, the intruder hastily disappeared.

For another similar holiday Edith booked rooms at a cottage near Coniston overlooking Brantwood, the home of Ruskin, whose books were among her treasures. Daily she watched the house to discover at exactly what time this shy, elusive genius, now in his seventies, emerged for his afternoon walk. Then one morning at breakfast she said: 'Today, Nancy, we're going to meet Ruskin!'

So it happened that the girls were standing in the road facing the gates when Ruskin appeared. According to Nancy, he looked at Edith, halted, and during a momentous interval of silence fixed her with his blue stare. And then, without so much as a glance at Nancy, he turned abruptly and hurried away.

'It was Edith's ravishing beauty that took his eye,' Nancy reported later, 'I wasn't in the picture at all!'

This same ravishing beauty had already brought many suitors – all, so far, rejected – through the gates of Fairview, the Rayners'new home in Fulwood. And here my grandparents had troubles enough to contend with. When Edith was eighteen her youngest sister, the delicate, gentle Henrietta, died after a lingering illness. Fairview, with its good-sized garden, was a far more expensive house to run than No. 58 Pole Street, while Alice's school fees still had to be paid. Added to this, the four-and-a-half-year-old Harold showed unmistakable signs of being a more-than-problem child.

It seems strange that two rebels should spring from such affectionate, industrious and conventional parents. At least, my grandmother never caused anxiety to anyone. My grandfather, possibly as the result of long hard years and family troubles did, towards the end, take to rushing out of Fairview, and boarding a tram in his vest and pants and a top-hat.

Fortunately Edith and Harold, who took after him in appearance, with their blue eyes, red-gold hair, and 'strong' noses, were likeable rebels. It was Alice, small, dark, vivacious, and destined to become a member of the Establishment, who was the most disturbed by the behaviour of her youngest brother.

From earliest days Harold was addicted to uncomfortable practical jokes, which were not always kept within the limits of the family. He would drill holes into pennies and sixpences, thread them, and place them in the path of passers-by outside the garden hedge. Then, crouching under the hedge on the garden side, he waited until someone stooped to pick up, perhaps, a not-to-be-despised sixpence. In the instant of eager fingers flexing to retrieve the coin, he whisked it away. Another day he ensconced himself in the attic from where he squirted the garden-syringe at top-deck passengers in the open trams as they swung round the corner of Fairview.

Jokes such as these Edith regarded not only as unsocial, but as completely unfunny. Whereas her nonconformity was constructive – because she rebelled against a social order of false respectability, Harold's was destructive and hindering. For one thing, it was impossible to keep him at any school. Indignant notes from headmasters were a source of embarrassment to my grandparents. After he had 'run through' every available day-school, my grandfather decided to send him away to Epworth, the Methodist school in north Wales. Before the end of the first term he was home again – the bad penny on the much-worn doorstep.

With a final throw of despair his father dispatched him to the naval training ship H.M.S. *Conway* (which stood in the Mersey) in the faint hope that there, at last, the boy might be disciplined. But not even the iron rod of the Navy could make him or break him. Once more he ran away.

Still only sixteen, the despair of his parents, Harold had learned much from life, nothing from books. It must have been a hard decision to ship him, as unmalleable stock, to Canada with the proverbial ten pounds in his pocket. How he was accepted by a Dutch farmer, married his host's daughter, and subsequently built up a flourishing grain business in Toronto, is another story.

Little could this 'reject' from H.M.S. *Conway* have guessed that his elder son was destined to entertain Queen Elizabeth II on board the flag-ship H.M.C.S. *Magnificent* during the Coronation celebrations. This son, Herbert, a vice-admiral in the Canadian Navy, was brought up by *our* Aunt Edith while he was being educated in England.

Of my father and Uncle Bertie, both of whom became doctors, I can only remark that they fulfilled their destiny in a less disrupting fashion. Ability, allied with energy and determination, seemed to course through the bloodstream of the family. The same maternal aunt who had once described my father as 'not good enough for your mother' was later to remark with understandable inconsistency: 'Of course, your father's a genius!' (A cousin, less charitable, described this as 'the Rayner kink'.)

Kink or no, he had flair – especially for diagnosis. He said that more often than not he could tell what was wrong as soon as the patient came into the room. So much so, that people from all over the country consulted him.

But he was never a glory-seeker. The achievement that pleased him most was his founding, in 1904, of the X-ray department, the first in Great Britain,[1] at Preston Royal Infirmary. Later he was appointed both honorary physician and honorary radiologist. And here he served for forty-two years, every day after his own work, so that he arrived home nervy and exhausted, and seldom before half-past nine. After he retired from this demanding work – without a pension because he was too old to qualify under the scheme – we heard many bitter indictments of the Welfare State.

One summer afternoon when we were out walking with Aunt Edith, as though to challenge her, he was 'going on' about the injustices suffered by the new-poor who had worked hard all their lives without reward. She turned to me with her characteristic smile: 'Your father doesn't mean half he says!' To him she merely nodded and refrained from quoting the parable of the labourers in the vineyard.

It is worth remarking that during the sixty years my father worked with X-rays – from 1900 until he retired from private practice in his 83rd year – he never wore protective garments of any sort. Whenever we demurred about the risk involved he only laughed: 'I don't give a damn – *fear* is the killer!'

Perhaps the high standard of work he set himself accounted for his keen and uncomfortable edges. Though the best of companions on a

1 The same year as that at King's College Hospital, London.

holiday, he was often irritable, cross-cutting as a saw, at home. As my mother remarked: 'His patients get the best of him; we have to put up with the frayed ends.'

His brother Bertie, two years younger, was a complete opposite with an equable and optimistic temperament. Dark and slight, like Aunt Alice, he would greet every cloudy morning as the certain forerunner of sun later in the day. But for all his easy manner, Bertie became a much-respected surgeon, with rooms in John Street, Manchester, where for several years he was senior surgeon at the Royal Infirmary.

Although, in one sense, the two sons outstripped their father, I believe my grandfather equally fulfilled himself in that most exacting role of family doctor – at everyone's beck and call, on duty night and day in a very poor neighbourhood. Yet he still found time for reading his favourite Shakespeare, Milton and Wordsworth, a taste for whom he passed on to his family.

Many times he took Edith and the two boys for climbing holidays in Scotland as well as the Lakes. Bertie, however, lacked the capacity for ecstasy which inspired the other three and transformed them, when walking among the hills, into radiant beings. Well they knew:

> Great things are done when Men & Mountains meet;
> This is not done with Jostling in the Street.

and they knew it even better than Blake, who was a man of the city.

That sort of mountain madness was moonshine in Bertie's eyes. His feet were always on the ground; his eyes less often on the stars. After one particularly exhilarating day, for instance, the four of them were trudging in silence the last, stony mile home when suddenly, round a bend, the Trossachs Hotel came into sight: 'That's the best view I've seen all day!' exclaimed Bertie to his father's extreme chagrin.

Often they climbed in Wasdale, attacking Scafell by Moss Ghyll, Deep Ghyll, and Piers Ghyll. Edith soon proved herself to be a fearless and skilful climber, almost as expert as her brothers. But my father became a near-professional. With intrepidity he tackled the bare rock-face (close to the famous Keswick brothers' climb) on Scafell. And when he was only seventeen he had given a lead to the leader of a climbing party up the Napes' Needle. Edith's mountain achievements, though less spectacular, were to continue alarmingly into her sixties, and will be heard of later.

When my grandfather died in 1916, at the age of seventy-four, Aunt Alice remained at Fairview to look after her mother who gradually went blind. Fortunately they shared a love of music; and in spite of her blindness, my grandmother continued to play the piano, while Aunt Alice, gallant and out-going, took to parish work and keeping White Wyandottes in the back garden. This refreshing normality made her totally different from Aunt Edith who was variously described by my father as 'a rum bird', 'a strange fish', or 'a one for wild-cat schemes'. My mother and her relations usually contrived to draw a veil over her unspeakable doings. This being so, I saw little of her in my early days, though I was occasionally taken to have tea with her in Winckley Square while my mother tactfully withdrew.

Although she wore sandals and looked different from other people I liked being with her, watching her animated expression as she spoke, or recounted the doings of Brer Rabbit and Brer Fox. She gave me something outside ordinary life. I think it was a sense of freedom. My first clear memory of her was in 1913, the year she set fire to Lord Leverhulme's bungalow on Rivington Pike, and was subsequently imprisoned under the 'Cat-and-Mouse' Act. (This was at least her sixth imprisonment.) Anyone who could convey to a child a sense of calm in the interim between such events must indeed have been a remarkable person.

Perhaps the most remarkable thing of all was that she, so singular, so apart from our world of pavements and parks, should have actually consented to be married. I learned afterwards how one of her many suitors had been so persistent that, for the first and only time, her will had given way to his.

It was a thirty-four-year-old doctor, Charles Rigby (he became my godfather and Uncle Charlie), who succeeded in persuading her to be his wife. Of all people he seemed to be the one for her. Tolerant, gentle in voice and manner, he was like her in many ways; and he shared her compassions, if not all her passions. With these needful qualities he remained devoted to her throughout a highly off-pattern married life. Perhaps they were affinities. At any rate, in the September of 1893, a month before her twenty-first birthday, they were married by her cousin, the Reverend C. W. L. Christien, in the bare little Wesleyan chapel in Lune Street.

II

Social work. The Brook Street Club. The 'Servant Problem'.
A post as housemaid. Adoption of Sandy.
Trouble in Winckley Square.

COMFORTABLE, domestic existence in Winckley Square, where Dr and Mrs Charles Rigby eventually went to live, was not Aunt Edith's idea of life. And from her husband's point of view, a wife with such a vocation cannot have been exactly comfortable to live with. Probably the surrounding atmosphere of prosperity still further stimulated her zeal for helping the poor and setting the wronged upon right paths. At any rate, these were the flags, the red flags (seen by her relations as red rags) which she flaunted in the face of satisfied middle-class society. Very soon, in the cause of women's suffrage, she was to brandish them at the Liberal Government, with a double flourish reserved for the prevaricating Mr Asquith.

In this state of mind, therefore, after a brief period of initiation, her first enquiry was into the conditions of working girls.

Full of enthusiasm, she visited mills, asking questions of managers and foremen as well as talking to the weavers themselves. In this way she led more than one employer to think along different tracks. Another venture was concerned with certain tailoring workrooms which were reported to be dark, stuffy, and insanitary. She went to see for herself, and discovered about twenty girls at work in a small, airless room lit only by a skylight, so grimed over that summer and winter alike went by unnoticed. In this twilight existence the girls, bent for long hours over dark material, suffered much. Their eyesight suffered even more.

Then, one day, the skylight was cleaned. A few weeks later a big window was let into a blind wall; and someone announced the good news of a mid-morning break for tea. The girls, whispering together, wondered if the tall soft-spoken lady who had shown such interest in their work had had anything to do with these changes.

True to her childhood custom, my aunt got into conversation with shop-girls, enquiring how many hours a day they worked, and how they were treated. But most of all she helped individual people who she considered had had a rough deal.

One of these was Mrs Burke, a flower-seller in Fishergate. At least, she sold flowers on a Wednesday, her Sabbath. The other six days were spent in cleaning, scrubbing, washing and washing-up after fat Sunday dinners in the houses of the wealthy. Over the exchange of flowers Aunt Edith learned, little by little, of the grim existence behind the romantic façade of flower-selling: violets and daffodils; roses in season. But Mrs Burke had a husband who beat her every night when he returned home drunk from the pub; and often locked her out – a treatment which continued throughout her pregnancy. No wonder her son, Johnny, was born mentally deficient and grew up to be quite unmanageable. My aunt promised Mrs Burke that he should be sent to a home. However, such places were not easy to find, and there was nothing suitable in Preston. It was only after weeks of enquiry that she found a place near Lancaster which would take the boy – if the committee voted him in. All her powers of persuasion were needed to get through the formal barrier of objections. Eventually he was accepted – on condition that he was provided with a new outfit of clothes. Undaunted, she raised the money for this purpose by a vigorous house-to-house collection.

Then there was Mary, an old body who for years had been 'in service' and was now too old even to look after herself. Hearing of her plight, Mrs Rigby came to the rescue. Not only did she install her in comfortable lodgings, but paid for them until the end.

Such actions in 'welfare days' would be matters of routine, or unnecessary because of State benefits and pension. At the time they were regarded by many people as extraordinary, even impertinent. 'The way Mrs Rigby goes prying into the affairs of the working class!' was one comment.

Mrs Rigby had also pried into the legal position of women of all classes, and thereby discovered many things she considered unjust. Although with the passing of the Married Women's Property Act (in 1883) the position had improved somewhat during the past ten years, women were permitted only a restricted share in local government, none at all in the government of the country. And while there was no law preventing women sitting on juries, nevertheless juries at that time were composed of men. Men commanded the State Church, and in the Civil Service women were admitted only into the lower ranks.

Most unfair of all were the divorce laws; and against these my aunt went to war. People today are apt to forget that until 1923, while a man might divorce his wife for adultery, she had to prove – in addition to adultery – bigamy, cruelty or desertion. Aunt Edith's first step in the direction of women's suffrage was her opposition to men's supremacy in matters concerning men and women together.

But for all her free thinking she held strict views on marriage, regarding it from the Christian viewpoint as sacramental. 'Even an unhappy marriage has its own purpose,' I heard her say; and 'There's as much to be learned from your opposite as from your affinity.'

Perhaps the contrast between her own understanding husband and the husbands of less fortunate wives spurred her on to win for married women at least a degree of independence. Even she, with all her freedom, felt the need for a life of her own, a place of withdrawal from Winckley Square. And the place she chose was a bungalow with a plot of land in Lightfoot Lane, Broughton. Here she grew fruit and vegetables, happy to be alone and feel herself in contact with the earth – this need for roots in the earth was to direct many future actions not understood by her neighbours. Apart from working the garden single-handed, she cycled nearly every day the four or five miles there and back. I wish I knew whether she had, by then, acquired a new bicycle!

This solitary work on the land not only produced cabbages, it fostered an idea which for some time had been forming in her mind. She wanted to start a night-school and recreation club for working girls whose lives were so drab and monotonous. At least she might fill a few gaps with some sort of pleasure, as well as education.

With this end in view she rented the first floor of the old St Peter's School in Brook Street, a dismal area of grimed red-brick houses, row upon row, surrounded by mills, and therefore a good centre for the girls to attend. To begin with about twenty girls turned up, but gradually the membership rose to over forty. They met two evenings a week for a 'get-together' followed by singing and games. Though my aunt had no capacity for needlework herself, she insisted upon two sewing tables, one 'plain' and one 'fancy'. She gave the girls lessons in hygiene; and soon had them doing physical jerks to music – much in the same manner as a music-and-movement class of today.

Meanwhile, Aunt Alice played the piano and two friends helped with the sewing classes and other activities, which were many, because Aunt Edith soon came to realize how much these girls needed mental, as well as physical, relaxation. At first the entertainment she provided in the form of concerts and recitals was a little beyond their reach; she had to learn to temper her enthusiasm to these shorn lambs.

When I spoke, much later, to three of the 'lambs' – aged between seventy-three and eighty – it was like getting to know Aunt Edith again. There was Nellie Harrison recollecting: 'Oh, she wer luvly – a big, tall woman – wi' goldy 'air an' *such* blue eyes you never saw! An' that smile – I can never forget it.' Nellie paused a moment, then: 'An' she spoke slow like, an' never raised 'er voice – it wer a treat ter listen to 'er. No, there's none like 'er these days,' she added with decision.

Nellie had started work as an eleven-year-old weaver's apprentice earning threepence a week. After a few months as a 'half-timer' she received two and ninepence, and at the age of twelve was promoted to the status of full-timer earning five-and-sixpence a week. At that age, then, children worked from six in the morning till half-past five at night, and six hours on Saturday mornings – a fifty-six hour week. I was thinking of my twelve-year-old daughter and all children of her age protected by the arm of the Education Act, when Nellie broke into my reckonings: 'At eighteen year old,' she said, 'I 'ad ter mind four looms, an' 1 got twenty-six shillin' a week. Out o' that I 'ad ter pay a tenter five-an'-six. I 'anded it all ter mi mother an' she giv mi sixpence a week spendin' money. I wer glad ter spend tuppence at t'club – it wer th'only fun we 'ad.'

Aunt Edith, who always opened the club meetings with the Lord's Prayer, welcomed girls of any denomination, indeed, of any religion or of none. They turned up in clogs and shawls, the only costume most of them ever possessed. In clogs, therefore, they would clatter to Moor Park to play cricket on summer evenings. 'She wer a great one fer cricket, though I didn't much care fer it mysel',' Nellie informed me. Cricket as played in clogs was something beyond my imagination.

And in the summer there were garden-parties. Owners of large country houses were cajoled by Mrs Rigby into opening their gardens to the club on Saturday afternoons. Many of the gardens chosen, at Broughton, Redscar, or Penwortham, were a good four miles from Brook Street. 'I suppose you went there by bus?' I enquired innocently, forgetting the gap in the years. 'Bus? No!' Nellie laughed at me, 'She marched us there, clogs an' all! We none of us 'ad shoes – any road, yer wer lucky t'ave a pair fer Sunday.'

Clara Millan, another club-member, described their reception at a country house where Mrs Rigby had had great difficulty in persuading the rather stiff householders to receive her 'Clogs Brigade'.

'They 'ad a most beautiful garden,' Clara began, 'an' Mrs Rigby 'ad arranged games fer us, but we never saw th'owners. An' another funny thing, we weren't allowed ter use t'family lavatory. I remember we went into a bedroom, an' we 'ad ter use chambers. Every so often a maid 'ud come in an' empty 'em. We weren't 'alf tickled at that!'

No doubt some householders would jib at the thought of clogs clattering along polished corridors and mill-girls' shawls laid across embroidered bedspreads.

Such memories rekindled Clara's devotion to Aunt Edith. 'I used ter think she wer an angel,' she told me, 'wi' that lovely skin an' golden 'air, and 'er blue eyes. She 'ad a way o' talking to you wi' 'er 'ead on one side – an' always wi' a smile.'

Through these somewhat inarticulate accounts my aunt's personality was lighted up afresh. Clara, in particular, seemed aware of dimensions beyond mere kindness and humanity. 'There was something about 'er,' she remarked, 'that was *special* – she understood us.'

One incident must serve to illustrate just how much she understood the girls and was therefore able to manage them. It happened that a new teacher, Miss Thwaite, engaged to take the sewing class, proved to be as sharp as her own needles. At any rate, she got properly under the skin of Maggie Sharrock, the brightest member of the class. Maggie dared to answer back; whereupon Miss Thwaite ordered her to leave the room. With a toss of her head Maggie obeyed and was followed, one by one, by the others, who clustered round her at the door. Defiantly they demanded their money back. Baffled by this rebellious behaviour, Miss Thwaite silently returned each girl her due of one halfpenny. Triumphant and seventeen strong, they repaired with this sum to the fish-and-chip shop at the bottom end of Brook Street.

At the next meeting after this incident Mrs Rigby, having led the girls as usual in the Lord's Prayer, asked them to sit down. There followed a significant silence during which she gained power while the girls grew more and more uncomfortable. Then she enquired what the trouble had been and listened quietly as first Maggie, and then the bolder of the others, related their version of the incident. Another powerful silence for reflection. Then, slowly, her attention was returned to the group and she began to speak: 'It was seventeen against one,' she reminded them, shaking her head reproachfully, 'and you behaved like naughty little schoolgirls. Did you never think of helping a new teacher over her nervousness?'

'She didn't go on at us,' Clara remarked, 'an' she 'ad an 'alf-smile on 'er face as she spoke. We wer all in tears when she finished!'

Aunt Edith learned that the more intellectual treats – such as Shakespeare recitals by Milton Rosmer and other celebrities – were not received with the enthusiasm she hoped for. After grinding days in the mill they were glad to relax and play childish games. 'I wer only thirteen when I first went,' Clara said, 'an' that wer the year it started.'

It was 1899. There can have been few clubs like it anywhere at the time; in the North it was the first of its kind. Besides offering advice in personal difficulties, and teaching the girls what they were ready to learn, Aunt Edith and her helpers often provided them with clothes and small luxuries. Because they worked such long hours in the heat and noise of the mill my aunt particularly encouraged games and sports; and every week she took them to the swimming-baths. At this time when most women in her walk of life were paying afternoon calls and giving bridge and dinner parties, the Brook Street Club was an herculean achievement. She was criticized, by some even ostracized, for not conforming to pattern. 'People looked at her askance,' one of her friends told me, 'and then when she left the club to start the local suffrage movement they said it had been a very good thing, and she was wrong to drop it.'

Before leaving the club for graver matters, however, my aunt made another attempt at more intellectual nourishment for the girls. Having left school at the age of eleven they were deprived and limited, and she longed to encourage them to express their thoughts and ideas, and so get to know one another better. With this aim in mind she started a discussion group, to provide an opportunity for developing personality and a feeling of citizenship.

So it was that the Arkwright Debating Society was formed (named after Sir Richard Arkwright, the inventor of the spinning-mule, who was born and brought up in Preston). My aunt would lead the girls into such forward notions as: 'Children should stay at school till the age of fourteen'. But though they showed interest in these daring ideas, only a few bold spirits – such as Maggie Sharrock – were able to express themselves. Nor did they respond when she arranged lectures by good, even celebrated, speakers. They preferred games, sing-songs, and good, plain sewing. Undefeated, my aunt turned her mind to a more suitable, but still cultural, form of entertainment – a performance of *Candida* by the Stockport Garrick Society.

In vain Aunt Alice demurred that the efforts of this well-known company would be wasted on the 'Brook Street' girls. 'And I doubt if they'll come all this way,' she said, 'and we haven't even got a stage!'

However, they were persuaded, and one Saturday evening most sportingly, they arrived. It was fortunate that they arrived punctually and in good humour because their expectations were to be fulfilled in a highly unexpected manner. Every resource of everyone present was tapped in the effort to arrange an improvised stage in that small upper room.

Soon it was discovered that the floorboards were both loose and articulate. After frustrated attempts at muffling the squeaks, it was finally accepted as a musical floor. Every board sounded its particular note, and long before the rasping, reluctant curtain was swept aside, each player had learned which board to avoid in crossing the stage.

Unfortunately this, like many best-laid of plans, was destined to 'gang agley' during the actual performance. To begin with, the play itself was too advanced for such an audience of such a period. Apprehension swelled during tense moments when inappropriate noises arose from the floor. Little gasps of nervous laughter fermented the audience to near-hysteria, so that Mr William Pitt with his Preston Light Orchestra, specially engaged for the occasion, had to rush impromptu to the rescue. Feverishly they dashed into difficult silences and camouflaged obtrusive noises with good, sound brass.

Well might J.H. Spencer, recalling the event in a Preston newspaper some forty years later, be prompted to write: 'I remember that the players behind the scenes were convulsed with merriment, and towards the end of the play they knew which boards were highly susceptible.' His report continues: 'These strange noises contributed to the liveliness of the performance without detracting too much from the play's interest.'

You might think that this venture would cool Aunt Edith's enthusiasm. But she was never one to be easily dismayed. On the contrary, full of hope, she founded the Brook Street Dramatic Society. Light comedies, farces, and dialect plays would probably have been within the scope of this raw company, but my aunt, who rarely sponsored anything lightweight, was bent on education. The play she chose for her new company's first production was no safe country comedy but, of all things, Ibsen's *An Enemy of the People*. At least she had the satisfaction of being the first producer of an Ibsen play in Preston!

During these first few years of the century Aunt Edith gave more and more thought to the position of women in all conditions of life. By associating with mill-girls she discovered the extent of injustices caused by lack of proper education. For example, she recognized some of them – such as Maggie Sharrock – as potential leaders. Clara Millan, in other circumstances, might well have been a teacher. Others could have been trained in administrative work while a weaver from Oldham, Annie Kenney, whom she was soon to meet, displayed the intelligence and determination of an MP. Even educated women were still looked upon as ornaments or as servants for the pleasure – and use – of man.

About this time an article was published which maintained that husband-catching was the end of woman's existence: 'The aim must be pursued with unceasing vigilance, the whole of woman's education, dress, manners, and thought must be subordinated to this one object, but they must never openly avow it.' This showed little advance on an earlier writer who regarded it as 'indelicate in a female to let it appear that she had married from inclination; she must always strive to make it seem that her physical and mental weakness had caused her to yield to force.'[1] More succinctly another inquired, 'What business have women turned forty to do with the world?'

It was a world not so far removed from this in which Aunt Edith indignantly found herself. Her background was that of class-conscious provincialism risen to its peak. But turning away from this world of appearances, she resolved not only to brighten the lives of the poorer people, but to fight until all women were recognized as citizens.

Happily Uncle Charlie – the 'long-suffering husband' – wholly sympathized with her campaign, if not with certain of its more eccentric experiments, such as her inquiry into the lives and conditions of maids. From her watch-tower in Winckley Square she observed that the servants (hateful word) were relegated, for the most part, to basements by day and attics by night, being allowed the freedom of the house only for purposes of servitude.

In the days before the 1914-18 war a good cook would receive, at the

1 Quoted in *The Case for Women's Suffrage*, by Florence Balgarnie.

most, two pounds a month; parlourmaids and housemaids were rated at something between one pound and thirty shillings. Weekly payments were not considered *de rigueur* and were only meted out to doubtful applicants known as 'temporaries'. For such women life at best must have been spare and bleak. Certainly they 'ate of the crumbs from the master's table'; doubtless they drank of his dregs, but this confirmed the fact that they were creatures apart, forbidden to partake of the iced cakes borne aloft upon silver cake-stands into drawing-rooms at four p.m. 'Kitchen cake' was bought in large slabs from the grocer, while 'kitchen tea' was Indian, strong and cheap.

Our family only arrived upon the scene when Aunt Edith was too immersed in 'Votes for Women' to consider details of domestic existence, so we escaped her vigilant eye in our direction. But I remember during the war accompanying my mother to Miss Cookham's Registry Office in Jordan Street. Miss Cookham, fat and blowsy, with bosom decked and jewelled, would smile us in and bid us be seated on horsehair chairs. Then, portentously, she lick-fingered her way through the Book. After a moment filled with the creaking of her stays, she would look up and begin to describe mysterious entities in a fruit-cake voice: 'Here's a nice girl. H.P. Twenty-four. Three years' reference. Quiet. Clean and willing worker. No followers.' Miss Cookham spoke with the authority of a medium. And then came an item of great importance: 'But she's asking two pounds a month!' I could almost see, beyond the veil of Jordan Street, a shadowy figure materializing in a dark corner and opening its mouth . . . 'C. of E., of course,' Miss Cookham added as she shut the Book.

My mother's refusal to employ a Roman Catholic ('They're such a nuisance with all that church-going!') seemed to me strangely at variance with her insistence that we ourselves should regularly attend matins as a possible means to salvation.

Remote from such goings-on, Aunt Edith never experienced what the ladies of Ribblesdale Place alluded to as 'the Servant Problem' because she treated her maids as equals. Too often they responded by not doing their work; and after a run of failures and changes, during which time Uncle Charlie suffered much, she eventually lighted on a housekeeper, Miss Tucker, who smoothed the rough places in their domestic life.

Uncle Charlie could have done with Miss Tucker to look after him when Aunt Edith was hoeing cabbages in Lightfoot Lane, making surveys into the lives of others, and, a little later, serving frequent sentences in gaol, when his situation became very bleak indeed.

But he had learned not to complain, since his one remonstrance had led to an even more uncomfortable situation. On that occasion he had demurred at having so often to fend for himself, and pointed out that, after all, he paid the bills, whereas she couldn't even earn her own keep.

'Do you really believe that, Charlie?' she had answered softly, and as softly disappeared from the room. And not only from the room but from the house.

Thinking she was trying to pay him back, Uncle Charlie wasn't unduly concerned by her absence – to begin with. But when she failed to turn up that night, and the next day, and the next, when none of her family or friends had news of her, he grew alarmed. At the end of a week he hired two detectives to track her down.

Another week went by and my harassed uncle began to wonder if he had been deserted for good. Eventually he was informed that his wife, calling herself Polly Sharples, had got a post as housemaid with a titled family in London. Abandoning his patients, Uncle Charlie took the next train, called at the given address, and asked to see Miss Sharples. He was shown into a small room adjoining the servants' hall. After a few minutes' angry-anxious waiting, in came 'Polly', high-collared, capped and starched. 'Edith,' he began, 'how *could* you do this to me?'

'I'm sorry, sir,' she replied primly, 'We're not allowed to receive followers. I'm afraid you'll have to go!' Relentlessly she carried this game through to the end.

But that particular game was already up because her employer, curious about the new housemaid, the only member of his household able to translate for him a letter written in French, had himself been making inquiries.

It happened that Uncle Charlie's mild protest had been made during the period of my aunt's concern for the treatment of maids. Having ascertained their position in middle-class households, she now wished to discover how they fared under the heel – or the spurs – of the aristocracy. In this connection it is worth noting that not so many years back footmen were paid by height rather than merit. So that a clumsy giant of six-foot-three received considerably 'higher' wages than a mere (though nimbler) five-foot-eighter. My aunt might well have wondered if housemaids were assessed by weight and parlourmaids by beauty. Possibly, as she was engaged without a reference (almost unprecedented in those days) this was the one occasion upon which she cashed in on her looks and dignity.

At no time did she aspire to domesticity. I never saw her carry a tray or cut bread and butter; and daily dusting she regarded as a waste of days. As for ironing, she would shake her head reproachfully at those rows of goffered frills on my petticoats and knickers. After all, she was a knickerbocker girl.

This being so, it is surprising that she remained in her new job for nearly a month. The tolerance of her employers must have impressed her and leavened her opinions of 'the privileged'. At any rate, on her return home she informed Uncle Charlie and her family that she had been very well treated.

In the meantime the servants' hall must have rustled with speculation at the entry of this alien bird into its nest. She, so graceful and athletic on a bicycle, in fields and among mountains, was slow, even clumsy, while moving about a room. She was born to live between hills and stars with a blue wind blowing. And her spirit was never to be confined – even in a prison cell. The world of furniture-polish was not her world; and I can imagine the upper-housemaid's comments on her carpet-sweeping.

If the role of housewife was never to be hers, neither, it seemed by now, and less happily, was the role of mother. Nature, who knew best, had decreed that such a pioneer should remain childless. But Aunt Edith refused to be let off. After twelve years had gone by without any sign of a baby, she decided to adopt one. Her contention was that every married woman in comfortable circumstances should share in this human task. All the same, I could never picture my aunt wheeling a pram or pegging out nappies. Often, indeed, I wondered whether married life, even with dear, kind Uncle Charlie, was really the life for her. However attached they might have been, however much respect, loyalty and affection went into their life together, she was not designed for bondage of any sort.

No doubt the shackles that bound her were elastic to the fullest stretch of the word; and he was the most forbearing of husbands. But she was born to ride a white horse, not arrayed as the fine lady of Banbury Cross, but like Joan of Arc, shining in armour, leading a procession towards the sun.

Mercifully Uncle Charlie managed to restrain her from adopting a baby in the first lustihood of its screaming period. Yet I daresay, even then she would have smiled into its red, furious face, saying soothing words in her low voice until it unpuckered, grew quiet, and smiled back.

Not until December 1905 did they formally adopt Arthur (named after my father but subsequently called Sandy) who had been born in May 1903. I have no memory of this strange alliance until about ten years later, for at the time my parents had not even met. I remember only being told that my aunt, as usual, had been much criticized for her unwarranted action. Criticized, also, when she took the six-year-old Sandy, wearing a tussore suit, to the grammar-school sports. In the first place, neighbours objected, she should not have dressed him as 'one of us', and secondly, the material of his outfit was, literally, unsuitable.

These criticisms, however, were mere whispers compared with the furore earlier aroused in the neighbourhood when one of the residents, sitting in the hawthorn-shade of Winckley Square gardens, observed Mrs Rigby rolling the newly-acquired Sandy in the dust – 'like the sparrows!' as she joyfully explained, 'they're so happy in their dust baths . . . we human beings are becoming a deal too artificial. Somehow we must get back to our natural roots!'

'Dust baths, indeed! Did you ever hear of such a thing?' With this story the attention of a next-day bridge four was wholly absorbed. 'She must be crazy. She oughtn't to be allowed a key to our gardens!' agreed the other indignant members of the tea-party.

So the episode ran the round of the Square until the last inhabitant to hear it learned that Mrs Rigby had been rolling the unfortunate boy in the gutter. From then onwards she was eschewed as more dangerous than crazy – she was lowering the whole tone of the neighbourhood.

When a year or so later my newly-married parents came to live in Ribblesdale Place a fellow-doctor's wife, calling on my mother, broke the fearful news that Mrs Rigby had taken to scrubbing her own front-door steps. 'And what's more,' this informant added, 'she has the child there too, scrubbing alongside, turning the place into a slum!'

In those days, when a 'lady' would sooner pick up a piece of bad fish than a scrubbing-brush, the idea of actually scrubbing one's door-step – and of being *seen* to do so – was associated with the regions of Back Silver Street. Not surprisingly my aunt made no headway in persuading her neighbours that menial work should be shared among all members of a household. And not only work. In Aunt Edith's house the maids had their meals in the dining-room and were treated as members of the family.

The courage, as well as idealism, that lay behind such actions was never guessed at. On the contrary, one family who lived a few doors away decided to show active hostility 'for the sake of the Square'. So it was that Mr and Mrs X called one evening and told Mrs Rigby plainly that her appearance and behaviour and, most of all, her way of treating inferiors as equals, was a disgrace. If she couldn't alter her ways, they implied, she had better leave the neighbourhood.

The temerity with which they rebuked the wife of a man so loved and respected as Uncle Charlie reveals more than anything the conventions of the day. The Xs represented others; they were well-connected, 'righteous' people, regular church-goers who felt it their duty to uphold the tone of Winckley Square.

How my aunt replied in words I don't know. But the following day residents of the Square were amazed to see the Xs' glossy front-door thickly coated with whitewash. It would be interesting to know whether they related this act to a certain passage in the New Testament.

A whole generation later such incidents still rankled. 'It was most distressing for your mother,' a relative on her side impressed me, 'having to put up with that sort of thing from her husband's sister. After all, *we* were carriage-folk!'

And 'carriage-folk' would never have dreamed of adopting a child of doubtful origin. When I first met Sandy (we were not introduced) he must have been about twelve years old – a pale, freckled, red-haired boy wearing a kilt and tunic with a black velvet cap. Perhaps there was something Scottish about him; my aunt generally had good reasons for what she did. All the same, he was unmercifully teased by his school-fellows. 'And no wonder,' my mother remarked, 'fancy dressing the poor child like that!'

And poor Aunt Edith, I sometimes thought, she could do nothing right. But for all that, Sandy grew up to love and respect his mother-by-adoption, and in spite of unusual customs he must have benefited from her influence. What is more important he grew into an extremely kind and gentle man, quiet, studious and good at his work. Although this experiment had its difficult moments, it cannot be regarded as a total failure.

Aunt Edith was too intellectual to be at her best with very young children, yet she had a most happy effect upon them – that calming, reassuring influence so lovingly recalled by her 'old girls' from Brook Street. It was the same with animals – recalcitrant horses and dogs in her hands were transformed into benign creatures. Even insects and plants responded to her touch. This side of her nature was to come to fulfilment during the years she spent in the country at Marigold Cottage. But first, a long, bleak, disturbing period has to be lived through.

III

Woman and man. Grace's relations.
The Pankhursts and the W.S.P.U.
Free Trade Hall meetings. First imprisonments.
Mrs Higginson and Beth.

A woman of smaller heart would by now have been driven out of Winckley Square. My aunt stayed on for ten years, not because she was thick-skinned but because, like a feminine equivalent of Sir Galahad, her heart was pure. And because 'the pure in heart' of the Beatitude is more accurately translated 'single-minded', it seems fitting here to complete this most apt version: 'Blessed are the single-minded for they shall attain reality.'

To achieve reality by my aunt's standards, however, required not only the strength, but also the courage of ten. It meant facing hostility, loss of friends and considerable hardship.

Always on the side of the underdog, it seemed to her that the National Underdog was represented by Woman or, rather, women, of all classes. While she rebelled because a working woman (with whose rights she was chiefly concerned) was considered less fit for a vote than her grown-up son, she found it equally wrong that the squire's wife should be denied the privilege enjoyed by his coachmen. And yet the women whose husbands were fortunate enough to employ coachmen remained obstinately ignorant of the fact that she was their champion also.

Through personal knowledge of women in the home, on both sides of the green baize door, and in workrooms, factories and shops, my aunt realized their pressing need for a weapon of attack, as well as defence, against their present situation. Yet when, inevitably, she became involved in the suffrage movement, her neighbours cut her in the street, tarred the stonework of her house and, as far as it was possible for ladies to spit, they spat at her as she went by.

When a neighbour, wife of a town councillor, crossed to the other side of the road on seeing her, and other acquaintances averted their eyes, my aunt took no notice. Instead she took a train to Manchester and joined the Women's Social and Political Union which Mrs Pankhurst had recently formed. Meetings were held at the Pankhursts' house so that Aunt Edith soon became friendly with Mrs Pankhurst's daughters, especially the lively and dominating Christabel. (Sylvia, an artist, didn't become involved for some time, and Adela, the youngest, later came to Preston and stayed at No. 28.) Inevitably she was introduced to Esther Roper (Secretary of the North of England Society for Women's Suffrage) and so met her friend, Eva Gore-

Booth, the poet, and other gifted and enterprising women.

Working with this forward-looking group my aunt was in her element. Uncle Charlie saw less and less of her; neighbours gossiped on behind her back. But what did she care, busily immersed as she was in activities which were to produce the Independent Labour Party? In fact, she became one of its first members, and was destined, also, to be one of the first expelled from it!

Though immensely strong-willed, Aunt Edith was never personally aggressive; I never heard her argue or raise her voice. Her aim was not merely to push women forward, but to restore to them what she believed to be their birthright by Christian standards. And for this end she was prepared to fight.

Long before joining the movement she had considered the way Christ treated women, remembering in particular His conversation with the woman of Samaria and His defence of Mary Magdalene and acceptance of her precious ointment. And had He not told His mother things which 'she treasured in her heart'? Moreover, she reasoned, He had appeared, that first Easter Day, not to His disciples, but to the three Marys.

Apart from this, she had absorbed the writings of an eighteenth-century Mary; Mary Wollstonecraft (described by Horace Walpole as 'a hyena in petticoats') who exalted women's place in the home along with the virtues of chastity and faithfulness in marriage, while pointing out that subservience to a husband must weaken a wife's character. Not that my aunt needed this last reminder. Indeed, she told my father that the local women, at least, were 'a deal sight too much indoctrinated with the story of Adam's rib!'

At this time, the beginning of the twentieth century, women had for so long been dependent on men that, paradoxically, they looked to men to set them free. My aunt held various meetings concerned with women's rights, and in this way discovered a few souls sturdy enough to tackle new ideas. One of these was Grace Alderman, a born feminist, who resented the complacent acceptance of men as the superior sex. Grace, when I talked to her many years later, tossed her head at the recollection: 'I could never see it!' she said, and went on to tell me how she had immediately warmed to my aunt's enthusiasm, especially when at one meeting she had opened the Book of Genesis and read through the story of the Creation. ' "Male and female created he them in the Image of God" – that's what it says. And the only Euclid I could remember,' Grace remarked, 'was that things equal to the same thing are equal to one another. Then we considered the Ten Commandments. If women are inferior to men, Moses should have made an easier set for us to keep!'

Having reached these conclusions, Grace soon found an opportunity of tackling the anti-women's suffrage Dr John Rigg whom she described as 'a good man and a friend. But still he thought that women should be guided by, and defer to, men'. In the new light of her reasoning this attitude seemed illogical to Grace who challenged him the next time they met with her own argument. It was some days after this that she observed Dr Rigg walking down Fishergate Hill: 'He crossed the road and came up to me, and said he'd thought the matter over. He was certain women were meant to keep the Commandments and therefore they couldn't be inferior to men.' Grace paused: 'If only the politicians had been like him!' And then, 'As for the cock-and-bull story of Adam's rib, that comes later in the chapter and in my opinion it's made up !'

By this time, of course, my aunt had gently, firmly, almost imperceptibly drawn Grace towards joining the suffrage movement. 'But before actually plunging in,' she told me, 'I gave the matter much thought. And if I'd realized what would be expected of me in Mrs Rigby's company, I might have drawn back. All the same,' she added, 'it was very galling to be a woman in those days. I was game for a good deal of discomfort, and discomfort we certainly got!'

Looking back more than fifty years, it seems unbelievable that the Liberal Government were still withholding from Eve the second apple of free choice ripened for her since the Fall – this one on a sanctioned tree. Yet through all ages artists, philosophers and poets, including Solomon, Plato, and Leonardo, have exalted woman beyond her own dreams. (Admittedly she got less than a fair deal from the writer of Genesis who might possibly have been on Gladstone's side.)

Plainly, if Boadicea, Joan of Arc, Queen Elizabeth, Florence Nightingale and Madame Curie had failed to convince man of woman's fitness to be a citizen, then no further achievement could prevail. Action, therefore, must prevail. Women were forced to become law-breakers in order to become law-makers. Mrs Fawcett's campaign for women's suffrage by peaceful means had been going on for more than forty years. It had made as much impression upon the rigid minds of politicians as a feather brushed against rocks.

After much deliberation along these lines Aunt Edith told Uncle Charles that she had decided to fall in with the militant suffragettes.

It might be helpful here to survey some of the old ground which she had carefully turned over. In the first place, Lord John Russell's Reform Bill of 1832 had put women more completely out of political bounds than ever before. This Bill had extended men's franchise from freeholder and freeman to the middle-class male householder. Trouble took root in that newly-planted word 'male'. In previous Bills the electors might legally have been women.

One of the first branches put out from this particular root was a pamphlet by a Quaker, Anne Knight, which resulted in the first petition on the subject being presented to the House of Lords. Shortly after this John Stuart Mill headed a band of women including Miss Beale and

Miss Buss (of Cheltenham Ladies' College) and the future Dr Garrett Anderson. But even these pioneers were unable to collect the hundred signatures required before presenting their petition to the Commons. Fortunately the sprightly Disraeli came to their assistance. Already he had made an eloquent speech in their favour; now he spurred them into collecting almost fifteen hundred signatures within a few days.

The wind was still against them. When John Stuart Mill moved his amendment (to the Representation of the People Act) to substitute the word 'persons' for the word 'male', he was defeated by a majority of well over a hundred. This was the work of Gladstone who, impassive, inflexible, was unchanged by change. And yet he had recently asserted: 'The essence of Liberalism is trust of the people qualified by prudence; the essence of Toryism is distrust of the people qualified by fear'. On the question of women's suffrage, he showed himself to be an extreme Tory.[1]

A little later a group of Scottish university women contested the Universities of St Andrews and Edinburgh 'on the ground that their names were on the register of the University, they were entitled to have been served with voting papers at the General Election'.[2] Judgement went against them. For seven years it was wings against a contrary wind.

Then, suddenly and surprisingly, towards the end of the Tory Ministry in 1904, Sir Charles McLaren carried his Women's Suffrage Resolution by a majority of 114.[3] About this time Arthur Balfour, the Prime Minister, when visiting his constituency in Manchester, was challenged by Christabel Pankhurst who asked why this resolution could not pass into law. In reply to her importuning he admitted: 'Well, to tell you the truth, your case is not in the swim!'[4]

The time had come to educate candidates before election to Parliament. Most helpful to the cause of women's suffrage was Christabel's knowledge of the law. Recently she had taken a law course at Manchester University which led not only to her degree, but to her passing out top of the lists.[5] (Being a woman, her previous application to become a law-student at Lincoln's Inn had been refused.)

Aunt Edith, by now a tremendous admirer of Christabel's courage and brains, hoped one day to see this dark-haired, lively young woman elected to Parliament. It seemed to her that Christabel, with her clear ringing voice, had been christened in heaven. Without doubt she was in part, though unconsciously, responsible for my aunt's metamorphosis from the gentle, almost angelic, creature I have portrayed into a decidedly

1 *The Case for Women's Suffrage*, by Florence Balgarnie.
2 *Ibid.*
3 *Unshackled*, by Christabel Pankhurst.
4 *Ibid.*
5 *Ibid.*

fiery angel.

As I have said, she had joined the Women's Social and Political Union at its inception in 1904. Inspired by Mrs Pankhurst who had declared, 'We must do the work ourselves, we must have an independent women's movement!' and inflamed by Christabel, she had flung herself heart and head into its activities, determined to lose no time in forming a branch in Preston. About this time she met Annie Kenney, the weaver from Oldham, and fastened upon her as the very one to help her launch the Preston branch. With a flair for public speaking and organization, and an understanding of fellow-workers' problems, Annie was to be the first woman elected to the Oldham Trades Council. Small and fair, sparkling with vitality, she proved to be one of the jewels of the movement. Already my aunt had been with her in February 1904 to a significant meeting held in the Free Trade Hall. After hearing Mr Winston Churchill affirm his beliefs in the principles of free trade, they received a surprise best expressed in the words of the *Manchester Guardian*:

> Miss Pankhurst asked to be allowed to move an amendment with regard to Woman Suffrage. The Chairman said he was afraid he could not permit such an addition . . . Miss Pankhurst seemed loth to give way but finally, amid loud cries of 'Chair!', she retired.

The Chairman read Christabel's proposal but said he was sorry he couldn't put it to the meeting. Christabel describes the following incident as her first militant step:

> ' . . . the hardest to me because it *was* the first. To move from my place on the platform to the Speaker's table in the teeth of the astonishment and opposition of that immense throng . . . was the most difficult thing I have ever done.'[1]

At any rate her action set the alarm for women's suffrage. While the Tory strength was ebbing the women banded themselves together to frame uncomfortable questions for the new Government. The extended franchise for men, they argued, had been won by means of violence, whereas in the case of women nearly fifty years of pleading had earned for them nothing more than friendly pats and foolish remarks such as: 'Dear little woman, what would we do without you waiting for us at home?'

Women had waited and worked far too long. It is difficult for us who have a vote to realize the helplessness of our grandmothers because in order to get a vote it is necessary to have at least a voice. Christabel, never a warmer of fireside slippers, determined to seize her chance at the big Liberal rally shortly to be held at the Free Trade Hall. She meant to

1   *Ibid.*

challenge the leaders with their professed ideal: *Government of the people by the people.*

Members of the Women's Social and Political Union met together to decide upon a course of action. After securing good seats for the meeting they got busy on a huge banner of white calico. Someone produced a tin of black stain for the lettering. The question was: what words would best convey their message? Suddenly one of the group pronounced the phrase which, for nearly ten years, was to be dinned into the ears of politicians: 'Will You Give Votes for Women?'[1]

This was the question to be forced upon the meeting. Christabel knew it meant 'Yes' for an answer or prison. And she knew it meant prison.

Aunt Edith, who had been in on all this, watched her and Annie set forth together as leaders on the first of many such ventures which were to be met for years with prevarication and refusal. Greatly excited, she took her place among the expectant audience in the crowded hall. Cheers greeted the speakers; the women waited, listening for the leaders to announce their programme including, they hoped, the business of women's suffrage.

The subject was never even mentioned. Towards the end of the meeting Annie stood up and shouted: 'Will the Liberal Government give votes to women?' No answer came. In that moment the Liberals were brought face to face with a new foe, neither Tory nor Labour, but the opposite, and opposing, sex. To continue in Christabel's words:

> 'Our banner was unfurled, making clear what was our question. The effect was explosive. The meeting was aflame with excitement. Some consultation among Chairman and speakers ensued, and then the Chief Constable of Manchester, Sir Robert Peacock, genial and paternal in manner, made his way to us and promised . . . an answer to our question after the vote of thanks had been made . . .
>
> 'Sir Edward Grey rose to reply without one word in answer to our question. The bargain thus broken on his side, we were free to renew our simple question: "Will the Liberal Government give women the vote?" The answer came then, not in word but in deed. Stewards rushed at us, aided by volunteers and accompanied by loud cries: "Throw them out!" '[2]

The scene which followed was to be repeated at meeting after meeting in town after town until the outbreak of war in 1914. Christabel and Annie, protesting violently, were dragged from their seats. They tried to assault the police in order to be arrested, because unless they were charged and imprisoned their efforts would be wasted, as Christabel's

1 *Ibid.*
2 *Ibid.*

previous action had been wasted. This time the challenge must be brought into court and into the newspapers.

Meanwhile, amid mounting excitement, the two women were dragged in front of the platform on the way out. For a moment Christabel managed to free herself. She stood up and addressed her question to Sir Edward Grey. 'I remember thinking,' she said afterwards, 'that suitably wreathed and attired he would have looked exactly like a Roman Emperor. Pale, expressionless, immovable, he returned me look for look. I was swept away through the side door which muffled the deafening tumult . . .'[1]

I have related this important occasion in full not only because it epitomizes the whole campaign, but because it confirmed my aunt in her militant course. From now on the gentle manner cloaking iron and fire was flung aside – at least for several years. And Uncle Charlie was faced with a new aspect to his wife's character, and with a new mode of life for himself.

To return for a moment to the Free Tade Hall, it is significant that after the women's dismissal the sympathy of the crowd was turned to them with cries of 'Shame!'

So determined were the police to frustrate Christabel's and Annie's efforts at assault – removing feet which would be stamped upon and fingers which might be bitten – that Christabel, the lawyer, was driven to her last resource. She was arrested and charged with 'spitting at a policeman'. Both women continued to be aggressive, refusing all sympathy and loopholes from police, magistrates and friends. They were determined to go to prison. And to prison they were sent. Winston Churchill himself offered to bail them out. But, satisfied at last in bare cells with bowls of gruel and scratchy garments, they remained adamant.[2]

This episode set the pattern to be repeated by hundreds of women, famous and unknown, throughout the country. Though Christabel's courage in making the first move was quite outsize, every demonstration of the kind reflected some bold, leading spirit. Such a one was Aunt Edith who herself had to go to prison before being able to kindle the interest of the women of Preston.

My grandparents were horrified to read in the local papers and in the *Manchester Guardian* reports of the behaviour of Christabel and Annie. Spitting at policemen; defiance followed by imprisonment – this was something right outside their conception of a gentlewoman's behaviour. Aunt Edith, on the contrary, was triumphant because the newspaper silence had been broken, and women without a vote were suddenly given

1 *Ibid.*
2 *Ibid.*

a platform. From now on, just as the General Election was drawing near, the Press became an ally.

Evasive answers from politicians prompted the Women's Social and Political Union manifesto which began:

> It has been decided to oppose Mr Winston Churchill at the General Election on the ground that he is a member of the Liberal Government which refuses to give women the vote.

And ended:

> Although the Liberals profess to believe in political freedom the Liberal leaders have always opposed Women's Franchise. It was a Liberal Government in 1884 which refused to give votes for women when the male agricultural worker was being enfranchised. The present Cabinet contains many enemies and no real friends of Women's Franchise.[1]

The Women's Social and Political Union would have equally opposed any Government which refused to give votes to women.

In Preston Aunt Edith cornered Harold Cox, the Liberal candidate, and faced him with the same question. There and then she tried to inspire a number of women to form a local branch of the Women's Social and Political Union. But the idea was too new for them. Guarded and suspicious, they realized, perhaps, that Mrs Rigby was a 'one' for new schemes which might lead them into trouble. As Grace put it, 'she was in a new thing as soon as it appealed to her. But I admit we were slow to follow her – at first.'

It was a picture in the *Daily Chronicle* that finally persuaded Grace and her mother to join up with Aunt Edith. At that time this was the only newspaper which ran a column for women; and it was written by a woman, Dr Sloan Chesser.

'I think it would have been after the big Liberal rally at the end of 1905,' Grace told me. 'Anyway, I was baking cakes at the time and Mother came into the kitchen with the paper – it was then the Press first began taking photographs – "Just look at this!" she said. Well, I looked, and if astounded could mean having the breath knocked out of my body, that would be just what I felt. What a picture! A group of women were being dispersed by the police. One woman lay prone on the ground and another was holding a horse to keep it clear. The policeman had his truncheon raised to strike this one down. Until then I'd thought England stood for fair play.'

Mrs Rigby, so Grace believed, was among that crowd. At any rate, the woman holding the horse, Patricia Woodlock, was a friend whom my

1 *Ibid.*

aunt invited soon afterwards to stay at her house and address a meeting in Preston.

It is possible that Grace was confusing this event with the first big battle with the police which took place in February the following year, after the opening of Parliament. No Woman Suffrage Bill had been introduced, though Keir Hardie had moved a resolution which might have been helpful. However, in order to prevent a division, it was deliberately talked out by a Liberal MP. Then it was that the Prime Minister, Sir Henry Campbell-Bannerman, declared that the Government had no intention of giving women the vote – at least, not yet. But almost in the same breath he said *sotto voce* to Christabel: 'Go on pestering people – these are only pinpricks!'

He was taken at his word. A small group of women stood at his door and knocked. But it was not opened to them. Whereupon the well-known suffragette, Flora Drummond (later known as 'The General') pressed a knob and miraculously found herself inside with Annie at her heels. They were arrested but not charged.[1]

Shortly afterwards when Lloyd George was pestered at a public meeting he tried to shift the blame. 'Why don't they go for their enemies? Why don't they go for their greatest enemy?' Immediately the women responded: 'Asquith! Asquith!' The Chancellor of the Exchequer was already regarded as the chief obstructionist. When he refused to receive a small deputation they went to his house with banners raised, but the police were there to receive them. A battle followed. Annie Kenney, captain of the band, and her two followers were arrested and sent to Holloway. It was the beginning of militancy in London. About this time a new name was minted for these women; 'suffragettes' was the brilliant idea of a journalist from the *Daily Mail*.

In No. 28 Winckley Square the first suffragette in Preston was planning her own campaign. Tactfully she called first of all on members of the Trades Union whom she hoped to ensnare. In this way one of her earliest victims was Mrs Higginson, owner of the local Health Stores, who has given me much information about this period in my aunt's life. Although Mrs Higginson was cajoled into attending suffrage meetings, she didn't join the militants for some years on account of her two young children.

Little did she realize that this first encounter with Mrs Rigby was to lead to ultimate imprisonment and hunger-striking. 'Before she called on me I knew her by reputation. Mrs Rigby was well known in the town,' Mrs Higginson told me. 'And as soon as she came into the room I recognized

---

1 *Ibid.*

authority in her. Of course, she came from a different world; and for all her homespun clothes there was nothing homely about her. She was stately and dignified.'

In spite of her efforts my aunt had little success, in 1906, with recruiting in Preston – 'unprogressive, self-sufficient Preston', as she was later to describe the town in the local paper.

In January 1907, at a meeting of the Independent Labour Party, she first met Mrs Hesmondhalgh, whom I will call Beth, and immediately seized upon her as promising material, along with a few other women whom she recruited after the meeting.

'She was so determined,' Beth told me, 'she even tried to get round my husband to persuade me. And then she sent Annie Kenney to complete the job. Well, I joined – half against my will – and the next thing I knew I was asked to face imprisonment!'

In Beth's words, my aunt's followers were to realize: 'When Mrs Rigby wanted you to undertake anything unpleasant or dangerous, she had a way of making you feel that *she* was doing *you* a favour!'

Beth, who was to prove loyal and courageous, undergoing hunger-striking and forcible feeding before her leader, told me something of her own life. 'I never knew my mother,' she began, 'and when I was five years old I got a stepmother. She certainly sent me to school with my school pence, but happiness she never gave me. My brother and I were so badly treated that my father put us in the care of a farmer's wife. Well, there was no more school for me after that – it was too far from the farm. In all my life I only got three years' schooling.'

Yet in spite of such a handicap, coupled with failing eyesight, Beth could write, at the age of eighty four, a lively account of her childhood, her working life, and the suffrage movement in Preston. When she was fourteen she went 'into service', and later worked as a winder in Samuel Slater's mill. 'I was there for twenty-three years without a break except for a spell of imprisonment, which they disapproved of because the Slaters were strong Liberals.'

Such women as these, my aunt felt, were a great deal more worth while than her neighbours in the Square.

Beth recalls the Sunday evening meetings which Mrs Rigby held on the top floor of No. 28. Meetings with suffrage questions taboo because on Sundays the members were encouraged to discuss domestic and social problems in a friendly atmosphere of coffee and cakes. In fact, my aunt conducted a sort of help-and-advice bureau as she sat cross-legged on a Persian mat, smoking endless Turkish cigarettes.

One evening a certain member stayed on after the others had gone home – to seek advice on serious 'husband-trouble'. Mrs Rigby was exceedingly helpful and sympathetic and, what was most unusual in one so reticent, confided that she herself had suffered the same sort of difficulty – though on different grounds.

I believe she was alluding to a clash following the adoption of Sandy which Uncle Charlie had opposed. In this considerable matter Nature and Uncle Charlie might have been the best judges.

However, Aunt Edith was able to offer sound advice to others on marital and various problems. By such means the Preston Women's Social and Political Union grew into a fellowship united by deeper bonds than those of politics. Its members were to become my aunt's friends and allies; she counted herself fortunate in having met them. Among the more wealthy women of the town, though a few supported the cause, hardly any became members. Most of them followed Mrs Todd – formerly Miss Rickward, headmistress of the Preston High School – who led the non-militants. It was not until Mrs Rigby was arrested and given the choice of a fine or a fortnight in prison, that they wondered why she chose prison.

IV

T HE more I have learned about my aunt, the more I regret that what
I knew of her was shadowed by prejudice. Looking back from the
time of her death, my father could say: 'Of course, she was years
ahead of her time'. I suppose those who accept the bars imposed by society
cannot help castigating others who break through. For my part, only a
child's innate sense of goodness in people preserved even an outline of her
true portrait. But, alas, shadows of growing up and worldly shadows
clouded it too often.

'Edith's too high-flown . . . Edith's not one of us . . . an eccentric . . .
disgraceful . . .' Such sayings sank into my mind. And my mother, so pretty
and well dressed, delicate as Dresden china, was not of her world. My
father, wholly engrossed in his work, regarded his sister as a crank. I grew
up, therefore, looking upon her as an oddity, and was made to feel
uncomfortable in her presence because of her 'funny' clothes and the way
people stared. But she was nice; she was real. As I grew older I began,
hesitantly, to admire her.

Only in writing this book, which has meant meeting those who knew her,
and discovering many unsuspected activities, has the portrait gradually
filled in and put on colour – more colours than I dreamed of at first. I never
knew, for instance, till I read Uncle Charlie's letter in the *Lancashire Daily
Post*, the facts regarding her first imprisonment. How she had got up at half-
past five one sleety morning in February 1907, to take part in a suffragette
procession from Hyde Park. This procession, several thousand strong, was
hoping for a response from the Government. But the Government was to
be set against the suffragettes for many years to come, so that the procession
resolved itself into a Women's Parliament, as these meetings came to be
called, at the Caxton Hall.

Here it was that Aunt Edith met Mrs Despard, whose rare spiritual gifts
she instantly recognized. Indeed, there was a personal affinity between
them; they viewed the suffrage movement rather differently from the
Pankhursts whom some people considered too autocratic. When, for
example, a little later on it was suggested that the W.S.P.U. should be run by
a committee, Mrs Pankhurst and Christabel were astonished; did not their
leadership rise beyond the need for re-election? And were they not firmer
and quicker in decision than any group could ever hope to be?
Undoubtedly. Yet this sharp point caused a division in the ranks, and

ultimately Mrs Despard broke away to lead the Women's Freedom League, another militant group which was run on democratic principles.

Meanwhile, she was chosen to lead a deputation to the House. My aunt, and Christabel and Sylvia Pankhurst were among the handful of women who accompanied her while many others pressed closely behind. At the doors they were confronted by rows of police who advanced upon them and beat them back. But the women were not to be so easily dispersed. Again and again they rallied their forces to press forward in a struggle that dragged on through the afternoon and into the raw February dusk. Every so often, battered and hatless, they retreated to Caxton Hall to recover their strength.

Some women against a strong force of mounted police armed with truncheons would have surrendered in the name of common sense. But their fight was of a different order. Some of them actually broke through the police guard and reached the lobby. Inevitably they were thrown out and arrested while hundreds more who had gathered in the square surged forward trying to force the breach. The police set upon them in another Battle of Parliament Square until the fifty-seven leaders, including Mrs Rigby, were arrested.

Next day they were tried and sentenced to prison or ordered to pay fines which, on principle, they refused to do. Mrs Despard and Sylvia got three weeks, Christabel, Mrs Rigby and a few others, two weeks, while the rest got seven days. The magistrate, Mr Curtis Bennett, ordered that these disorderly scenes be stopped. Whereupon Christabel, in her clear, round voice, replied: 'That depends not upon us, but upon the Government. There will be more scenes if we do not get the vote which is our right!'[1]

On 15 February a short leader appeared in the *Lancashire Daily Post*:

The venerable Mrs Despard will be treated as a first-class misdemeanant. Most of the others will undergo the usual rigours of prison discipline. We hope the suffragists now dealt with will be allowed to serve their full term without any amelioration of their conditions. There is no reason why they should have exceptional treatment, and when it is given they only regard it as a sign of weakness.

The only woman from Preston and district to be imprisoned was Mrs Rigby.

In answer to this leader Uncle Charlie, one of the best-loved doctors in the town, immediately replied:

Sir, I believe this to be greater brutality in words than anything that has been done in deed by any suffragist now in prison. Edith

1 *Unshackled*, by Christabel Pankhurst.

Rigby from her childhood has given every ability that she possesses
. . . to help her sister women. For at least ten years . . . she has
given every day and all the day to the tasks of visiting, organizing,
and studying . . . the cause of distress among her sisters. No one but
myself knows the hours she has worked at it with . . . singleness of
purpose [undaunted] by opposition, contempt, loss of friends, or
anything else . . .

She has been a teacher at a large Mothers' Class at St James's
Church, secretary to the Preston Ladies' Health Club, and is now
connected . . . with the Socialist movement in Preston . . .

She is no criminal, but one who has worked might and main for
the betterment of her sisters. She never did a wrong, consciously, to
any human being, but she is in prison. She is a woman of education
and energy and pursues certain methods [having] tried every other
method without result. She is rewarded by prison.

You, Sir, know her, you know of her works, her self-sacrifice, and
you think her well rewarded by prison, and would have it used to its
greatest severity. A gentler, truer, better-hearted woman never lived.
Because she thinks the mothers of this country ought to have a voice
in its management . . . prison is her reward. The infant mortality
today is terrible. Women who bring up children are excluded from
any representation in the Government . . . prison for those who
wish things altered.

Are women slaves? Is this a free country? Have women no brains?
. . . when they want a voice – prison, aye, and plenty of it.

On Saturday morning last Edith Rigby left her comfortable home
at 5.30 a.m. to take part in a procession from Hyde Park. She
tramped through the mud and wet . . . to show her faith in peaceful
methods – as did thousands of others.

There was no mention in the King's speech that any notice was
taken of them though the government knew all about it. Prison is
the place for such women.

I am the husband of Edith Rigby, and so can speak of her . . . It
is the truth . . . these women you think worthy of stripes are
martyrs. Do you, Sir, try to realize what they are giving up for this
cause, and I am sure that you will repent and apologize.
February 5th, 1907

> Charles Rigby,
> 28 Winckley Square,
> Preston

(This letter appeared on 18 February.)

Aunt Edith, already a prison visitor at Preston gaol, by no means
regarded herself as a martyr. On the contrary, Wrong-Side-of-the-Bars

country proved to be illuminating and an opportunity for genuine observation. Being truly on the side of the angels, her adventure began with a rare coincidence: the first morning in chapel she was amazed to recognize the chaplain as none other than her erstwhile comrade, Mr Caulfield, recently transferred from Preston gaol.

Equally surprised, but considerably more pained, was Mr Caulfield, who visited her cell later in the day, somewhat in the spirit of the righteous confronting a fallen angel.

'I'm sorry to see you here,' he began reproachfully.

'Why sorry?' she replied, 'I'm proud and glad to be here!'

The day after her release she confessed that she'd had quite a clash with the chaplain: 'When he first visited me he thought I was rather too jubilant about being in prison,' she said. 'However, next time he came with a lecturing air; he said we were law-breakers, and pointed out the great need today for reverence and control.'

She paused, recollecting the exact conversation before continuing: 'I asked him how the newspapers were dealing with this rebellion of ours and he replied that they were tired of it. On his third visit,' she went on, 'I challenged him: "Mr Caulfield, which papers do you read?" When he told me he read the *Daily Mail* and the *Lancashire Daily Post*, I informed him that the papers were full of our revolt, examining the question in every possible way. "Therefore," I pushed the point home, "your statement was quite incorrect." Then I asked him a few questions regarding the laws of the country, whereupon he quickly departed!'

No doubt the sureness of her ground, the quiet manner in which she spoke affected him as once, years ago, it had affected her Brook Street girls. However, she was so greatly distressed when this incident was reported in the *Lancashire Daily Post* that she wrote a letter profoundly apologizing for what she had revealed 'in the intense excitement of the morning of release' and 'after the abnormal strain of the preceding hours with a brass-band welcome and breakfast speeches.'

Though Aunt Edith never allowed a lie to pass unchallenged, she was the last person to show anyone up in a bad light; and she hated personal publicity.

Only because she had been a local prison visitor and had worked for prison reform, was she persuaded to answer further questions relating to her own experience. One thing she reported was the deplorable organ-playing at prison services: 'I felt the need for some good music,' she said, 'and also for talks on human subjects which would give prisoners the chance to ask questions and explain their difficulties.'

All her past objections to the prison service were fortified by her recent experience. They were to be strengthened further by the many imprisonments still to come.

'Prison is hopeless as a place of reform,' she told a Press reporter. 'You have to do what is right because you are made to and they punish you if you don't. As for strengthening the will and spirit, there is none of that to be got there. But I was very struck with the discipline among the wardresses. One was bound to admire the loyalty to duty and the good tone of the staff in relation to one another.'

As to the food, she remarked that it was wholesome, 'Better than I expected and fifty per cent better than in tramp wards; and the same applies to the beds. All the same, prison food has a stodging effect on the mind. One has time for writing but no energy for it. And then I realized what a terrible thing it was to be forbidden to talk to people who were serving a long sentence. There was never a time for conversation. It was always: "You cannot talk here"; "Remember where you are"; "Remember you are in chapel".'

Lack of music in prison was made up for by brass bands at the gates which greeted the thirty women released early on 27 February. Playing 'Men of Harlech' and 'As We Go Marching Home' they headed a procession of two or three hundred who had fallen in to welcome the suffragettes and marched with them towards Holborn and a good breakfast.

Among the letters opened at the breakfast-table there was one containing a cheque for fifty-seven pounds – one for each prisoner. After the bacon and eggs and coffee came a resolution calling upon the Government to accept Mr Dickenson's Bill to give votes to women on the same terms as men. Mrs Rigby, who replied for the prisoners, began by saying she was glad they had been in prison and had received strict treatment with no privileges. 'Prison is a grimy, serious institution,' she said, 'a new experience for many of us who have never known cold and hunger. It's good for us all to experience conditions which are quite beyond many people's social horizon.'

Speaking of the prison system she continued: 'it is well administered but inhumanely ill-directed. I've come out a firmer socialist than I went in. And I feel the burden of womanhood heavy upon me because women are at the bottom of the scale in a country where they've no share in the Government.' She hoped that one day Miss Pankhurst would be an MP. For herself, she was resolved to become a town councillor. 'And all women,' she ended, 'long to be of more service to the country. God help the Women's Revolution!'

Before returning home she spent a few days in Reading where by a seemingly inspired chance she met a twenty-year-old girl who was profoundly impressed by her sincerity and courage. This was the lovely, golden-haired Charlotte Marsh, destined to be one of the stars of the W.S.P.U. and to carry the cross at Emily Davison's funeral,[1] and who

1   Emily Wilding Davison threw herself in front of the King's horse at the
    Derby in June 1913.

eventually became vice-president of the Suffragette Fellowship. But it was her encounter with Edith Rigby that inspired her to join the movement in the first place.

In Preston the following week a meeting in support of women's suffrage was called at the Assembly Rooms. Expectation rustled through the audience because Mrs Edith Rigby, newly released from prison, and Miss Annie Kenney were to be the speakers. Mr Williams, the chairman, having professed himself in favour of the movement, pleaded for a fair hearing for the two women. He was referring to an explosive meeting of the previous week when Annie Kenney had been nearly shouted out of the hall. No wonder he felt apprehensive as he called upon Mrs Rigby to speak!

She stood up and looked around the room for a few moments in silence. 'We liked her at first sight,' Grace told me afterwards. 'It was obvious that she didn't feel at home on the platform. She seemed almost shy; and yet she was firm and sincere.'

After an interval she began, slowly and emphatically: 'I want to tell you plainly that it was not on impulse I took part in the recent suffrage rebellion in London. No one regretted more than I that such methods had to be used.' Here she reminded her audience of the long, empty years of peaceful pleading under Mrs Fawcett's leadership. 'The other women imprisoned with me were of the same mind,' she went on, and the audience murmured, eager for prison details. But Mrs Rigby, never one for dramatization, kept strictly to bare facts.

'There were fifty-seven of us sent to Holloway – rather a handful for the warders who were nearly worked to death in sorting through fifty-seven lots of belongings. They put five of us – I was one – into a cell four yards square. We were there from half-past four until half-past ten. At least it gave us the only chance we had for a talk!'

'My fellow-prisoners,' she resumed, 'were not rebels but thoughtful women ready to risk life itself in our just cause. Prison is not a comfortable experience, but you mustn't think we regard ourselves as martyrs, or feel sorry for ourselves, indeed . . .' she broke off with a smile, 'far more courage is needed to stand up here before you tonight! Those who have spoken at street-corners, outside workshop gates, and at by-elections, meeting obloquy and derision, are the true heroines – not those who have just done seven or fourteen days in prison.'

She sat down to a friendly response.

Annie Kenney, the next speaker, nodded to her and came to the front of the platform. Grace describes Annie as 'small and fair and very wick. She'd lost one finger at work in the mill. And she spoke much more quickly than Mrs Rigby. Her strong Lancashire dialect was most effective. Full of punch and pith she was,' Grace went on, 'with a salty sense of humour that soon had the audience in laughing agreement. "The way we're going," Annie declared, "we'll see lads of twenty-one making laws for their own mothers!" '

At the end of the meeting Mrs Rigby appealed for volunteers to form a committee for a Preston branch of the W.S.P.U.. As always, she got round people so that a week later the committee was formed with herself as secretary, Mrs Alderman as chairman, Miss Ainsworth as treasurer and nine other members, four of whom – Mrs Burroughs, Jenny Jackson, Grace and Beth – were to face imprisonment.

Annie, who was staying at No. 28, helped Aunt Edith to organize this new branch. Together they visited committee members and others who might follow suit, charging them with the enthusiasm necessary to take part in deputations and processions, and also to risk and accept imprisonment. My aunt had difficulty in persuading anyone to let a room for their weekly meetings. Eventually a sympathetic dentist agreed to hire them his waiting-room during the evenings. It was over the bookshop, later stoned in an anti-suffragette riot in 1909, because the manager, Mr Pass, was the husband of a committee member.

When the understanding with the dentist came to an end they met temporarily at No. 28. 'By this time we were taboo,' Grace told me. 'No one would have us until a tea-merchant in Glover's Court took pity on us and let us have his top floor.' Here the committee of twelve set to, scrubbing, painting and polishing. While some members made curtains, Mrs Rigby bought a set of spindle-back chairs; and with Arthurian foresight she also acquired a round table for meals as well as for committee meetings.

When completed the room looked more like a retreat than a rebels' den. 'And as for our leader,' Grace assured me, 'she was dependable, straightforward, and always kind.' The meetings held here were happier than those which subsequently took place at No. 28, where there were occasional murmurings at my aunt's autocracy because of her resolve that Uncle Charlie's routine should not be upset. At five minutes past nine promptly, no matter to what stage the meeting might have progressed, Mrs Rigby would stand up with a cool: 'Well, ladies, it's the doctor's supper time. I must go. You may stay on and finish what's to be done. Don't forget to close the front door behind you! Good-night and thank you!'

Whereupon she would vanish and be no more seen. 'Could you beat it!' exclaimed one of the group, 'and she calls herself democratic – why, she's a downright autocrat!'

'Then you tell her so at the meeting', another member suggested. But no one dared question her authority.

Prominent people who came to Preston to speak about women's suffrage were invited to stay at No. 28. One of these was Keir Hardie, leader of the Independent Labour Party, who reminded his audience of the subject's right to petition the King, an admission he was later to extract from the Speaker of the House of Commons.

'Keir Hardie, my God, imagine having *him* to stay!' I remember my father's comment. Yet this bearded man with his direct gaze strengthened my aunt's decision to take part in yet another deputation the following October, after the opening of Parliament.

Already her watchful eye had lighted upon two promising members of her committee – Mrs Burroughs, a tackler's wife and mother of four sons, and Jenny Jackson, a weaver with the grit of Annie Kenney. Accordingly, with these two, she set forth for the W.S.P.U. at Clement's Inn, now buzzing with excitement of battle. Christabel, the chief organiser, seemed to live here with her mother and Mrs Tuke as secretaries, and Mrs Pethick Lawrence as treasurer, who with her husband was at this very moment launching the suffragette paper: *Votes for Women*. The women were waiting, almost on tiptoe, to hear if Mr Dickinson's Bill had passed its second reading. Soon came the news that the Bill had been talked out by a Government supporter.

Once again Aunt Edith, with her two companions, joined the deputation of petition and protest – this one led by Viscountess Harberton. The pattern repeated itself with the women being met by police mounted outside the House. Determined to get inside, they pierced the navy-blue flank of the law. Some of them succeeded in reaching the doors behind which men sat and calmly talked out women's rights.

Along with Mrs Burroughs and Jenny Jackson, Aunt Edith was among those arrested. She was sentenced to two weeks, the others to seven days, in Holloway.

When news of the release of Mrs Burroughs and Jenny reached Preston the weavers in the 'red-and-green' mill where Jenny worked conspired against her. On the morning of her return, the moment she was seen approaching the gates, they formed two lines and spat at her as she walked between them. How Mrs Burroughs fared I do not know, but Jenny had to find work elsewhere.

From now on a major part of the suffragette policy was to oppose Government candidates at by-elections. Mid-Devon, Newcastle, and Leeds had already witnessed Liberal defeats so decisive that the *Daily Mail* reported: 'Everything else paled before the last efforts of the suffragettes. It was picturesque, brilliant, triumphant.'[1]

In spite of this, when Parliament assembled in February, 1908, the King's speech proved to be, as far as women were concerned, the King's silence. Whereupon delegates from more than a hundred towns assembled for a three-day conference at Caxton Hall. Mrs Rigby, the chief representative for Preston, was accompanied by Beth, Grace and

1 *Unshackled,* by Christabel Pankhurst.

Mrs Towler, a prim ex-schoolteacher who was also a tackler's wife with four sons. 'They were very well-trained boys,' Grace observed, 'her house was always in order, so it was quite a thing for her to leave home and risk imprisonment. Anyway, she spent a whole week baking for her family – she baked enough to keep the five of them going for a fortnight!'

On this occasion about fifty women were recruited to storm the House of Commons while Mrs Rigby, chosen to carry the petition, laid her own unusual plans for the day. Mary Phillips, a London organizer, along with a friend, received orders to meet Mrs Rigby at a certain address which, to her surprise, turned out to be a haulage contractor's. When they arrived about ten women were already assembled. Without delay Mrs Rigby indicated that they were to bundle themselves into a furniture van – to give the appearance of a removal. A driver was waiting to lock them in. And thus, huddled like sheep, black sheep, they endured a bumpy and suffocating journey to the House. The moment the van clattered to a stop (at St Stephen's entrance) the driver ran round to the back and unbolted the doors. Like a twentieth-century edition of the Trojans bursting forth from the belly of the Wooden Horse, the women surged out behind Mrs Rigby. Brandishing the petition like a torch, she urged them to force their way into the lobby. Police rushed at them, driving them back and back into the crowd which pressed towards them like an oncoming tide. Helpless, they were tossed about as though by the breakers of a stormy sea. Trying to fight their way out and free of the police, many women were badly injured. Mrs Rigby had both wrists severely twisted and her thumbs bent back. Another woman, a Yorkshire journalist, was treated with even greater brutality. Small and delicate-looking, she was almost torn in pieces when the women tried to rescue her from the police. Like a hare among a pack of hounds, she was barely alive on arrival at Vine Street Police Station.

Suddenly a police inspector blew his whistle: 'Arrest them all!' he commanded. The four hundred policemen called out for the occasion rounded up the women like cattle. Before going into Court for their trial they were warned to expect six weeks' solitary confinement. 'We refused to believe it,' Grace told me, 'we thought they were trying to frighten us. But we had a nasty surprise when it proved to be true. Mrs Rigby got a month in the third division – she was an old lag by now!' Grace heard 'her' policeman remark angrily: 'These sentences are a damned disgrace to the country!'

Being in the third division meant that Aunt Edith was separated from her companions and treated as a criminal, dressed in a kind of sack with sleeves, and fed on skilly. She must have made a good impression, however, because in a week's time she was promoted to the green dress of the second division.

She never spoke to me of her prison experiences – perhaps because my mother was appalled by the thought. A mention of that period in my aunt's life, and Mother's face would become blank, as though a blind had suddenly been drawn down. It was Grace who explained to me that the worst part of imprisonment was not the bad food, hard beds, lack of air and exercise; not even the loneliness, but the fact of being locked up like a dog in a kennel. She couldn't bring herself to go through it again.

'I can never forget the noise of the cell doors banging,' Grace said, 'all along the ground floor, all along the middle floor (mine) and then all along the top floor – for meals, visits by Matron, Governor, Medical Officer, and the magistrates who were all men in those days. I thought I should go mad!' She went on to describe her exercises in the cell: 'Four paces forward, four paces back, five if you went diagonally. And all the time the sound of the prisoner above doing the same thing. I took to pacing in my stocking-feet to spare the one below.' Everyone was delighted when Mrs Rigby joined the company. 'Though we weren't allowed to speak, her calmness was reassuring. And we could sneak a few words at exercise time in the yard. We were made to walk single-file, in silence, on flagstone tracks. At half-time the wardress shouted "Reverse!"; that was our chance for two words.'

Aunt Edith and Grace, being unable to knit, were made to sew mail-bags. Fortunately my aunt's reflective nature helped her to benefit even from this experience. She admired the pigeons flying like shuttles in front of the tiny windows; for her, at least, they carried green leaves of promise. And the Governor's white cat, glimpsed along the corridors, was another source of delight.

After a fortnight had gone by Mrs Towler became extremely agitated thinking of her family who, by now, would have eaten every crumb of her baking. So great was her distress that Mrs Pethick-Lawrence was asked to bail her out. This done, she fled home to Preston and put her oven on.

Aunt Edith, who was the next one to be released, waited in London to welcome the other two. After their previous failure to storm the House of Commons, she determined that all three should now see over it in an orthodox manner. To this end she arranged for the first Labour member for Preston to escort them. All went smoothly until, by a strange chance, they ran into Harold Cox, the Liberal member. Aunt Edith, having already skirmished with him at home, smiled graciously and introduced him to Beth and Grace; 'We've just come out of Holloway!' she announced with pride. Mr Cox, bewildered at the sight of these haggard, unkempt ex-prisoners who, in truth, resembled hospital cases, swallowed, nodded his head, and bolted.

Undeterred, they enjoyed the tea to which Mr McPherson, the Labour member, thoughtfully invited them. 'We were terribly hungry,' Grace told me, 'and the plate of tea-cakes was replenished three times! I hope the poor man was able to afford it, because MPs weren't paid in those days.'

The holiday was still on. Next day Aunt Edith took them to see *Hobson's Choice*, a singularly appropriate choice after their recent experience. And finally, as a last treat before returning home, she entertained them to a Prisoners' Release lunch party at which she instructed Beth to answer questions in her broadest Lancashire.

Home again was by no means rest again. But this time the prisoners were received with enthusiasm, even with pride, so that Aunt Edith was prompted to write to the local paper:

A year ago, February, 1907, three of us from our native town of Preston – unprogressive and self-sufficient Preston – decided to go to prison and thus arouse our town to interest in our movement. Now, in March, 1908, we have a large and crowded suffrage demonstration to welcome four of us released prisoners.

I am one of thousands of women who are glad to have taken a part in this movement, who have found that they have gained more than they gave – as is ever the case when serving a noble cause in true chivalry.

Could other women know how wonderful it has been to meet local and national workers, to feel the comradeship . . . which women from the North have given to those from the South, and have received again; which women who have what is idly called 'worldly advantage' have given to others with sadly limited chances, and have received again.

The power of working together for the development of womanhood, and thus of motherhood, and of humanity, revealed through our movement . . . is not this prophetic of the great spiritual strength inherent in our race when women are no longer in subjection?

Do not these things repay one a thousandfold for the painful publicity and personal suffering?

Edith Rigby

This letter embodies the ideals of Mrs Despard with whom, as I have already indicated, my aunt had much in common. These two were fighting more than a practical battle; they had a vision of a juster world where men and women worked together towards a common good.

When Mrs Despard (a devout Roman Catholic) stayed at No. 28 my aunt discovered her to be a woman of great charm, as well as a deep thinker. Tolerant and broad-minded, she looked on religion and science as separate ladders pointing to the same truth. As for politics, she felt they could not properly be divorced from religion. 'Everywhere,' she wrote, 'we have the same principles: man, woman; mother, father. It is only when we reach the sphere of what is called politics that woman disppears altogether and the man is seen dominating alone.'[1]

Eventually she left the W.S.P.U. to lead the democratic Women's Freedom League while Aunt Edith, though agreeing with her principles, remained loyal to the Pankhursts. For one thing, the Preston branch of the W.S.P.U. was flourishing and putting forth new leaves every day.

Looking back over sixty years there is something comic, and yet moving, about these Housewives of England, newly emerged from the mob-cap chrysalis, banding themselves together to fight for their rights. Probably all suffragettes were concerned, not merely with getting the vote, but with raising the status of women in every field. And for this purpose a vote was essential. It was because Aunt Edith involved herself in the social and human problems of her own group, apart from political aims, that membership and funds steadily increased from the day it began. With all her 'Brook Street' fervour she arranged parties, discussions and recitals.

Three very gifted sisters, Patti, Sissy and Amy Mayor, helped with entertainments. For example, when my aunt engaged Henriquetta Creighton, the Spanish prima donna from the Carl Rosa Opera Company, to sing at a concert, Sissy, an understudy for the company, also sang, while Patti danced and Amy, a concert pianist, accompanied.

It was through her interest in their mother that my aunt 'discovered' these talented sisters. Mrs Mayor had originally been employed as nursery governess by a wealthy family in Winckley Square. Though her employers had not been unduly harsh, only exacting from her what was usual at the time, the young Agnes (as she was called) had worked long, hard hours. An idea of her working-day, which had so enraged my aunt, may be given by an advertisement which appeared in 1862 and was later quoted by Lord Kilmuir when unveiling a memorial to Christabel Pankhurst:

> 'Wanted, a young lady who has had the advantages for a situation as governess. To sleep in a room with four beds, for herself, four children and a maid. To give the children baths, dress them and be ready for breakfast at a quarter to eight. School 9-12 and half past two to four, with two hours music lessons in addition. To spend her evenings in needlework for her mistress. To have the baby on her knee while teaching, and to put all the children to bed. Salary £10 a year, and to pay her own washing.'

From this soul-crushing existence Agnes was eventually rescued by marriage. My aunt, hearing of her experiences, went out of her way to help her and to encourage her daughters.

Patti, who was the same age as Aunt Edith, became a well-known artist

1 *Woman in the New Era*, by C. Despard.

whose pictures were often exhibited. When I met her some years ago (in her ninety-first year) she told me how she had once painted Annie Kenney, against a flaming sunrise: 'She was that sort of person. And I'd have liked to paint your aunt,' she added, relapsing into silence. As I got up she roused herself to ask: 'Did you know she was very beautiful? I can see her now, standing on the edge of the baths, arms raised, ready to dive. She looked like a goddess. And she could swim like a fish under water; we used to throw in pennies for her.'

One of Patti's pictures, *Portrait of a Half-Timer*, so caught my aunt's imagination that she suggested having it reproduced for Preston's W.S.P.U. banner. This was the banner soon to be carried in the biggest of all the women's processions in Hyde Park.

My aunt had a happy flair for scenting out gifted people and encouraging them to their own, and everyone else's, benefit. For instance, in spite of fundamental differences, she saluted Mother's musical talent and introduced her to Amy Mayor. Before long these two were playing together at concerts.

Perhaps here I should say something about Mother, who repre-sented the world Aunt Edith opposed, and to whom, so far, I have done less than justice by presenting her in a wholly reactionary light. Admittedly she was High Anglican and Conservative (how astonished she would have been at any hint of deprecation!) and to cross the threshold into Aunt Edith's world would never have occurred to her as in any way desirable. Yet she did the usual 'good works' – Child Welfare, League of Pity, N.S.P.C.C. and so on, out of a genuine compassion for those who were deprived and handicapped. But always I was aware of a barrier between 'them' and 'us'. Perhaps she was afraid, in the way the 'haves' are so often afraid, of being challenged by the sheer weight and numbers of less-privileged people. And though she was kind, even tender-hearted, she would not allow herself, for instance, to be lenient with the maids. 'Give them an inch,' she would say, 'and they'll take an ell!' Whereas in Aunt Edith's household there was no question of division.

In common with our neighbours, and in keeping with the times, Mother lived by the 'silver standard'. No silver candlesticks, tea service, or trays could have shone more brightly. While through the mists of youth I dimly remember that Aunt Edith's equivalents were of pewter, brass or wood.

All the same, Mother was extremely thrifty. With true Lancashire economy, she'd never buy a pound of sausages if three-quarters would do. One of my earliest errands was to buy half a pound of Blue Band margarine because it was a penny cheaper than some other make and would, at a pinch, pass for butter.

She was the sort of person who could dress herself on almost nothing, contriving with odds and ends and bargains to appear the prettiest woman in the room. I was immensely proud of her beauty, especially when she came to visit us at school. Her shining fair hair, fairer than Aunt Edith's, and wild-rose complexion provoked comment everywhere.

For two seasons before her marriage Mother had played with the Hallé Orchestra under the direction of Sir Hamilton Harty. Occasionally she played in Arthur Catterall's String Quartet and at one time belonged to the Brodsky String Quartet. Had she not married, she would certainly have become a professional violinist. And had she only realized it, the world Aunt Edith and the suffragettes were fighting for would have welcomed a married woman who also followed a profession.

In those days when many people played an instrument of some sort, 'house quartets' and local orchestras were common enough. From earliest childhood I was accustomed to hearing such music – pleasant, inconsequential, ordinary. My father disliked the sound of Mother's violin practice; either it irritated him or disturbed his patients. So she never played in our house. Until one day, some years later, in a fit of gaiety (he must have been away) she took out her violin and treated me to a solo.

I think it was a dashing fragment of Tartini she gave me – something brilliant and gay. I can never forget it. The gooseflesh streaked up my spine as I listened. This was different. This was music, light and quivering as butterflies, yet balanced and strong. Poised, flickering in sunlight on a top note. Then dashing down steps to a deep, dark, swollen well. There it lay, pulsating in darkness, before twitching awake and leaping up a ladder of air . . . And Mother looked happy and alive as the music poured through her. Indeed, she used to say that anyone who'd never played in a great orchestra had never really lived.

She was every inch an artist, with her curving-back thumbs and fine sensitivity. What a pity the two opposites – she and Aunt Edith – were not quite opposite enough to meet! If there *is* a heaven beyond this heaven-and-hell, I'm certain there must be a circle of dancing-grass where they have already met. With her practical, as well as musical, abilities Mother would have been invaluable to the W.S.P.U.!

In common with all suffragettes, Aunt Edith regarded the replacement of the Prime Minister, who was friendly towards them, by the hostile Mr Asquith as a disaster. In spite of further suffragette victories at by-elections in Peckham and North West Manchester, and the favourable turn of the public tide, he demanded proof that the majority of women were behind the movement. Not even the request of sixty Liberal members for facilities for a Woman Suffrage Bill convinced him. All his subsequent hedgings and hintings were preludes to refusal. Nothing was ever to convince him. Even the biggest and boldest demonstration of the whole campaign – arranged by the Pethick-Lawrences – left him indifferent. For this occasion militants and non-militants flocked together in Hyde Park. Under the aegis of the W.S.P.U. alone seven processions emerged. Bands played in the sunlight; banners of purple, green and white fluttered in the wind. Here it was that Patti's *Portrait of a Half-Timer*, inscribed with the words: 'Preston Lassies Mun Hev the Vote!' was flown by the Preston group. On this proud occasion Bernard Shaw, who favoured women's suffrage, complimented Patti on her portrait, and walked some of the way beside her in the procession.

As for the Prime Minister, his answer to this 'great cloud of witnesses' was merely: 'I have nothing to add.'

Further demonstrations were held in the north. In Preston Aunt Edith worked without respite, holding meetings indoors and out, exploring every new possibility. With the co-operation of fellow-members she drafted a petition to be signed by all women ratepayers in the town. This entailed weeks of trudging up and down streets, knocking on door after door, and endless explaining in order to collect signatures.

Eventually the petition was presented to the Corporation, and only five men voted against it after Dr John Rigg's summing-up: 'This is a constitutional method. If we refuse we are driving them to militancy.' He, at least, had learned something from his conversation with Grace.

Cabinet ministers, unhappily, were not so easily converted. After the opening of Parliament in October (1908) with the true-to-form silence on the subject of women's franchise, a large gathering was held in Trafalgar Square. Here it was that a leaflet, *Help the women to rush the House of Commons*, was scattered among the crowd whose fringes hid no other than Lloyd George. It was the ominous word 'rush' which alarmed the Government and resulted in the arrests of Mrs Pankhurst, Christabel, and 'General' Drummond.[1]

Lloyd George, called in as an unwilling witness at their trial, was thoroughly trounced by Christabel. And when Mrs Pankhurst asked if he did not think these disturbances would stop if women were given the vote, he replied: 'I should think that is very likely.' While they were still in prison he addressed an Albert Hall meeting on the question of women's suffrage. But instead of coming to the point he retreated into govern- mental wool of 'ifs' and 'buts'. Whereupon he was not merely heckled, but severely hen-pecked. Ruffled as a beaten bantam-cock, he retired. And from this moment he refused to allow women into his meetings.

I report this incident because Lloyd George's decision – to be taken up by other ministers in other places – was destined to penalize many suffragettes, my aunt not least of them.

1 *Unshackled*, by Christabel Pankhurst.

V

*Hunger strike begins. Lady Constance and a dinner party.
Churchill meeting in Preston, 1909. In Walton Gaol.
Population census. Black puddings for J.H. Thomas.
The Derby statue. Burning of Rivington bungalow.*

THE following year Uncle Charlie was invited by be my godfather.
Perhaps my parents hoped that Aunt Edith would be absent from
the ceremony (she was actually in gaol when the date was fixed)
because by now she had begun in earnest to be an uncomfortable relation.
Two aunts from my mother's side had consented as godmothers
to assist Uncle Charlie in protecting me from 'the devil and all his wicked
works'.

All the same, to Aunt Edith's way of looking, baptism was significant as
'a means of grace and a hope of glory' and meant more to her than to most
godmothers. As it happened, she was released in time to be present, and I
like to think that she stood near me, an 'off-the-recording' angel. No doubt
she enjoyed the christening cake and half a glass of champagne (especially
after prison fare) because she entered into everything in her temperate
manner.

Although there were no frills in her life, she managed to have a great
deal of fun (a word she would not have used) from her many causes and
enthusiasms. At this moment she gladly joined the W.S.P.U. campaign of
pestering ministers. When, for instance, Mr Haldane, the Secretary for War,
travelled from Euston to Preston, there she was on the platform to greet
him: 'Will you give women the vote? Will you? Will you?' I can imagine him
brushing her aside and telling her to put that question to the Prime
Minister – an enraging piece of advice for a suffragette who was already
attempting this very thing.

In the intervals between taking meetings and breaking into them she
frequently travelled to headquarters in London where the storm was
gathering force because Mr Asquith would neither listen to questions nor
receive deputations. And along with other suffragettes she chained herself
to railings in Downing Street – all to no effect because the Votes For
Women Bill failed to come to a second reading. It was an artist, Miss
Wallace Dunlop, who made some headway by stencilling on the walls of St
Stephen's Hall these words: *It is the right of the subject to petition the king, and
all commitments and prosecutions for such petitioning are illegal.*[1]

After being charged with wilful damage Miss Dunlop refused to pay a

1   *Unshackled*, by Christabel Pankhurst.

fine and was sent to Holloway for a month. When her request to be treated as a political offender was refused she fasted for four days and was then released. Meanwhile, she created a new pattern; from now on suffragettes realized that hunger strike was the unspoken order.

Undeterred, they interrupted meetings with even greater determination than before. In Birmingham, for instance, where Mr Asquith was due to speak, two women climbed on a roof, threatened the police with slates, and hurled a brick at the Premier's car. The Government now adopted sterner measures. Avoiding the choice between giving women the vote and letting them starve, they began to feed them by force.[1]

Women were barricaded from Lloyd George's meeting in Newcastle, a performance to be repeated when Churchill came to Preston in December 1909. Some time between these two meetings Aunt Edith invited to No. 28 two women who had been imprisoned at Newcastle and released without being forcibly fed. There were Lady Constance Lytton and Mrs H.N. Brailsford, wife of the journalist. There was an outcry among the suffragettes against preferential treatment for the privileged; not for one moment did they believe the medical report which alleged ill health.

My father wrote a stinging letter to the paper in defence of medical integrity, while my aunt was set on discovering the truth for herself. She agreed with Lady Constance, who had been absolved on account of a heart disorder, that the authorities would not have cared a fig for the heart of a working woman.

With this in mind Lady Constance disguised herself as a char-woman, called herself Jane Warton, and travelled to Liverpool in order to protest against the forcible feeding of three women in Walton Gaol. After no more than shouting her protest and throwing a few stones in the Governor's garden, she was arrested and imprisoned. And she was proved right – nobody bothered about Jane Warton's heart.

For four days she was forcibly fed and suffered grievously on account of her condition, till one of the doctors became anxious. Meanwhile, her sister, Lady Emily Lutyens, appeared at the prison gates and demanded Lady Constance's release. When the prisoner's identity was revealed there was a rare flutter in the national dovecotes. Already Lady Constance's health had been seriously undermined. As far ahead as 1911, when she agreed to speak at the Preston Guildhall, she was unfit to face a large audience. Knowing this, Aunt Edith thoughtfully suggested a small meeting in the Mayor's Parlour, and welcomed her to No. 28 by arranging a dinner-party of suffragettes to meet her. As usual on such occasions, the

1 *Ibid.*

hostess and her guests wore the ceremonial long white dresses and white corded ribbons edged with purple and green. Except for the 'Votes for Women' slogan in large black letters across the front, Mrs. Rigby, with her shining hair and deep blue eyes, might have been playing the part of Demeter. At least some goddess of the grape-harvest was suggested by the white robe and suffragette colours – purple for loyalty, green for hope and white for purity – of which my aunt wholly approved.

During the course of dinner Lady Constance read out part of a letter from her brother, the Hon. Neville Lytton, which raised hopes of the Conciliation Bill being passed on its second reading. This jubilation, however, was soon to be dashed by heavy governmental waves which totally wrecked the Bill.

To return to November 1909. After the release of Lady Constance from prison, my aunt was immersed in arrangements for the impending visit of Winston Churchill to Preston. At the same time civic precautions on a giant scale were being made to keep all women out of his meeting, arranged for December 3rd in the Public Hall. Down the length of Fox Street, Fleet Street and Wharf Street, barricades, like the walls of Troy, rose to music – at least, they rose to the tune of ten thousand pounds supplied by ratepayers. Had Churchill's V sign originated in 'Votes for Women' all would have been well!

But all was very far from well. The battle in progress was between Men in Authority – on the Town Council, in the police force and in politics – and women alone. While the women's headquarters were the W.S.P.U. rooms in Glover's Court, their camp was the ever-accommodating No. 28 Winckley Square. Already entrenched were Mrs Brailsford, Mrs Massie, an organizer from Kensington, and Miss Margaret Hewitt, a national organizer. All three were eager to support Mrs Rigby and her followers in gate-crashing Churchill's meeting.

There was much work to be done in arousing public sympathy or, often enough, antipathy. With Mrs Massie's help Aunt Edith stuck 'Votes for Women' posters in prominent places such as the Reform Club and the Public Hall, which already spoke for itself through boarded windows and covered skylights. So impressive were these fortifications that people drove in from surrounding villages to gape at them.

Against this Goliath Man-in-Authority the suffragettes resorted to the tactics of David. From outside the Public Hall and other important buildings stones were flung which produced the satisfactory crack-and-tinkle of glass. From inside the G.P.O. David, in the form of Mrs Massie, removed a stone from a sling of brown paper. It whistled through a window with truly shattering results!

But not till Wednesday, December 1st, was the suffragette campaign opened in earnest with a meeting in Market Street addressed by Margaret Hewitt. Daringly modern, she wore a jaunty hat and a trace of lipstick, and was in no way deterred by the hail of dirt and abuse which greeted her reference to a mass meeting of suffragettes to be held outside the Public Hall on Churchill Night.

The next day Aunt Edith enlisted the help of Beth to stick more posters alluding to Mr Asquith as Mr Double-Face. But, alas, the sticking-paste proved ineffective; probably they had neglected to use boiling water for their mixture. Frustrated, they retired to No. 28 to reconsider the matter. After a few moments' silence a slow smile lit Aunt Edith's face as she turned to Beth: 'We must each carry a potato in our pockets,' she decided, 'with our message attached. Then, if we're arrested tomorrow, we can fling them through a window in protest!'

This impish delight in schoolgirl tricks ran curiously parallel with high-mindedness, and saved my aunt from coming anywhere near being a prig. Another favourite activity, in keeping with her love of play-acting, was her passion for dressing up, which she practised upon every possible occasion. In fact, the next morning, the Friday of the Churchill meeting, came another opportunity.

With the idea of discovering a way into the meeting, she attired herself as a shrimp-woman wearing the traditional cotton sunbonnet, print dress and apron. Bonnet and dress were of pale lilac, as though faded by sea air, and she wore a woollen shawl pinned across her chest. Carrying a shrimp-basket, she sallied forth to the butter-market which adjoined the Public Hall.

Chatting with stall-holders and customers, she looked more the part – from lilac bonnet to black boots – than the owners themselves. At least she succeeded during the afternoon in getting into one of the crush-rooms of the hall where a minor meeting was in progress. But I suspect the whole scheme was partly an excuse for dressing up and mingling with the market-women. On another occasion she went out with Beth, long after midnight, with the intention of cutting certain telegraph wires. For this purpose they adopted the unexpected guise of midwives, the last people, one would have thought, to cut their own means of communication.

But to return to the evening of the Churchill meeting. When it grew dusk no fewer than a hundred and fifty police were parading the streets and guarding the doors outside the Public Hall. A huge, hostile crowd was huddled alongside the barriers. Eventually the men, like sheep, were let through; the women were barred. Resenting this, some of them butted the suffragettes who were the cause of such a division. 'They pelted us with horse-droppings,' Beth told me, 'and became so rough and noisy that the police raised one of the barriers to let us through for protection. Some of us went up Fox Street to the next barrier. I climbed on top of this one and began to address the crowd in my loudest voice.'

Almost immediately the police hauled her down and bundled her into the waiting Black Maria. Whereupon Aunt Edith leapt up into her place. Her speech from the top: 'We are here to stay!' was even shorter than Beth's. She too found herself in the van, soon to be joined by Mrs Massie and Mrs Worthington, another member of the W.S.P.U. The four women were trotted briskly to the police station.

Aunt Edith and Beth held their potatoes in readiness. After they had been charged with resisting and obstructing the police Beth slyly put her hand into her pocket. 'Shall I?' she whispered. A policeman grabbed her hand and the potato: 'No you don't! We've just had that clock mended.'

Before being allowed home they were thoroughly searched. Two potatoes confronted them on the Bench next morning.

While they were being questioned at the police station a riot – mob-fighting and shop-window breaking – was going on in the town. Indeed, at this moment the boot-shop of Mr Pass (already mentioned as the husband of a W.S.P.U. member) was being raided. His daughter escaped from the crowd into the arms of the police who also came to the rescue of other suffragettes. Several women were pulled about like so many lengths of rope and Mrs Tuson was driven to seek refuge in the house of a parson. For the police that night many issues must have been confused!

Next day Mrs Massie was fined two pounds or given a month's imprisonment. The others had the choice of a fine or a week in prison which, with the exception of Mrs Worthington, they preferred. Mrs Rigby, when invited to make a statement, declared: 'English women refuse to be taxed without representation!'

This time, however, she didn't get her own way. My grandfather, gravely concerned lest his daughter should be imprisoned in the local gaol, called on my father, who agreed that her fine must be paid. Her presence in Preston gaol, where she had so recently been a visitor, would have been too embarrassing. Accordingly they set out for the police station and my grandfather paid the required five shillings.

'And mighty indignant Mrs Rigby was at having her fine paid!' Beth commented. 'She said they'd no right to do it without her consent. Anyway, she went out, really angry, to plan some further damage.'

Not only angry, she was disturbed because Beth, whom she had persuaded into the movement, would be sent to prison, which now meant hunger-striking and forcible feeding while she herself went free.

Her concern was justified. Beth was made so ill by the forcible feeding that when the doctor ordered her release the authorities dared not risk her being seen by the crowd waiting at the gates. She was sneaked out of prison in the dark of an early morning.

If Aunt Edith was 'mighty indignant' at having her fine paid, my father and grandfather were 'mighty upset' at her goings-on in their midst. The ladies of Winckley Square looked away at her approach while pitying 'poor Doctor Charles'. As for my grandfather, he believed that she was a pawn in the hands of W.S.P.U. organizers. And my father, remembering Miss Hewitt's lipstick, complained bitterly to a news-reporter: 'It's that little painted Jezebel who has led my sister astray!'

At that very moment his sister was planning her revenge for the unauthorized payment of her fine by taking a train to Waterloo (Liverpool) where Churchill was due to speak that evening, Saturday, 4th December.

By nine o'clock she was to be seen standing on a chair outside the police station in Church Road. After she had addressed the crowd a policeman lurking in the shadows observed her get down from the chair, walk over to the police station and throw a white object at one of the windows. And then, because the window remained intact, she ran up to it and smashed it with her fist. Immediately the watchful policeman arrested her. After being charged with wilful damage, her case was tried at Islington Police Court the following Monday. (The 'white object', by the way, was proved to have been nothing more formidable than a handkerchief filled with coppers.)

She began her term of fourteen days in Walton Gaol by refusing food and drink. On the fifth day, when threatened with forcible feeding, she replied: 'When we are treated as political prisoners hunger-striking will cease. And when we are given the vote there'll be an end to disorderly behaviour.'

Hunger-strikers who resisted forcible feeding were usually held down by four wardresses while a doctor put a gag in the prisoner's mouth and inserted a tube down her throat. Then a fifth wardress would rapidly pour in liquid. My mother, her disapproval overcome by curiosity, once asked Aunt Edith how they had treated her.

On this occasion, it seemed, she had been made to sit on a high-backed wooden chair; then she was wrapped like a mummy in a blanket which enclosed her in the chairback – a far simpler method. After tilting the chair backwards, the doctor inserted a tube up her nose while a wardress poured in beef tea.

Not only the victims but the doctors revolted against the treatment. Letters appeared in the Press and a note to *The Times* pronounced the Government's definition of forcible feeding as 'hospital treatment' to be 'a foul libel . . . Violence and brutality', it continued, 'have no place in hospital treatment.'

The following item appeared in the *Preston Guardian* in February 1910:

Mrs Rigby, whose sentence of fourteen days' imprisonment in connection with Mr. Churchill's visit to Waterloo expired on Monday December 20th, was released on Saturday the 18th. She fasted for five days, after which she was forcibly fed. She notes that the result is to harden the throat and make the passage of the tube more difficult while the bodily distress is great.[1]

The Governor, Matron, and doctor tried to weaken her resolution by telling her that the forcible feeding case had gone against Mrs Leigh[2] and that the hunger-strike was at an end. There was a pause for a few seconds while Mrs Rigby says she felt as if the ground were slipping from under her feet. Then she answered: 'In our opinion the judges of the law are wrong.'

There is a saying that a woman will do anything for a man but nothing for a cause. That belief has now been pretty thoroughly exploded – voluntarily, for a cause. The most delicately nurtured women have endured discomforts, trials, and pains which few men would care to undergo.

On the day of Aunt Edith's trial Mrs Alderman, Grace's mother, appealed at Preston Police Court against the imprisoning of suffragettes in the third division. 'If they are given the option of a fine,' she rightly objected, 'they should never be put lower than the second division.' The magistrate's clerk merely repeated the orders of the Government. 'Then my friends are treated as common criminals?' she asked. 'That is so,' he replied coldly, 'intentionally so.'

By no means all suffragettes were able to face imprisonment; some of them after a few days found it more than they could endure. In such cases the bailer-out-in-chief was Mr Pethick-Lawrence who, with his wife, was unfailingly generous of money, time and trouble. On more than one occasion these two were the guests of Aunt Edith. Whenever either of them had to address a local meeting they made use of her ever-open door.

Christabel, Sylvia and their mother were also included among her distinguished suffragette visitors. My father was both amazed and disapproving of such hospitality. What was she doing, for instance, inviting George Lansbury, Victor Grayson and Mrs Ramsay MacDonald and her children to stay at her house?

The answer was, in the main, discussing the next move to irritate the Government. At this particular point in 1910 the suffragettes registered a strong reaction to the population census which was to take place the following year. A steep decline in the female population must have been subsequently recorded, because all the members of the W.S.P.U. refused to fill in the forms. 'We count for nothing in the eyes of the law,' they argued, 'so why be counted?' Many small battles were waged on this score. To give one example, the official who called on Mrs Alderman and Grace was extremely put out when they handed him a form bearing only the names of their two male lodgers. Householder was there none. He

1 Probably the reason why she was fed through the nose.
2 Mary Leigh, a well-known London member of the W.S.P.U.

started to bluster and warned the two women that they were liable for a fine of five pounds. Grace laughed at him. 'Why,' she exclaimed, 'we're only females! What d'you want with *our* names?' Before the man could reply she told him to be off, calling after him: 'Anyway, we'll have our five pounds' worth of fun!' No more was heard of the matter.

Most of the other Preston members arranged to be away from home that day, while those who remained met for a social evening at a tailor's workroom. By dint of songs and cups of tea they managed to stay awake and away from home all night.

Meanwhile, membership was still growing, apart from many new sympathizers who dared not join the militants for fear of their husbands' displeasure or, perhaps, in dread of being sent to gaol. Prison seemed to hold no terrors for Aunt Edith. Indeed, at this period her visits there were so frequent that she felt it only right to hand over the reins of secretaryship to a woman with other ambitions.

Her place was taken by Miss Bamber, science teacher at the Convent School in Winckley Square, who, at one of the first meetings of the new committee, announced that she had no need to go to prison for the W.S.P.U. Her work (in school, one presumes) she considered to be sufficient sacrifice.

Before long, however, she was to make an even greater sacrifice by marrying a Mr Bowtell. But she had no intention of relinquishing her maiden name and announced that she wished to be known as Mrs Bamber-Bowtell. She began a fashion for double-barrelled names – another woman's protest against losing her own identity along with her surname and sometimes, also, her independence and job.

Aunt Edith, who revered Christian names, was always known as Mrs Edith Rigby. Why should a woman wait for widowhood, she asked, before having her own name fully restored to her?

Being a suffragette revealed another facet of her character, a sort of puckish streak which seemed strangely at variance with the Christian idealist. Perhaps her private censor released some latent power to work – even havoc – in a new cause. And every new cause she took up with her whole heart; half-measures and compromise were not for her. Nor did she feel the need to confide in anyone unless she required an accomplice for such ventures as cutting telegraph wires. Quietly, with her slow, inward smile, she got on with the job.

During the next few years her capacity for escapade seemed boundless, but a clash with Mr J.H. Thomas, the Labour MP, led to an unexpected episode. Already set against him because he opposed the suffragettes – at least, until the return of a Labour Government he would not consider giving women the vote – his disagreeable manners still further inflamed her.

Therefore when she set forth to hear him speak at the Free Trade Hall,

Manchester, on Easter Monday, 1913, Beth, who accompanied her, must have guessed at some dark purpose behind this trip. And the purpose proved to be even darker than she imagined because Aunt Edith went not to hear Mr Thomas's words. After listening for some minutes to what she considered his offensive remarks, she could contain herself no longer. Suddenly she stood up, put her hands in her pockets, and pelted him with black puddings. This debt of honour discharged, she turned away in disgust and left the hall which by now was in an uproar.

Speechless with laughter, Beth followed her as she elbowed her way through the half-cheering, half-jeering crowd. 'Heaven knows how she managed to produce black puddings on Easter Monday,' Beth exclaimed, laughing at the recollection, 'because she never went near the shops on Saturday. She must have got them on the Thursday before Good Friday, so they couldn't have been too fresh.' 'But,' Mrs Higginson shrewdly remarked, 'they were more derogatory than tomatoes and eggs.'

Not to be outdone by her companion, Beth, this same day, broke into the I.L.P. Conference which was being held in the Y.M.C.A. rooms in Peter Street. These rooms belonged to a one-time pub, so that the doors were fitted with the usual brass handles. Beth, who had come prepared for action, produced a padlock and chain from under her coat; she wound the chain around those accommodating handles before locking the men inside and shouting: 'Locked like rats in your own trap!' Little did she know that this door was their only exit.

No wonder both she and Aunt Edith had been expelled from the I.L.P. for similar tricks after the Easter Monday activities in 1907. These two preferred to bait politicians rather than roll hard-boiled eggs down grassy slopes – an old north-country custom practised on that day.

While I could understand the fanatical zeal which led my aunt to burn down Lord Leverhulme's bungalow and to put a bomb in the Liverpool Cotton Exchange, I was astounded to hear of her throwing black puddings at an MP. And in a public hall at that! Indeed, more than once I have been obliged to revise my original portrait of her by adding scarlet streaks to the 'spiritual' blues and lavenders.

But of one thing she was wrongly accused. Contrary to 'kitchen- gossip' she did *not* tar the statue of Lord Derby in Miller Park, though admittedly she made the necessary arrangements. This act of defiance followed the defeat of Mr Dickinson's Women's Franchise Bill and a triumphant leader on the subject in the *Lancashire Daily Post* (May 7, 1913). In the same edition a headlined column announced Mr Asquith's strong opposition to the Bill, while Sir John Compton Ricketts, the Liberal member, was reported as saying that women in Parliament could be of no benefit to the community. All this was more than my aunt could endure.

At the same time her Labour sympathies were strengthened by Philip Snowden's reply to Sir John: 'All this talk about the mental inferiority of women is nothing but colossal conceit on the part of men. I am not appalled,' he went on, 'by the prospect of the country being governed by them'.

From now on, Aunt Edith determined, this 'colossal conceit' should suffer reverses at her own hands and in her own town.

So it happened that on the following Sunday morning, May 11th, the ladies of the town, parading in Miller Park as usual after matins, were confounded by the sight of huge crowds gathered around the familiar figure of the fourteenth Lord Derby, now sadly bespattered with tar and looking remarkably like a well-spotted Dalmatian.

According to the *Lancashire Daily Post* the statue was 'defaced by a gross act of vandalism . . . Someone', the report continued, 'has spattered the body of the statue with some black viscous fluid resembling diluted tar which has blackened the trunk, arms, and legs, and splashed the polished granite base . . . It was suggested that a syringe had been used by someone not tall enough to spray the head. This fact, coupled with the small footprints in the grass, indicated – not surprisingly – that the culprit was a woman, or two women'.

At six o'clock that same Sunday morning a ranger walking through the park had observed something white fluttering from a nearby rose tree. (Later this was found to be a luggage label pasted with a newspaper-cutting: *Will the Government yield to force?*)

An hour after this a certain Mr Dewhurst was gazing appalled at the woebegone statue. Immediately he raised the alarm, and reading back it appears that the Mayor and entire Corporation were raised from their beds. At any rate, the Town Clerk, the Chief Constable, the Borough Surveyor and many other officials hurried to the scene of outrage. News of it spread like a bush-fire until hundreds of people flocked into Miller Park to gape at this figure of tragi-comedy.

Was not this the Stanley who, as prospective Tory candidate for Preston, had declared that he did not want 'fustian' to vote for him? And when 'fustian' took him at his word and he was not returned, removed himself and his family to Knowsley Hall as a token of noble contempt for the 'lower element' in Preston?

Although Aunt Edith was not one to rejoice even in the fall of the mighty, she must have felt a certain justice in this reply. And she rejoiced openly to read in the newspapers that after fruitless attempts to remove the tar-stains 'it was considered advisable to cover the figure with a white canvas sheet, pending further efforts'.

To her entire satisfaction these further efforts expended on 'less conspicuous parts of the figure' all resulted in failure and at a cost of two hundred pounds. It was left to time and the rains to wash away the black marks from this Stanley whose ancestor had called postmen bloodsuckers and blackmailers for demanding a rise in wages from eighteen shillings to one pound a week.

Fortunately for the Corporation's pocket, the reward of fifty pounds offered for news of the miscreant was never claimed. The suffragettes were able to keep secrets. In later years, after the affair had blown over, my aunt, whose idea it was, took the blame. Only two months after this episode she burned down the wooden bungalow of Sir William Lever (later Lord Leverhulme). This was his 'pleasure-house' high up on the slopes of Rivington Pike, and surrounded by exotic gardens in which grew almost every known variety of conifer and flowering shrub from Japan to the far West. Terraces, fountains, rock-gardens and lawns responded to Sir William's midas-touch, while on the lower slopes grazed wild animals such as llamas, kangaroos and deer.

My aunt thought this sort of thing should happen only in the dream-life of a Kubla Khan. Yet in fact solid as gold this Soap King of Port Sunlight had almost achieved Xanadu in his 'gardens bright with sinuous rills,/Where blossomed many an incense-bearing tree'.

Although, ironically, he was personally in favour of women's suffrage, he was also a Liberal lord in every sense of the word and therefore an obvious bull's-eye which my aunt, only fourteen miles away, could not resist. As Johnny Miller, Rivington's oldest inhabitant, once observed to me – for we were neighbours on the flanks of the Pike – 'Aye, it wer Mrs Rigby 'oo burned down 'is first bungalow'. And then, lowering his voice so as not to hurt my feelings: 'She wer a bit of an eccentric, yer aunt, but she made a proper job o' it. Wi mi own eyes I saw it blazing away brighter 'n Bonfire Night!' Johnny shook his head and smiled: ' 'e took care ter build t'next one o'stone!'

This upland retreat reflected Lord Leverhulme's originality and his genius for entertainment. Aunt Edith heard of shining cars speeding up the Pike on roads newly laid for the purpose, of dinner-parties, week-end parties and balls. The Prince of Wales himself had visited the bungalow and Lloyd George was a not infrequent guest, a fact which quickened her determination to destroy the place.

With this idea she went one day to Rivington to reconnoitre. It was late May or early June, and the bare hillside seemed to have put on a second snow of blossom. Red deer and fallow deer raised their heads as she passed. While admiring them and the pedigree herd of Shetland ponies – along with the kangaroos and ostriches – she observed that these animal were better housed and fed than many people in the land.

All the same, she paced up and down the road above the bungalow with some misgiving, because she liked to encourage such enterprises as the making of gardens and animal-breeding. And after all, these pleasure-gardens had evolved from a small boy's idea of cutting bars of soap into pieces and selling them (as Sunlight Soap) in acceptable packets – to give only one instance of William Lever's inventive mind.

But in her eyes the bungalow expressed capitalism rather than commercial genius. As such and in protest against the Liberal Government, it must be destroyed.

She lingered on until it grew dark. The gardens with their rock- pools and statues and flights of steps shone under the moon while the music of violins mingled with voices and laughter. It was like a page from a fairytale.

Returning to Preston she decided that a large keg of paraffin would be required for the job. Questions assaulted her like bees storming a foxglove. Where could it be stored without arousing suspicion? How to transport it up the Pike by herself?

The first problem was solved by Albert Yeadon, a member of the I.L.P. who was in sympathy with her aims. Through consulting him she found an ally for her scheme. She was welcome to store as much paraffin as she pleased in his wardrobe. (I got this information from Mrs Yeadon who told me gleefully how a large keg had been smuggled into their house and gradually filled.) Somehow Aunt Edith discovered that the bungalow would be empty on the night of July 7th. She then hit on the idea of being driven over to Rivington – with Albert and the keg of paraffin – by her husband's chauffeur, himself called Charles. After arranging for Albert to call early in the morning of the 7th, in order to stow the paraffin in the back of Uncle Charlie's Humber open tourer, the three of them set off at midday.

On arriving at Rivington my aunt ordered the unsuspecting Charles to stop near the old pub 'The Black Lad' (since pulled down) and gave him a shilling for a pint of beer and a sandwich.

With Charles safely out of sight, she and Albert lifted the keg from the car and between them they carried it uneasily up the steep slopes of the Pike. Just short of the bungalow my aunt stopped and ordered Albert back to the car: 'I must finish this job myself,' she said firmly, 'I can't have you involved any further in our work'.

Reluctantly Albert obeyed. Very soon my aunt was pushing her way through the thick bushes surrounding the gardens. After walking twice round the place to make sure it was empty, she laid and lit her paraffin trail. The weather was fine and dry so that the grass crackled into flame as she brushed it with a match. This done, she ran downhill hoping to reach the car before the damage was apparent.

All had been accomplished within an hour and the waiting Charles (who afterwards became our chauffeur) wondered what she'd been up to. Years later, reminiscing, he told me the whole story. 'She'd such a smile on 'er face as she climbed into the car,' he said, 'an' she seemed mighty pleased with 'erself. I guessed she'd been up to no good!'

After dropping Albert in Preston, Charles was ordered to drive on to the 'Bull and Royal'. 'An' there we stopped,' he went on, 'to pick up a friend of your aunt's – a lady by the name of Pankhurst. I drove them to the station, an' when I got home the missus told me off for being late for dinner!'

In fact, Charles's wife was at that time 'doing' for the Rigbys. Both she and her husband were agreed that they'd never in their whole lives met anyone like Mrs Rigby. 'She wer always dressed so strange and spoke so strange, and,' added the observant Mrs Charles, 'you should 'ave just seen 'ow the ladies o'the Square dodged out of 'er way – it wer comical ter watch!'

Meanwhile, the inhabitants of Rivington were watching something not so comical. The blaze from the wooden bungalow was a rare sight to see from their back gardens. And the spectators experienced that thrill of pleasure so often to be found in the disaster of others. 'I was in the kitchen,' a neighbour told me, 'when my mother shouted, wild with excitement, that the bungalow was whirling up in flames.'

News of the fire reached Sir William Lever as he sat at dinner, the guest of – ironically enough – Lord Derby, who was at the same time entertaining King George the Fifth and Queen Mary during their tour of industrial Lancashire.

Aunt Edith made no attempt to hide herself away; she gave herself up to the police.

All over the country at this time suffragettes were damaging property and burning empty houses. In the Manchester City Art Gallery the glass from several pictures had been smashed, yet during this critical year no single person was injured.

By no means all women sympathized with these methods. In Preston, as elsewhere, there were angry scenes condemning them. For instance, at a meeting in the market square the suffragettes were sworn at, spat at, and bombarded with fish. Cockles and mussels, aimed at faces and eyes, drew blood but not tears. In the midst of this battle a Quaker lady remonstrated with Miss Bailey, a W.S.P.U. member and one of my aunt's admirers. 'You must have patience,' she begged. 'you'll never get what you want this way.'

'What good'll patience do?' Miss Bailey rounded on her. 'Men got the vote by force. Ireland is getting Home Rule by violence. Fifty years of patience have got us nowhere!'

Hardly any of the better-off women, mostly Liberals and Tories, joined the militants, so Miss Bailey informed me. 'And the non- militants, led by Mrs Todd (ex-headmistress of the High School) could never get a meeting; their campaign was too "milk-and-water". As for us, we got grand, full, lively meetings – even if they did break up in disorder now and then! Your father was dead against the suffragettes,' she added, 'he thought his sister had lost her senses.'

The Government replied to such scenes with further arrests and longer sentences of imprisonment. While murder was being committed – and condoned – in connection with the Irish Home Rule dispute, Mrs Pankhurst, for demanding the vote, was tried at the Criminal Court and sentenced to three years' penal servitude. In prison she refused food, yet for some reason she was not forcibly fed.[1] Possibly her dignity and calm protected her from this outrage.

The Home Secretary, Mr McKenna, now knew that the only alternatives to forcible feeding were to let the women die (and they were willing to die) or to give them the vote. Then he hit upon a diabolically bright idea; to release them after as many days' fasting as they could live through, and return them to gaol, when sufficiently recovered, for a further term of starvation. In this way a sentence might drag on for months, even years.

It was under this 'Cat-and-Mouse' Act, as it came to be called, that Aunt Edith was imprisoned after burning the bungalow on Rivington Pike. Once again her loyal husband took up his indignant pen and wrote appealing for justice to the *Lancashire Daily Post*:

> Sir, The re-arrest of Mrs Edith Rigby for the fourth time, as chronicled by you, must be my excuse for troubling you. She has again gone to prison and hunger-striking like a sheep to the slaughter. And this will have to be repeated at least fifty times if her sentence is to be carried out. Mr McKenna must be greatly pleased at this success – one woman to be fifty times without any food for as many days as the conscience of the medical officer will allow . . .
>
> Years ago I wrote in your journal that English women were free women . . . and would not submit to injustice. My words are being borne out by their deeds. They will not tolerate the present conditions. They will have the vote. You may torture them but that does not deter them. You and your party . . . have brought in this Act of Torture.
>
> I wonder if you are satisfied with women being repeatedly brought to the verge of death, then liberated, afterwards brought back to the same torture? Even their gaolers pity them, but they have no power. It is you and your party who are responsible . . .
>
> You may say she is sentenced for an outrage . . . Had women been treated with justice, there would be no outrage . . . You are outraging your principle that taxation and representation should go together . . .
>
> It has been thrown in my teeth that I should have restrained Edith Rigby. How have the powers that be, with all their forces, restrained her? By torture.

1 *Unshackled*, by Christabel Pankhurst.

I have never met a person who does not believe that some women ought to have the vote . . . I could wish that the women would go on household strike and let men be placed as I am. I am told that the State is but a bigger house; it must be managed on the same principles. Take the wife from the home, and I know from practical experience how it works; there is chaos . . . If your wives were taken from your homes for a few weeks you would realize it was time to give them justice. The country needs their help as much as the home needs it. By giving them justice their will be no need for an act such as the 'Cat-and-Mouse' torture. The energy that has been shown in trying to get the vote will be expended in benefiting the country . . .

A state of unrest is felt on all sides; lawlessness is increasing with new methods. Why? Because you are denying women justice.

September 11th, 1913

Yours etc.,
Charles Rigby.

VI

Bomb for Liverpool. 'Cat-and-Mouse'. Escape to Ireland.
Disguises. Tobacco factory girls. Vegetarianism.
Outbreak of war. Change of tune.

THOUGH Uncle Charlie was won over to her side, the family disapproval of my aunt deepened. Her name was rarely mentioned, and then only in undertones which told me that she was a fanatic. I suppose every wholehearted Christian must be seen in this light. At any rate, while expediency and common sense are safeguards against anti-social behaviour, single-mindedness in pursuit of the truth must lead away from what is, supposedly, the 'normal'. In our desire to be like others how we toil after the average, the commonplace and the undemanding!.

As I said at the beginning, Aunt Edith was not like other people. She wholly accepted Christ's teaching and was prepared to practise her beliefs regardless of the cost to herself and others – as Uncle Charlie's letter has just made plain. I, on the other hand, lacking the courage for this uncompromising way of life, have often asked: 'Where does Christianity end and common sense begin?' This in relation to selling one's possessions and giving to the poor, forsaking father, mother and brothers for the Way and the Truth . . . and to those tremendous injunctions to deny self, lose one's life, and to 'take no thought for the morrow'. And for many more which seem beyond our limited capacity for good.

For my aunt, apparently, Christianity never did end. And if, to our way of looking, common sense never really began, she was gifted in the highest degree with uncommon sense. Perhaps what I have light-heartedly painted red and described as her puckish streak is, in fact, entirely compatible with Christian behaviour. Certainly in her eyes the burning of a rich man's bungalow would be compatible with the overturning of moneychanger's tables. As for the clash with J.H. Thomas, he had been offensive and offending. What were a few black puddings compared with a millstone round his neck and being cast to the bottom of the sea?

From the use of black puddings, however, Aunt Edith graduated to bombs. My father, who deplored all her suffragette activities, considered the bomb in the Liverpool Cotton Exchange the most dastardly. But he might have known that the bomb in question – intended to wake up the cotton-trade to women's need of the vote – was harmless as a crackerjack, if a great deal more noisy.

Even so, it was a difficult assignment requiring both secrecy and co-operation. Beth was my aunt's chosen accomplice, but the two were never seen to meet, and never corresponded. All their fellow members were kept in the dark. Aunt Edith, dependable as ever, knew a man who would make a bomb guaranteed to explode with a maximum of noise and minimum of danger. After giving him the order she instructed Beth to call at his house with a suitcase.

A few days later Beth duly called. Anyone who happened to be watching the house must have been surprised at the brevity of her visit, because within a few minutes she emerged, still carrying her case, rather in the manner of an unaccepted guest. But now, had the spectator realised it, her case was loaded in every sense of the word.

Rapidly she walked down Friargate in the direction of home when, looking up and across the road, she was dismayed to recognise a friend who was also a detective. There was no escape; he smiled and came over to her, offering to carry her case. 'Are you off for a week-end with this heavy thing?' he asked as he took it from her. 'Oh no,' Beth hastened to reassure him, 'I've just been getting some new material.'

'You'll be having a suit of armour by the feel of it!' he exclaimed as he walked beside her, carrying the case in his right hand. Arriving at her front door he set it down on the step. 'Mind you make a nice outfit!' he teased her and hurried away.

This was the suitcase which Aunt Edith took by train to Liverpool in December, 1913. She was followed by a detective who watched her open it outside the Royal Exchange and immediately arrested her.

Once again, just before Christmas, she found herself in Walton Gaol and on hunger-strike under the 'Cat-and-Mouse' Act. Greatly distressed at this new charge for imprisonment within a few months, Uncle Charlie went to see her and implored her give up the hunger-strike for health reasons. But though by now weak and ill, she held out against his arguments. 'God is with me in this cell,' she assured him, 'as near to me as in church.' There must have been times when my uncle would have welcomed a more elastic form of Christianity! Her last words before he left were to give Sandy 'a child's Christmas'.

After four days without food or water, by which time she could hardly stand, she was released. Uncle Charlie drove her home where friends were waiting to look after her. She must have recovered with remarkable speed because when, a week later, the police came rattling on the front door, she made a lightning exit fom the back, wearing workman's clothes and mounted on Pegasus, as she called the bicycle which Albert Yeadon had lent her.

What happened next nobody knows, but somehow she escaped to the west of Ireland where she remained in hiding for several weeks. Indeed, for months at a time Uncle Charlie had no idea where she was. And when Nancy (Annie), her school-friend, now married to Percy Watchurst, a

Methodist minister, wrote him a letter of sympathy and inquiry he replied:

> 28 Winckley Square
> Preston
> January 3rd 1914

Dear Annie,

Thank you very much for your note of sympathy. As you say it is a difficult business to decide, but for me there is only one course and that is to back Edith. I know her perfect sincerity and love of justice; she feels it to be the only course her conscience allows her to follow, is willing to suffer contumely, blows, loss of friends and kindred, starvation and so on to prove her sincerity, and she has suffered, never you fear, to see her as I have – almost a shadow, scarcely able to stand, with the smile of an angel and the courage of a lion, a front as undaunted as any hero that ever lived. Then I should be the veriest villain on earth if I was not willing, and thankful also, to be able to back her with every power I've got. I think her little short of an angel, and I'm so sorry I cannot do more to help her. I've to be passive, I must keep the home together, look to the boy, and be able to afford her shelter and help whenever she needs it. I do not have the moral courage to face what she has done, I doubt if I could do it for any cause. It makes me so ashamed and I feel so unworthy of her, and I know how many a time I've made it harder for her, because, partly, of my difficulty in seeing it in her light. But I'm perfectly and absolutely sure she is right, and I believe the cause is gaining daily, and before this year is out the vote will be won.

I don't know where she is, we can communicate with each other, but where she is or what she is doing I know not beyond this; she is engaged in a work of the greatest importance, working daily, not engaged in militancy, and she has promised me she will not do this without giving me due warning and asking my consent (which I should not withhold). She says she is gaining strength, is happy, would much like to see us, but will be away four, or more, months, but hopes to spend next Christmas with us. This is about all I can tell you.

A cause that has people like her at its back is bound to succeed, and there are many such, and they will do more yet if necessary . . .

I hope you are keeping well, and that the New Year will be as happy and prosperous as possible. Kindest regards to Percy and yourself.

> Yours faithfully,
> Charles Rigby.

During my aunt's absence from home her well-laid plans went ahead. Before setting off on the Liverpool expedition she had instructed Miss Reeder, another loyal friend who managed a haulage contractor's business, to carry off a similar type of bomb to Blackburn and put it in the mouth of a certain cannon. (Here, because of the opposition of the clergy, one might be forgiven for imagining a clerical canon. In fact, it was a relic from the Crimea, mounted in the park.)

I had the whole story almost from the cannon's mouth. In other words Miss Reeder described how she had accomplished this curious mission. 'To begin with,' she said, 'I had somehow to get the bomb to Blackburn – by hand, as it were. Well, I decided that the best thing would be to hide it in my muff, because I had to go by tram, and I thought no one would notice it that way. Even though I took a friend with me – for moral support – I felt very self-conscious sitting there with everyone staring at me. But I felt far worse when we went past Blackburn Police Station and a crowd of policemen got in! Wasn't I relieved to get off at the park gates! After we'd found the cannon we walked around for a while till the coast was clear. Then I popped in the bomb, as your aunt had instructed, and lighted a fuse. We made off as fast as we could but before we'd gone half a mile there was a terrific explosion. Everyone was terrified – they thought the Germans were on us!'

Encouraged by her success, Miss Reeder then made her way to the Blackburn Rovers Football Club. To her relief the place was empty, so she had no difficulty in laying and lighting a fire on the grandstand. As soon as it crackled into a promising blaze she made a hasty exit and returned, again by tram, to Preston. Here she got hold of some acid which she poured onto the greens of Fulwood golf course. 'And d'you really think this sort of thing helped your cause?' I asked her.

'I'm certain,' she replied, 'we wouldn't have got the vote without the militants – at least, not nearly so soon. The war was an excuse to save the Government's pride. After withholding it for so long and breaking so many promises they were really bound to give in. When war came they made *that* the reason. But the truth is, they dreaded any more disturbances!'

Aunt Edith, meanwhile, after a blank interval in Galway, was next heard of in a house in Evelyn Street, Deptford. From here she got in touch with Christabel who, after her mother's imprisonment, had fled to Paris. And from Paris, using Annie Kenney as her go-between, Christabel continued to give orders as before. For one thing, she suggested a meeting in Preston to be arranged by local members now that Mrs Rigby was officially 'off the map'. The new secretary, Mrs Higginson, with the help of her committee, advertised the meeting in a highly original manner. 'We dressed ourselves in long purple gowns and wore black lace masks,' she told me. 'Then we became sandwich-board men and paraded along

Fishergate and all the main streets.' These boards announced that the meeting would be held in the Public Hall where the chief speaker would be John Scurr MP. After his name huge black letters spelled out the cryptic words: AND ANOTHER.

By now Mrs Rigby was more than a local celebrity. She was in league with the chief suffragettes, and had been in prison at least as often as the leaders of the movement. At this moment when she was wanted for re-arrest there was much speculation as to whether she would dare to come out of hiding. The police had cats' eyes at every mouse-hole and not even the suffragettes themselves believed that 'Another' would dare to materialise just now.

Shortly before the meeting was due to begin W.S.P.U. members gathered at the Public Hall to welcome guest speakers. 'We found every ante-room, every corner and corridor blocked by policemen,' Mrs Higginson told me, 'and there were plain clothes men watching the entrances while dozens in uniform paraded the streets.' This was a mouse-trap indeed. Mrs Rigby's friends grew apprehensive and hoped she would stay away.

They had not yet got the full measure of her. Fully restored to health, she was prepared for battle. But none of her friends recognised the fashionably dressed woman wearing a pink-feathered hat who slipped through the police guard and made her way to a seat in the front row. Indeed, they wondered who was this stranger with an over-generous bust (it was a cushion underneath her bodice) and glittering pendant earrings. And, playing her old game, my aunt was hugely enjoying herself.

Her friend, Miss Ratcliffe, at present living at No. 28, had preceded her into the hall in the guise of a pig-tailed schoolgirl. Because she was a judge's daughter Miss Ratcliffe was using an assumed name. (After the ending of the suffrage movement, by the way, she entered a convent and became a prioress.)

Meanwhile, Amy Mayor was distributing leaflets advertising the two speakers: Mr John Scurr MP and (as the sandwich-board women had foretold) 'Another'. In due course Amy came up to the 'society lady' on the front row. The face under the feathered hat looked up at her with a sly smile. Amy, fluttering with astonishment, passed rapidly along the row.

It was an unusually quiet meeting. Mr Scurr, after receiving the full attention of his audience for about half an hour, announced his pleasure in calling a surprise speaker. To everyone's more-than-surprise the jewelled being in the front row stepped up onto the platform and began to speak. Apprehension rippled over the audience: there was no disguising Mrs Rigby's voice.

Like clockwork beetles policemen appeared from every corner and crevice of the hall. One W.S.P.U. member, the redoubtable Mrs Pass, knocked off their helmets as they ran up the steps to the platform. Someone shouted: 'Ratepayers, look what you're paying for – Beef, not Brains!'

By this time people were standing on their seats, stamping and shouting. Several women, including Miss Ratcliffe, were arrested. Later, in the police-station, she was accused of scratching a policeman. 'What!' she exclaimed, 'I scratch a policeman with these?' She held out her kid gloves in derision.

Not even Mrs Pass was charged with hindering the police. They wanted only the one woman who had evaded them for too long already. Everyone except Mrs Rigby was allowed to go free. Once again the mouse was hurried back to her cell.

However much my aunt enjoyed these goings-on, she couldn't have possibly enjoyed imprisonment. My father had hoped that she would break away from the militants to join Mrs Todd's 'milk and water' campaigners and so spare herself and her family all this discomfort and suspense. But she remained adamant.

I often wonder how the ten-year-old Sandy fared at this time in the hands of come-and-go housekeepers. In fact, the sum of his memories of my aunt during this period is telling: 'I remember nothing of her, except that she was in prison a lot!'

All the same, to dwell for a moment on his situation, he does remember sunny afternoons of play in Miller Park, and he was happy enough at the old Preston Grammar School in Cross Street, a stone's throw away from Winckley Square. If Aunt Edith's care of him lapsed temporarily through pressure of events, she made it up to him in later years. Uncle Charlie suffered more from sketchy meals, the vagaries of maids, and, worst of all, constant anxiety. A doctor's work under such conditions proved to be a greater strain than he yet realized, and people wondered how his marriage endured under these trials. This is perhaps explained in Grace Alderman's words: 'There was deep love and understanding between them. All the many times we met at Winckley there was never a hint of jangling or discord in their relationship'.

Not only did my uncle put up with this erratic household, he was obliged to retire for years to the fringes of Aunt Edith's life. Yet he never doubted, as did some, that these struggles had been worth while. As for my aunt, she rejoiced because women had now proved their determination and integrity, and also because the suffrage movement was to provide an army already organised and eager to serve the nation.

In any case the non-militants, with their invitations to 'Bring your knitting' to meetings, could never have been for Aunt Edith. She was born to answer a challenge; the suffrage movement enabled her to fulfil herself in many ways.

If opportunities for excitement, plotting and dressing up were gladly seized upon, her main incentive was genuinely the 'fight for right'. Along with a joyful capacity for escapade went the courage to follow a course through to the end. She was made of the uncompromising stuff of martyrs – as none knew better than Uncle Charlie.

But she never let this campaigning interfere with 'first things'. For instance, when her mother began to go blind, she made a point, every week, of going to see her and reading to her. If she happened to be away (or in prison) she sent one of her colleagues instead. And apart from family duties she kept her place on several committees concerned with the public good, though her appointment as prison visitor was allowed to lapse.

Health, both mental and physical, was ever to be one of Aunt Edith's concerns. Not for nothing did she pay frequent visits to the Health Stores which were owned and run by her suffragette friend, Mrs Higginson. I remember my father's scorn when he heard she had become a vegetarian. 'The human gut was never designed for vast quantities of lettuce and bran like a rabbit's!' he exclaimed as he vigorously dissected his breakfast bacon.

My aunt's decision, however, was based as much on moral as on health grounds. It was a prelude to, and linked in some way with, her budding interest in anthroposophy – inspired by Rudolf Steiner – which was soon to reshape her life. In any case, this was a turn in keeping with her nature. She had always rebelled against any form of cruelty to animals, birds and even insects. The sight and smell of a slaughter-house revolted her. Apart from this she believed that the eating of meat strengthened the baser, animal passions. But before embarking on her next and 'higher' phase of development, I must return to complete the earlier picture as she emerges from a stormy background of black and scarlet.

Some time before the outbreak of war she started singing classes at No. 28 to stimulate members of the W.S.P.U. to further efforts. By now my aunt had a Dutch woman, Marie Byvoets, living with her who helped to run the house. Miss Byvoets was a gifted pianist. And in this connection I must point out that Sandy was not forgotten: my aunt persuaded her new friend to give him piano-lessons, as well as playing accompaniments for the W.S.P.U. singers. From now on each meeting opened with the singing of some appropriate song – such as 'The March of the Women' – to keep them in good heart.

This was needed when, for example, in December 1913, Mrs Pankhurst was imprisoned on her return from America. It seemed that no further effort could now prevail over the Government's antagonism. The W.S.P.U. naturally denounced this act of injustice as a scandal, especially while Sir Edward Carson, Mr Bonar Law and other male law-breakers in connection with Irish Home Rule, went free.

Shortly after this, letters were sent by suffragettes to all churches asking for prayers for their sisters in prison. In Preston one of the only three clergymen to reply wrote: 'Had I been at home I would have put the Chief Constable and his staff to work to free the Church from the brawl made by you.'

And yet only three days earlier the Bishop of Kensington, presiding over a meeting of the Anglican clergy, had strongly protested against the forcible feeding of suffragettes. This in spite of the fact that the previous May suffragettes had placed a bomb of 'an extremely dangerous type' near the Bishop's throne in St Paul's, thus provoking another Bishop's 'thanks to God for taking care of His cathedral against the machinations of some miscreant who tried to wreck it last night'.

Not only the Government and the Church, but women themselves were divided on the whole question, to the extent of dissenters forming a National League for opposing Woman Suffrage. Even today some people maintain that the militants actually delayed the end for which they were fighting.

By their burnings-down and breakings-in they had by now become more than merely a nuisance to the ordinary citizen. Everyday life was disrupted by their campaign. But if the suffragettes did set some ministers against them, their more gentle predecessors had drawn a complete blank. Mary Wollstonecraft's *Vindication of the Rights of Women*, published in 1792, which had perfectly stated the case, lay 121 years behind on the shelf.

Aunt Edith followed Mary Wollstonecraft in all directions leading to women's further education, along with fuller responsibilities. As I have already implied, the suffrage campaign played a comparatively small part in her wider purpose of helping the poor and the oppressed. It was during the suffrage period, for example, that she took up the cudgels for the girls who worked in Woods' Tobacco Factory. Trouble began when the girls employed here were ordered to start at seven, instead of eight o'clock in the morning. The place wasn't paying, so the foreman told them, and unless they agreed to the extra hour they'd find themselves out of work. Frightened of losing their jobs, they meekly gave in.

Had conditions been good this extra hour would have been bad enough. As it was, windows were sealed and doors opened only to admit fresh supplies, so that the whole place reeked with the heavy fumes from baking tobacco-leaves. The health record was appalling; even the girls who were not off sick felt ill at work. And no wonder, when all were suffering from some degree of nicotine poisoning.

My aunt approached one of the firm's directors, but making no headway with him she put the case to their chief customer, the Co-operative Wholesale Society, who agreed to boycott the tobacco unless working conditions were improved. Where persuasion had failed a threat succeeded. The extra hour was knocked off and some degree of ventilation installed.

This sort of thing was constantly happening so that my aunt resolved to form a trades union of women workers in Preston. With this idea in mind she called on Will Margerison (of Margerison's White Windsor Soap) and suggested that his women workers might belong to such a union. However, according to Miss Bailey, he insultingly opposed the scheme and told her to mind her own business. Undaunted by this refusal, she approached Mr Woolley, the first Labour Mayor of Preston, who welcomed the idea of protecting women workers and compensating those who were sick and out of work.

About this time Miss Bailey, then manageress of a café, recalls hearing a knock on the door one evening while she and her sister were having supper. Her sister went to the door and remained conversing on the doorstep for about ten minutes before returning with a leaflet. She held it up for her sister to read: *A single person is weak while a union is strong.*

'Whoever is it?' Miss Bailey asked curiously. 'You were stuck there talking long enough!'

'She didn't give her name,' her sister replied, 'but she was ever such a nice lady. She spoke slow like, in a soft voice. It was all about forming a union for women workers.'

The caller, of course, was Mrs Rigby, who shortly afterwards formed the Preston branch of the National Federation of Women Workers.

When war broke out in 1914 all suffrage activities came to an end, and the women turned to any sort of work that might help the country. Everyone thought there'd be a blockade and that England would starve. 'The first thing that happened,' Miss Bailey told me, 'was food-hoarding. I remember the rush on the Health Stores; the women went mad buying sacks of flour and sugar. Poor Mrs Higginson was sold out in no time. But my father wouldn't let us buy. He said we must take our chance with the rest.'

A great many women, particularly cleaners and those privately engaged, found themselves out of work. And members of the W.S.P.U. had to be directed into new channels. Aunt Edith, never lost for an idea, observed that this was a wonderful year for fruit. By the end of August orchard trees were rich with ripening plums, damsons, apples and pears.

This fact, coupled with the possibility of a food shortage, inspired her with a scheme for a privately-run jam factory.

First of all she put an advertisement in the paper for fruit, free for the picking. When several farmers responded, she set out with Mrs Higginson in her pony-trap and called upon each one in turn. Many a loaded orchard was put at their disposal. Ladders and buckets were provided by co-operative farmers; the two women did the rest. And anyone who has picked an orchard of plums or damsons during a heavy fruit season knows that 'the rest' is very hard labour, because fruit-picking is a compulsive occupation. Between them they reckoned to gather more than a hundred pounds of fruit during an afternoon.

More pickers were needed, so my aunt rounded up several followers and persuaded them to help in what she called a 'national emergency'. September came and the fruit turned red and purple, yellow and gold. Plums were gathered first, then damsons, apples, and hard hazel-pears to fill the skip-baskets given by millowners. Rusting hedgerows yielded great hampers of glistening blackberries. Marrows were harvested, and unripe tomatoes and cauliflowers for chutney. And one basket was packed full of orange-red rose-hips to make into jelly.

The W.S.P.U. rooms in Glover's Court resembled a scene from *Goblin Market* with sweet, ripe fruit piled on every shelf, heaped on the floor. Pans, basins and scales were lent by members and friends; and many women were employed to clean and weigh fruit and sugar – demerara at threepence three-farthings a pound, which seemed an outrageous price to the women who had so recently bought it at twopence.

Miss Bailey was put in charge of the entire concern. This meant organizing the women and working like a bee herself; weighing, boiling and bottling. In this art she was so well instructed by the brother of Annie Kenney that a bottle of her 1914 vintage-year damsons was exhibited, in perfect condition, at a show held in 1956.

Such an enterprise was a happy example of my aunt's imagination working towards co-operative good. Not only were many women given the work they badly needed, farmers were proved generous, and also the gas company, who put in gas stoves and rings free of charge. Finally, someone lent a shop, rent-free, in the Arcade, and customers were able to buy excellent pickles and jam at sixpence a pound. If the original idea of providing work and using fruit was wholly fulfilled, a great deal more was achieved in the matter of human relationships.

After a spell of hard, unpaid work under my aunt's guidance, Miss Bailey could say of her: 'She was a wonderful woman, so keen on doing good. There ought to have been a monument to her'.

But a monument was the last thing Aunt Edith would have wanted. She, who disliked speaking in public and any form of display, preferred to work in secret. Nor did she write letters unless absolutely necessary. All this has increased the difficulty of tracking her footsteps, so many of which lie hidden in the sand.

Meanwhile, though war-work for women was seriously begun, the vote was not yet won. For that they had to wait until February 6, 1918, by which time they had stepped into nearly all jobs until recently held only by men.

The year 1914 saw militancy at its height: no meeting, theatre, restaurant, court or show of any kind was safe from this plague of women. 'The worst fight on record since the movement began is now raging in Holloway,' wrote Mary Richardson on her release, after a long spell of forcible feeding, to be operated on for appendicitis.[1] The war between women and the Government had come to its climax on the eve of the First World War.

Many suffragettes were surprised and aggrieved, therefore, when Mrs Pankhurst and Christabel declared a truce. 'How can we fight for a Government which has been torturing us?' their critics in the movement demanded. Mrs Pankhurst replied that they were not fighting for the Government but for the Country. In spite of ill-health she spoke to women on the home-front and men on the war-front. She advocated military conscription for men; work in munitions factories for women. And foreseeing a food shortage, she pressed for the introduction of rationing.[2]

So successful was her campaign that when Lloyd George became Minister of Munitions he actually begged her to organize another of those once-dreaded women's processions, to demand the right to work in munitions factories. The procession, which ended in yet another deputation to Parliament, largely overcame the prejudice of MPs.

At last the Government opened its arms to women. It also opened its coffers, supplying money for organizations, banners and bands. Participants in this final procession of the W.S.P.U. must have been moved by the irony of a remark from a Liberal Cabinet Minister: 'I never knew we had such women!'

He would have been even more surprised had he foreseen that within a year or two it was the presence of women in munitions factories which prevented the men from going on strike. They refused to down tools and leave the soldiers at the front without arms. It is even possible that victory might not have been achieved without their help.

Because of this many members resented the arbitrary way in which Mrs Pankhurst and Christabel closed down the women's movement at the end of 1914. A dissenting group gathered under the leadership of Charlotte Marsh who, two years later, with the backing of a small

1 *Unshackled*, by Christabel Pankhurst.
2 *Ibid.*

committee, formed the Independent W.S.P.U.. This organization threw out no more than six local branches, one of which was Preston, again under the aegis of Mrs Edith Rigby, who had originally inspired the young Charlotte with her own ideals.

The new forward-looking group organized women at home and in war-work, besides battling (peaceably) towards the vote and further emancipation. Such efforts were urgently needed, as may be judged by a war-time speech of an overseas MP declaring that the salaries of women in the Civil Service should be limited to two pounds a week, no matter how responsible their work. He continued: 'Anything more would be wasted in the purchase of theatre tickets, toilet articles, dress, powder and perfume'.

Whereupon a Lancashire newspaper correspondent pertinently replied:

'There appears to be no satisfying the confirmed opponents of feminine independence. First, they blame women for 'under-cutting' by offering to do work quite as well and more cheaply than men . . . and now they want to make undercutting compulsory.

The basis of this new charge appears to be that women waste their money on luxuries. Some do, others don't. And surely those who are justly accused of 'theatre tickets, toilet articles, dress, powder and perfume' can retaliate with cigars, billiards, drinks, football matches, clubs, and a dozen more traditional masculine indulgences?

But quite apart from such *tu quoques*, the whole principle of payment according to expenditure is manifestly absurd. How does a Cabinet Minister spend his five thousand a year? And a High Court Judge his five thousand?

Are we to cut Mr Balfour's salary on the ground that he smoked too much tobacco last year, or dock Mr Justice Darling of one hundred pound for excess music-hall tickets?'

Even when, belatedly, nine months before the Armistice was signed, women were given the vote, it was by no means on the same terms as men. Only women over thirty who were local government electors (or wives of such electors) were put on the register, which accounted for about eight million women as against thirteen million men. And even this grudging gesture was made partly because the insurance companies had warned the Government of their refusal to continue to pay for the fires caused by the suffragettes. Before the outbreak of war these were costing them as much as £40,000 a week.

It was not until 1927 that Mr Baldwin introduced a Bill, which became law in July 1928, granting the vote to women on equal terms with men. However, no woman was elected to Parliament in the first General

Election after this victory, though a few, including Christabel, made a last-minute attempt to get in. It was too early for the new régime, and not enough time had been allowed for preparation.

The first of the very few women to sit in Parliament during the early years was Lady Astor. Mrs Pankhurst put up as Conservative candidate for Whitechapel, and no doubt she would have filled the post extremely well. But the strain and suffering of battling years had to be paid for; she was obliged to withdraw on account of illness.[1]

Aunt Edith's ambitions to become a town councillor were already bent in another unforeseen direction: work on the land. This was to be her war effort, a reaction, perhaps, to too much excitement and too many journeys and imprisonments. At any rate, early in 1915 she was looking for a freeholding where she could keep animals and grow fruit and vegetables. Before very long her search was rewarded by the sight of two white-washed cottages surrounded by gardens, an orchard and about five acres of grass. They could be made into one. This was near Howick, about a mile down a sandy lane off the Preston-Southport road – at that time a green and wooded area which seemed half-asleep in the heart of the country.

After the railings of Winckley Square she needed no rose-coloured spectacles with which to view this small estate. It was April; the orchard shone with pink-fisted apple-blossom, and with the whiteness of pear, plum and damson. In a corner three beehives gleamed in the morning sun. A five-barred gate opened into a yard where a cherry had spilt its petals. After the grim years of anxiety and privation she must indeed have echoed Yeats with his dream-cabin of Innisfree: 'Nine bean rows will I have there and a hive for the honey-bee'.

There and then she decided to take Marigold Cottage.

1 *Ibid.*

VII

Buying a pony. Miss Flanagan and Grëtel.
The bees. Miss Tucker. Sandy and Herbert.
Stars and sunrise. Contrast with Ribblesdale Place.
The Watchursts. Rudolf Steiner.

WITH her eyes turned to new horizons, Aunt Edith lost no time in joining the Women's Land Army. From now on she wore breeches and a farmer's smock and cut her short hair even shorter. I have vivid memories of this period, memories in which breeches and leggings seem curiously at variance with gentle admonitions and a hedge-rose complexion.

'What a pity to dress up like that when she's so good-looking!' I overheard one of Mother's friends remark. 'That wonderful colouring would get her anywhere.' My aunt's purpose in life, however, was not to 'get anywhere', but just to be her very strange self.

All the same, her odd appearance often caused me painful embarrassment. On one occasion, which has bitten deep into memory, she took me by train to St Annes-on-Sea to try a horse for her new trap. I went to the station with Mother who looked as usual, what I can only describe by the ridiculous word 'dainty'. After waiting for a few moments on the platform, I was suddenly transfixed by the fearfully masculine figure advancing towards us. Not only was my aunt wearing sandals with breeches, but a man's jacket and, worst of all, a man's hat over wispy, home-cut hair. This sort of thing is nowadays so common that my dismay cannot possibly be appreciated.

At the time, even with land-girls about, her appearance always caused comment. On that particular train journey I shrank back and back into my corner seat to observe the amazement and disapproval of our fellow-travellers. However, once arrived at our destination – the stables – my sense of proportion was restored. What a sensible get-up it proved to be! Aunt Edith, who had never learned to ride, insisted on mounting the spirited dark-brown whose paces she had come to try. His name was Donald, and his owner demurred that he was a hackney, rather nippy and unused to the saddle. Undeterred by these objections, my aunt pursued her intention to ride him on the shore. Whereupon I, to my delight, was lifted on to a stolid, tub-like pony while the owner bestrode a lanky chestnut. And down to the sea we clattered.

All went well at the trot, though Donald's forelegs, in ominous spinning-wheel motion, seemed to turn higher and faster with every stride. Then, ill-advisedly, the chestnut broke into a canter. This was too much altogether for Donald. I had a view of his hind-legs kicking up with a flourish, and of my aunt's hard landing on the sand. Unhurriedly, a little unsteadily, she picked herself up while Donald was being retrieved. I glowed with admiration to see her remount and jog determinedly home. Donald, however, was turned down as a too-erratic performer, and eventually a thirteen-hand bay cob, Nutty, was found for the trap.

In the meantime a great deal of work was necessary to make the cottage habitable and the land more productive. One of my aunt's first decisions was to wash 'Marigold' to the colour of its name. I can see it now – donkey-brown thatch and orange walls glowing in the afternoon sun. When I first went there Aunt Edith was wearing the inevitable breeches and a holland overall. She had been digging and her boots were clabbered with mud. In the distance a tall, lanky woman continued to turn over the potato-patch. Aunt Edith led me to be introduced to Miss Flanagan whom she described as her right hand. Uncle Charlie, by the way, took a different view of this helper, who received thirty shillings a week while the 'Marigold' project was losing two pounds. All the same, he felt compensated by having his wife at last, safely rooted in the soil.

Miss Flanagan straightened her back and scraped the sandy river-soil from her boots. 'Nice to meet you,' she nodded briskly, 'and now, how about a cup of tea?' We walked back to the cottage and my memory of the conversation becomes blurred in the haze of a September afternoon with the sun polishing green apples and picking out dark clusters of damsons. As we passed the beehives in the orchard an aggressive gander hissed at us and flapped his wings.

We paused at the door of a shed to inspect pyramids of Kerr's Pinks and Arran Banners, my aunt's favourite potatoes – I suspect on account of their processional names and colours of magenta and cyclamen. A few sacks were filled, ready for market, with these pink beauties, and around them two kittens chased in a twirl of black and white. I remember tall clumps of Michaelmas daisies which seemed to magnetize those handsome black velvet butterflies with their tartan border of scarlet and white. Aunt Edith explained that Red Admirals were attracted by the colour of lilac. As she spoke she picked a bunch of the daisies for me to take home. 'Put them by your bedside,' she said, 'and gaze at them for a few moments before you go to sleep.' Then, with a reassuring twinkle at my questioning glance: 'Mauve is a good colour to sleep on!'

After that first dimly-remembered visit I went many times to 'Marigold'. No matter how busy my aunt was with the planting and cutting, picking and storing, she never seemed to be in a hurry. There was always time to show me something interesting or something new – a kitten, perhaps (though she disliked cats) or a hedgehog. And there was always time for talk and a leisurely tea.

Yet no one could have been more fully occupied; she worked harder on the land than Miss Flanagan, besides coping with the business side and actual sale of produce. Apart from this she employed one or two land-girls, including Miss Ratcliffe, the judge's daughter who, as previously mentioned, had for some time lived with my aunt at No. 28.

Another unexpected helper was Grëtel, a German fraülein who had been engaged with the primary purpose of teaching my aunt the language. War or no war, Aunt Edith was determined to visit Germany at the first possible moment in order to meet Rudolf Steiner in person. Meanwhile, with Grëtel's assistance, she learned to read his books in the original.

Among my aunt's many visitors to 'Marigold' were Mr and Mrs Yeadon. Although Albert (who used to work for a coffin-maker) had been sacked because of his association with the suffragettes and Mrs Rigby in particular, he bore no grudge and she, for her part, felt no sort of guilt on his acount. But Uncle Charlie went out of his way to make amends to the all-too-co-operative Albert. For example, one afternoon on leaving the cottage he drove to the Yeadons' house bearing propitiatory jars of honey and a huge bunch of sweet-peas. 'It's a great thing for Edith to part with these!' he smiled as he offered them up. 'She likes to sell everything these days.'

In truth, because of her expanding enterprise, she had already bought a second and larger pony, a dappled mare called Bramble. And twice a week she drove Nutty, the bay – so named because he shone like a polished hazel-nut – into Preston with fruit, vegetables and honey in season. In order to carry the largest possible load she attached a wicker-basket to the back of the trap. Three more beehives had been acquired, making half a dozen in all. With typical thoroughness my aunt made a study of the life of the bee, even to the extent of taking Maeterlinck's classic as her foundation.

Though I loved watching the bees at work in a haze of sun, and listening to their humming, which made a hot day seem even hotter, I was terrified of them at the close quarters of the hives. The way they blundered and thudded around those miniature front-doors before making an entry, and shot out again, zooming like bombers, was wonderful – but only from a distance.

At swarming-time the sight of Aunt Edith alarmed me. Wearing gloves and a floppy hat, armed with nets and veils, she resembled a sea-enchantress about to descend to the ocean-bed in search of stinging flowers. Such precautionary garb suggested danger. But she assured me that one only gets stung if one is afraid. And that was the first article of her personal creed.

Always a campaigner, from now on she determined to bring good food to as many people as possible. By 'good' food she meant food that was vital, unforced and full of natural salts and sugars. In those days vitamins were almost unrecognized and white bread and sugar were the rule.

Not so at Marigold Cottage. There it was wholemeal bread and honey for tea. As I listened to my aunt's talk of bees gathering nectar from the sun-warmed clover-field, I believed I was scooping liquid sunshine from my plate. And we never peeled apples and pears because of the 'sunlight in the skin'.

All vegetable waste was added to the compost heap: artificial manures and fertilizers were unheard-of. Indeed, 'getting back to our roots' as a means to health and happiness was one of my aunt's basic themes. One of the first things I remember about 'Marigold' was the 'privy' at the bottom of the garden. I was unused to such an inconvenience and complained that I couldn't find the chain. 'Oh, we don't have that sort of thing here!' my aunt told me. I then inquired if there was any disinfectant. 'Disinfectant,' exclaimed Aunt Edith in a shocked voice, 'and destroy all that good living matter!' Then, observing my look of dismay, she went on more gently: 'Did you not know, dear, why my strawberries are so big?'

At tea that same afternoon I was grateful for the honey which enabled me to refuse the strawberry jam freshly made by my aunt's housekeeper, Miss Tucker. And now I've mentioned Miss Tucker I must pause to describe this enigmatic creature who was an essential background to Aunt Edith's life. I don't remember when she appeared on the scene, but I think of her as always being there. Without her presence my memories of 'Marigold' must surely have been less idyllic. At any rate, Miss Tucker, who was shaped like a cottage loaf, materialized and remained as the good housekeeper who did all the chores and produced all the meals, waving aside my aunt's offers of help as 'a hindrance' (which they certainly were). She never changed – except to become more like a cottage-loaf – and never left until some thirty years later when, like a true disciple, she followed my aunt out of this world.

Athough Miss Tucker lived an essentially background life, she shared meals with us at the round table – which my aunt still insisted on – in the window.

Plates, cups and saucers of delphinium-blue were thicker than those we used at home; and the crumbly wholemeal bread was cut and laid with butter far more amply than I had been accustomed to. Besides honey there would be a pile of fresh fruit and a slab of Miss Tucker's oatmeal parkin. Even the tea-cloth, which matched the curtains, was of brightly-coloured homespun, like my aunt's dresses.

This roots-in-the-earth life made the world of lace and silver and china tea-cups seem brittle and unreal. It was so much simpler, all eating together, than the distinctions I had grown up with between nursery tea, kitchen tea and, far removed, drawing-room tea with its distant tinkle of laughter and china.

Miss Tucker never spoke during meals. She sat, hairy and formidable, in a cloud of herself, only smiling with an effort when Aunt Edith, whom she adored, addressed her as 'dear child' or, in playful mood, 'Carinthia'. Even her reply to praise would be brief and grudging. Now I realize that she was intensely shy and didn't understand children. But at the time I found her repelling; I couldn't understand the bond between her and my aunt, which was deeper than one of employer and willing slave.

As for Mother, she couldn't bear Miss Tucker's ungracious manner, her silences and grunts, and her unprepossessing appearance: she was pale and podgy, and she wore thick, *pincenez* glasses over small, deep-set eyes. All the same, I'm sure my aunt was right when she described Miss Tucker as 'a gallant little body'.

Almost as reserved and difficult to know was Sandy, of whom I had only brief glimpses during school holidays. I remember, for instance, dusty days in August before he embarked on a few years at Trent College. This, by the way, was a surprising departure because the idea of a public school seemed to be at variance with Aunt Edith's educational ideals. Perhaps she found the task of bringing up a single boy not so easy as she had expected. And the relationship was made more difficult by Sandy's unusually shy and retiring nature. It would be about this time, or a little earlier, that she bought him the Scottish kilt and cap – so much in keeping with his sandy hair and freckles – that caused him such distress at the hands of his school-fellows. At any rate, however much went underground in his mind, he remembered nothing at all of his doings at 'Marigold'.

It was my cousin Herbert, sent over from Canada to be educated in England, who told me of a certain holiday episode concerning them both. Though Sandy was well on in his teens, the ten-year-old Herbert, a practical joker like his father, managed to lead him astray.

On this particular occasion Herbert, after negotiating the slope of the cottage thatch, planned to give his aunt a fright, chiefly because he'd never seen her put out. To this end he arranged that the pair of them should settle on the roof-top until she returned for tea from her work in the field. At a given signal they were to 'shoot the thatch' onto the ground immediately in front of her.

Shortly before tea, therefore, they took up their perch on the roof. Having miscalculated the time they had more than an hour to wait while impatient behinds were well-polished by warm straw. Aunt Edith was occupied with spraying fruit trees; but eventually she was to be seen approaching in her usual leisurely fashion. As she neared the front-door Herbert (future vice-admiral) gave the order, and they shot, more precipitantly than planned, to the path below. Undismayed, because apparently unnoticing, Aunt Edith continued her course, calm and slow as a barge on a canal. It took a great deal more than that to ripple her composure!

Although Sandy had no recollection of such pranks, he did remember being taken by my aunt to the Moor Park observatory. Thus, apart from his work as an electrical engineer, he owed his one great interest, astronomy, to her. In the potato-field at night she would discourse on the stars and the moon, stressing the influence of the moon upon the tides and the growth of seeds.

At some point in her study of the heavens astronomy descended into astrology. My aunt had a faculty for character-reading and guessing people's birthdays, though 'guessing' is not the word she would have used in this connection. According to her, certain personal characteristics resulted from the position of particular planets at the time of birth, 'a fact which, being an Aquarian, you'll find difficult to accept,' she would tease me. 'Aquarians seek the truth, but must arrive at it by way of reason.' She went on to explain that this is a very hampering process because reason brings argument against brick walls: 'And it takes a deal more than reason to see through *those!*'

When I was older she tried to lead me into even deeper waters or, perhaps I should say, up to higher levels of consciousness. But I was too ignorant to be anything but incredulous of things I could neither see nor touch. I couldn't enter her world, not even if I stretched up to the farthest star.

Stars, moon and the sun, to her way of looking, were interwoven with the fabric of grass and trees in a world where all growing things, including ourselves, are related:

A leaf of grass is no less than the journey-work of the stars . . .
And the running blackberry would adorn the parlours of heaven.

Whitman's poetry was also part of her creed. This feeling for relationship with the earth, always strong in her, has been expressed in many ways already: in her love of the mountains, her need for a life in the country, and in her baptism of Sandy in the dust of the Square gardens. And she saw the sun as a symbol of the Light of the World. The ancient sun-worshippers, she maintained, in doing homage to the Life-Giver, unconsciously worshipped the same God as ourselves. So that druids' circles, cromlechs and so on had fired her imagination long before coming upon Steiner's interpretation of these things.

Meanwhile Herbert, now a day-boy at the nearby Hutton Grammar School, served as her next pupil in this direction. At the age of ten he was taken by night to the potato-field and made acquaintance with the stars; not a bad beginning for a sailor. But more than this, my aunt determined that once at least he should watch the sunrise on Midsummer morning. Accordingly, on Midsummer's Eve rugs, pillows and a compass were assembled in the newly-shaved hayfield where they spent the night.

Herbert's only comment, when I later inquired how the night had gone, was a good-natured complaint of the cold. There had been a heavy dew to soak the rugs long before the sun rose over Preston murkily huddled in sleep. But Aunt Edith was satisfied that Herbert had seen for himself the miracle – 'like a ball of fire' – breaking through the east. She would have been pleased to know that in later years, watching the dawn from the bridge of his ship, he often recalled his first 'hayfield' sunrise.

Eagerly she fostered his own desire to become a sailor, and soon after his fifteenth birthday he left Hutton for the Royal Naval Training College at Dartmouth. But he continued to spend his holidays at 'Marigold' until the time came for him to leave England for active service with the Royal Canadian Navy. And whenever he spoke of 'our' aunt, his voice would take on a quality of warmth and affection as he smiled back at her exploits, much in the same way as she once smiled at his own.

During the 'Marigold' years I also swam under the influence of her particular star. But I was pulled two ways: between life there and my formal existence at Ribblesdale Place, with which she was so much out of sympathy.

At home, with my younger sister Elaine, we lived by the clock rather than the calendar as at 'Marigold'. Our time was divided between long hours playing in the nursery and brief intervals of sunlight in the garden – half an acre of rockery, lawn, asphalt and flower-beds. In the afternoons we were taken for walks in the park by our nurse. Treasured interludes with Mother were confined to the hour after tea, except on Nurse's day off. Then, sometimes, there would be a thrilling expedition through the park, across the Old Tram Bridge, over the Ribble, and away into the magic of woods and fields beyond.

Although I adored Mother and was happy enough at home, I longed to escape from the gritty town, and even from the park with its formal flower-beds cut and coloured like jigsaw puzzles. Unlike my more maternal sister, I grew bored with dolls while devoting hours to a wooden farm. At this time my dreams were all of horses and the delectable countryside into which they carried me. The moment I heard the clatter of hooves beneath the nursery window I would leap on to the ottoman shouting 'Bay!' or 'Chestnut!' as my guess might be. A pony spelt freedom and leafy lanes with a farm in the background. I even longed to drive away in the milkman's float.

Mother despaired of my rebellion and sulking: 'I don't want to go in the park. I want go into the *proper* country!' The Old Tram Bridge provided the only solution by bridging not merely the Ribble, but the two opposing worlds which I thought of as 'made' and 'real'. 'Marigold', undoubtedly, was 'real'. And so I felt myself pulled between the red-brick world of silver and starch into which I had been born, and the roots-in-the-earth life to which I belonged.

This conflict was intensified by Mother's disapproval of Aunt Edith's ways. And because I loved Mother and admired my aunt I was baffled. Nearly everyone seemed to fit into Mother's pattern of life, whereas Aunt Edith belonged, in a very real sense, outside. Who else among our family and acquaintances would appear in public dressed like the milkman?

Such questionings, never voiced, were barely conscious at the time. Present delights filled my days at 'Marigold'. For instance, the joy of riding bare-back in the paddock a fat, sun-warmed pony was unclouded by thought. This was Nutty who grew lazy on too many 'between days' so that I was welcome to ride him whenever I pleased.

Sometimes my aunt would saddle Bramble and ride with me accompanied by her fox-terrier, Spotter – so named not on account of his tar-spot but because of his magnet nose for rabbits. I can see him now, hind-quarters sticking out of the burrow down which his head and shoulders are sunk, a hail of soil flying upwards from clockwork forelegs.

My aunt had a flair for naming not only animals, but also things. Because her tool-shed had a stained-glass window she referred to it as 'Ecclesiastes'. And her particular spade was known as 'Adam'. 'Why "Adam"?' I onced ventured to inquire. 'Because he spent the years outside the garden digging,' she answered with her slow smile. 'But you use your spade for digging *inside* the garden,' I pursued with childish doggedness. 'Not the Garden of Eden,' my aunt replied as she selected a wooden hay-rake from three iron-toothed companions. '*This* garden grows thistles.'

She was wearing a greenish trilby hat, white linen smock, and black leggings, which seemed rather a hot costume for hay-making. The rake, however, was for Miss Flanagan. This year my aunt had borrowed a hay-rake machine on which she clattered up and down the shining fields. In the heat of elation among thick waves of falling grass, she would fling her hat to the ground and charge onward, a conqueror with flushed cheeks and hair flying in the wind. She reminded me of Boadicea, Britain's Warrior Queen, who figured largely in my history book.

My aunt not only cultivated the land and sold good produce cheaply, she welcomed dozens of people – friends and strangers alike – to 'Marigold'. Several ex-suffragettes came to the cottage for a rest, although, as Mrs Higginson crisply remarked, they were all expected to pull their weight. A W.S.P.U. members' tea-party actually meant arriving at half-past two and getting down to a long session of weeding or fruit-picking. On several occasions Beth and Mrs Higginson were roped in for this sort of thing. After stripping rows of currant bushes they considered they had earned their tea. Albert and Mrs Yeadon, arriving one afternoon for a quiet sit in the sun, were presented with hoes. With these they scuffled paths and all the flower-beds before retiring, blistered, hot and hungry for a tea of oatcakes and boiled eggs.

During this period Mrs Higginson was a frequent visitor to the cottage, and before long my aunt was asked to be godmother to her daughter, who was named Edith May in Mrs Rigby's honour.

There always seemed to be someone staying at 'Marigold', but the family whose name, Watchurst, appears most often in the visitors' book, I never met until later. There are so many Watchursts – Annie, Nancy, Lewis, Dudley, Beryl and Joan – that I was baffled. Only through writing this book have I sorted them out and discovered that Nancy was the Nancy (Annie) Taylor, my aunt's friend from Penrhos College days. And Lewis, the eldest son, introduced to me as Jimmy, I met by chance at a party some years ago. By that time he was president of the British Rotarians, a leader of groups, lecturer and former lord mayor. I had no idea he had any connection with Aunt Edith; only through the course of conversation did we discover our common bond. He told me how he had been drawn to her by her integrity and loftiness of mind – quite apart from her friendship with his mother. It was she, of course, who led him into the path of Rudolf Steiner. And Steiner's ideas were to form the basis of his Rotarian lectures and of his whole policy as president. Some time later I came to hear that these lectures and his leadership had been considered so outstanding that it had been no easy task to appoint his successor. In fact his sister Beryl told me that he was embarrassed by his success. Having been guided all the way, he felt unworthy to receive such credit and praise.

Of all the Watchurst family only he and Beryl responded to anthroposophy, which seems to appeal to a certain reflective, searching-for-truth nature. Because Lewis had been introduced to the subject at 'Marigold' he was chiefly interested, to begin with, in Steiner's methods in agriculture. On the other hand Joan, his younger sister, found the subject quite alien to her more direct, outgoing outlook.

Nearly every school holiday, from the age of twelve, Joan found herself at 'Marigold' in company with Herbert, who was about the same age. Together they spent many happy hours – as my aunt, with thoughts towards ultimate matrimony, intended that they should. One day, when they were about thirteen, she took them by train to Southport. Herbert, now extremely good-looking, suggested that he and Joan should occupy the next (empty) compartment to Aunt Edith. She looked at him gravely. 'Provided that you do nothing together that you wouldn't do in front of me,' she said, 'I see no reason why you shouldn't.'

Their solo journey at least taught Herbert that kissing a girl was a far less exciting business than he had imagined.

Another day they were allowed off alone, with adequate money, to Southport fairground. But they overspent on the swings and round-abouts and were reduced to booking two half-fares home, though Joan by now was six months over age. Aunt Edith discovered their deception, and Joan, at least, never forgot the lecture they received on the wickedness of cheating and defrauding. They were made to apologize to the stationmaster and pay him the money owed to the railways.

Then there was the day when my aunt invited two distinguished, 'chauffeur-driven' ladies for tea. They must have been subscribers to one of her charities because this was the only occasion when Joan remembers 'silks and satins' at 'Marigold'. Aunt Edith, not quite at ease, gave Herbert her large, leather-encased watch with instructions that the pair of them were to remain out of sight for two hours.

This injunction was obeyed to the letter. After the 'silks and satins' had been received by my aunt (in her homespun) and were observed by the children, from a nearby tree, to rustle into the cottage, Herbert said to Joan: 'Aunt Edith hates these dressed-up people, doesn't she?' When Joan agreed that this was true he suggested that it would be doing his aunt a favour if the ladies were to be annoyed in some way.

Whereupon, armed with large clods of earth, the two of them climbed the friendly thatch. At the moment when Herbert judged the ladies to be eating scones and honey around the fire – for it was a cold day – he dropped the first clod down the chimney. Several others were to follow, heavy enough to ensure the tea-table and fine draperies being covered in soot.

The escapade was all too successful. An hour earlier than reckoned on, and in great haste, the ladies departed. Aunt Edith, half-smiling through her indignation, impressed upon the children the wrong of causing distress to others – even if those others were well provided for. But she was far less concerned than over the affair of the railway-ticket.

Such an unfashionable standard of values struck her off the lists of local hostesses. In any case, her habit of speaking the truth must have made her an uncomfortable guest; I couldn't imagine her wasting time dressing for dinner in the ordinary social way, or being caught up in the wheel of entertaining. And yet, although she spoke her mind – when asked – I never heard her condemn, or even criticize anyone.

Not suprisingly she had no small-talk or gossip, nor was she ruffled by provocative remarks. For instance, I remember Mother taunting her after she'd objected to some cottages being built beside her boundary fence: 'Well, Edith, you're a socialist; you should be glad that poorer people than yourself are able to build in such a pleasant place!'

I can see her now, head on one side, carefully considering the justice of this remark. She must have owned herself beaten because she made no reply. But then she's always understood the admonition: 'There's a time to speak and a time to keep silence'.

Tolerant and unselfish herself, she assumed the same qualities in Uncle Charlie. Fortunately for her, he not only possessed them but was additionally blessed with a broad sense of humour, enough to save them both from many an awkward situation. He put up with the 'Marigold' project by treating the whole thing as a joke and inviting his friends to 'come and have tea with us on our sanded floors!' He used to pretend that his wife was turning him into a veterinary surgeon.

Though not in the least a countryman, he made the best of muddy weekends in the winter, of hands blistered by the hay-rake in summer. He helped with the apple-picking, worked with spade and hoe, and collected the eggs. But lest I seem to set him up as a saint (which he almost was) I must relate a certain incident of one wild, wet April afternoon. It was a Saturday, a day of slamming doors and straw blowing in the wind, and my parents had taken me to tea at 'Marigold'.

Uncle Charlie had been sweeping out the stable, and when we arrived he suddenly appeared round a corner, hatless and dishevelled, wheeling a steaming barrow-load of manure. Mother darted out of the rain into the house. My uncle, with a most rueful smile, set down the barrow in front of my father. 'Arthur,' he confided from a deep well of feelings, 'I'm a fool, nothing but a blooming fool!'

As to how he reacted to his wife's unfolding ideas on religion and philosophy, I can only guess that he suffered them in silence. It would be about this time that she became dominated by Rudolf Steiner's anthroposophy, which he described as 'a path of knowledge to guide the spiritual in the human being to the spiritual in the universe'.

Later on I will speak more fully of Steiner's study of the invisible world through the world of nature, which he called 'spiritual science'. But in all ways, by searching into the spirit of man as into the nature of a star, by revelations concerning human purpose and destiny, anthroposophy seemed to offer my aunt an open glove into which to put her hand.

How she first came to hear of Steiner I don't know, but one of the poets who lighted her way towards him was Blake: 'When the doors of perception are cleansed, then we shall see life as it really is – Infinite'. And being in tune with the Infinite, the happenings of her life seemed to occur when she was ready for them: opportunities for social work; the suffrage movement; and now a period for rest, reflection and further growth at 'Marigold'.

Sometimes after tea, as we sat round the table, she would talk about rhythms and cycles – of the moon and tides and seasons, rhythms and cycles repeated in the lives of animals and man; work and relaxation; digging and dancing; the to-and-fro and rise-and-fall of movement, whether of limbs at play or leaves in the wind. When she was 'on this tack', as Herbert nautically expressed it, her eyes seemed to become bluer

The author with her Aunts Alice and Mary outside Fairview, Fulwood,
her grandfather's house and surgery, in 1912.

Few photographs were ever taken of Edith
Rigby. The camera was anathema to her and
she would hastily absent herself if it seemed
that she was likely to be photographed.
Often, too, she would dress herself in some
disguise – which she loved to do – and it is
quite likely that there are photographs on
which she does appear, but anonymously.

One of the rare occasions on which Edith Rigby allowed herself to be
photographed. Probably taken during her visit to America in 1931.
Edith is on the extreme left of the picture, wearing her customary sandals.

Emmeline and Christabel Pankhurst in prison uniforms,
22nd December 1908. Edith Rigby was never photographed during her
many stays in prison, but she would have been attired like her friends the
Pankhursts. Edith often went on hunger strike and was force fed, and
each stay in prison took its toll on her health.

Local suffragettes appear in court in Manchester, 1913.
From left to right: Miss Annie Briggs, Miss Evelyn Marrosta,
Mrs. Lillian Forrester and Mrs. Baines.

Opposite (top): The First Women's Conference, 1907.
Mrs. Selina Cooper is fifth from the left on the back row;
Mrs. Pankhurst is ninth from the left on the front row.

Opposite (bottom): Lancashire and Cheshire delegates of the Women's
Franchise Deputation to the Prime Minister, 1908.
Edith Rigby was part of this deputation but, as usual, had made herself
scarce when the camera appeared.

Mrs. S. J. Cooper with fellow suffragists
on campaign in the North-West of England in about 1910.

Lancashire Marchers on a suffrage procession from Manchester
to London, June 17th 1911. This photograph was taken at
Scone Girls' High School, Stratford-upon-Avon.

Above: Lord Leverhulme's
bungalow at Rivington which
was the object of Edith Rigby's
incendiary activities. All that
remained of the bungalow
after the fire were a few
masonry pillars.

Right: The statue of the Earl of
Derby in Miller Park, Preston,
which was pointed out, coated in
tar, to the author as another
example of her Aunt Edith's
evil-doings.

Above: 28 Winckley Square,
Preston, home of the suffragette
Mrs. Edith Rigby.

Right: The author, Phoebe
Hesketh. Mrs. Hesketh is well-
known as a writer of published
prose and poetry and has written
several books based in her native
Rivington.

and her gaze more remote, as though she were looking beyond you into far horizons.

Most of this talk washed over our heads as it certainly washed over the head of Sandy, now training to become an electrical engineer, and with little time for poetry. I can only look back and recognize something Wordsworthian in my aunt's passion or, more truly, reverence, for nature. Wordsworth's sense of people in relation to their environment seemed part of her consciousness. Her father's introduction to the Lake country and its mountains – with his pocket-Wordsworth for guide – had borne more fruit than he could have foreseen. Because it was as much through Wordsworth's feeling for nature, and man's place among its beauties and terrors, as in Blake's vision that my aunt received a foretaste of Rudolf Steiner. So that anthroposophy, like everything else, came to her at the right time and in the right place, while she was reflecting on these things.

To us, anthroposophy had an intimidating sound, and we never really tried to understand it. I remember, for instance, one afternoon when Aunt Edith called to see my father at Ribblesdale Place. She had just returned from Steiner's headquarters at Dornach and was obviously 'walking the sky'. At any rate, unable to contain her enthusiasm, she began unfolding the mysteries of speech rhythms and colour vibrations. Then, looking at me, she broke off with an understanding smile.

'I can't make moss or sand of a word she says!' my father exclaimed after her unobtrusive departure.

He was not the only one to be baffled by this turnabout from the red vibrations of her suffrage days to the blues – or at least lavenders – of her youth. Even her loyal suffragette friends were dismayed and could make nothing of the books she left them on the subject.

Even so, a handful of followers attended the meetings which she held in the St John Ambulance Rooms. One evening she invited Joe Williamson, prospective Labour candidate for the Fylde. After attempting, as briefly as possible, to explain Steiner's interpretation of the miracles, Mrs Rigby resorted to her own words and described the first miracle, the changing of the water into wine, as a speed-up in the natural processes: 'Water drawn into a grape, warmed by the sun and fed by the cosmic rays *is* wine – given time to ferment!'

She impressed upon them that Steiner was a scientist who made a study of sprriritual truth through the processes of nature, and who, from boyhood, had been able to see the spiritual world inwardly. In vain she strove to express the inexpressible. At the best of times my aunt found it difficult to clarify her thoughts; not because they couldn't be put into words, but because she seemed to think by a different process from the rest of us. On this particular occasion, before giving up hope, she looked towards Mr Williamson and asked for his opinions. She might have been warned by his blank gaze, for he bluntly replied: 'It's as clear as mud'.

Here I can't resist adding that, had my aunt been retaliatory, she might have answered: 'Mud in *your* eye, Mr Williamson!'

Finally, even Mrs Higginson, always ready for new ideas, briskly summed up the opinions of my aunt's friends: 'After the vote was won she gave up all her good works and took up with Rudolf Steiner.'

VIII

Burning the hives. Tea at Rose Cottage.
Stolen apples. Book choices. War interlude.
Brock Cottage. Christmas at 'Marigold'.
Botany excursions.

MRS Higginson's judgement, though understandable, was not accurate, because my aunt continued, in one form or another, to do good works all her life. Each new venture was taken up with such zest that you felt here, at last, was the end for which she had been born. Every time it proved to be nothing of the sort because she was continually losing herself in some new role and emerging as a slightly different person.

At 'Marigold' we believed that she was growing permanent roots in good, plain soil. But no, never for one moment did she become earth-bound. Though her feet were on the ground, her quest was always 'over the hills and far away', as may be seen by the following letter, written after staying in the wooden holiday hut near Ulverston which Nancy Watchurst had built for her family. The letter also reveals the feyness for which she was so harshly criticized:

Marigold Cottage
(no date)

Dearest Nancy,

This won't be the letter that the heart has written to you before the ruck of the day descended on me. (I hoed 8 fruit trees this morn.) But it can bring instant word of gladness at having seen you all three looking so right in that adventuresome 'Venturesome Castle'. If ever there was one builded in thought and heart's stirrings, and aimed for no mere appearances but to house your best and dearest in a place they could rejoice in – mountain, lake, and sea. That then, is the Great Peace, and not fairly to be called Hut or Cabin, but St Famille or Casa Giocosa, or that teasing name: the Peascod [because eleven people had been crowded into four small bedrooms].

My next (!) 2 places are to be Peaseblossom: Cobweb. It is very like that the clouds will disappear, all rays of joy from the children's hearts will warm them off. You know, child, I never thought a hut could be built at that price which would be worth it, but yours is a great surprise and seems to me a wonderful thing. You are now due for easier times there: my word, it must have been uphill work since Easter! Everything speaks of careful, wise thought, all to the one end:

for the growing men and women to spread their wings from. If only mothers and fathers could help their children more in the most difficult time of all: leaving the nest, there'd be fewer pitiable things and crimes than there are. What *is* morality but love service? You see, it was never in my power to help Sandy like that: so the Great Father has helped him.

Do come and see me next time you come up. And I hope Beryl and John will come and have a night with me on the way to school and work.

Best love from
Edith

I now see the 'Marigold' years as a necessary period of adjustment, almost a fallow period, in spite of hard work, between my aunt's social and suffrage activities and the more mountainous years ahead during which she travelled much, on land and sea, as well as in spiritual realms beyond our understanding.

Meanwhile, the practical side of her nature found ample scope. There were bad seasons and crops alongside the good, and she accepted potato-blight with the same equanimity as a glut of apples. One summer the bees got a disease and had to be destroyed. So she made a pile of all six hives in the corner of the orchard and, adept at this sort of thing, sprinkled them with paraffin and set them alight – as though making an offering to the gods.

She watched the blue smoke weaving among the apple boughs with a curious expression of melancholy triumph. Indeed, I was far more distressed than she by this drastic action. No more honey for tea, I thought, no more pleasureable fear in approaching hives and watching the industry of the bees. And no more wonder at the swarming-time activities. I sat down on an overturned basket and wept.

My aunt, who was sweeping round the bonfire, rested her brush against an apple tree. 'I think a certain young person needs the company of another young person,' she said kindly. 'We'll drive out in the trap and have tea with the Goldburns.'

The Goldburns, mother and a daughter my own age, who lived in an ivy-covered cottage, had been taken under my aunt's wing. Sometimes she invited Marjorie, a pale child with peat-brown hair and matching eye, to meet me at 'Marigold'. But so far nothing had blossomed between us, in spite of Aunt Edith's remarks that Marjorie had no father and badly needed a friend. In each other's company we grew more and more silent; I longing to be off on my own, to the river or for a session in the stable, and she, no doubt, longing to get back home. So on this occasion I went unwillingly upstairs to brush my hair and wash my face. As I looked from the window I could see orange-bright eyes still glowing among the wood-ash where the orchard pile slowly smouldered away. Funny we should be going to visit the Goldburns . . . My aunt called to me in a hurry; she had stuck a jay's feather in her trilby hat to denote that she was going out. At that moment I heard hooves in the yard and went outside to see Miss Flanagan leading Nutty in the trap. Aunt Edith climbed in and took the reins. My gloom evaporated when she handed them to me. This afternoon she was in spanking form, enjoying the drive as much as I and enlivening me with 'pony-talk'. 'We might mate Bramble with an Arab stallion, and produce a real "classy" creature,' she suggested with a twinkle. Among animals, at least, she permitted class distinctions.

We arrived at the cottage all too soon. Mrs Goldburn, a grey widow in black alpaca, greeted my aunt and thanked her for a bunch of sweet peas. Marjorie hid behind her mother's skirts. There was none of the expected: 'Now, Marjorie, say "how d'you do!" and shake hands'.

Over the tea-table my aunt endeavoured to strike a spark by asking her about school, but could elicit nothing more than: 'S'allright,' 'Not so bad,' and 'I dunno'.

Whereupon her mother hastened to fill the gaps, talking volubly about her husband who, it seemed, had recently died and left her with little enough 'to make ends meet', which word from then on I interpreted as 'meat'. Nevertheless, there were potato-cakes and a slab of sticky parkin on the table, and the tea came strong, dark-coloured as the earthenware pot.

It was an uncomfortable meal. Marjorie sullenly consumed a vast number of potato-cakes while her mother's voice ran on without pause, the words tumbling over one another, awkward with dialect. But Aunt Edith listened – as she always did when most concerned – with her head on one side. I dreaded lest she invite the two of them to spend a day at 'Marigold', but thank heavens my aunt's idealism was sometimes tempered with the common sense she was supposed to lack

Be that as it may, I often marvelled at her knack of dissolving difficult situations or riding over them with positive enjoyment. Whereas my parents seemed always in the throes of some domestic problem or decision – such as whether to dismiss a first-class housemaid for stealing sweets – my aunt approached similar matters with intuition and a sense of humour. For instance, there was the time when she caught two boys taking apples from her orchard. It was a wet September afternoon and the boys, idling down the lane after school, spying around the garden and fields, found everywhere deserted. Whereupon they entered the orchard and helped themselves liberally to the red-cheeked Worcester Pearmains till their pockets and school-dinner baskets were full. Curiously enough my aunt seemed to have a reserve eye of eagle quality, and few such happenings escaped her notice. Visions and dreams in no way impeded her sight of here-and-now. On this occasion, donning a mackintosh and wellingtons, she plodded through the wet grass to the orchard and caught the boys, literally, red-handed. Their containers full, they had settled down under dripping boughs, to a long juicy munch. 'Do you like apples?' my aunt inquired as they gazed at her in dismay. Their mouths being too full for articulate reply, they merely nodded. 'Well, come along with me,' she said in an ominous voice. It says much for her command that they obeyed rather than dashing away through the hedge.

In the kitchen she ordered them to empty their pockets and baskets on the table. Grëtel, who was watching with fascination, declared: 'Der Anblick war wirklich sehr eindrucksvol!'

Soon the table was covered with the good red fruit set out neatly in rows. Their task done, the boys plainly were expecting a severe telling-off before being sent home. Aunt Edith merely surveyed apples and boys in turn as though assessing their relative values. After a few silent moments she gazed thoughtfully at the boys. 'And now,' she insisted in her gentlest voice, 'you may eat the apples!'

'Wot, all *them*!' exclaimed the larger boy as he twisted his cap around in an agony of anticipation. 'Yes', she replied, 'and then you'll learn how enjoyable stolen fruit can be!'

Grëtel, who told me this story with relish, related how at a certain point in their ordeal Aunt Edith had relented. But at least her orchard was never again raided.

Delinquency in children, she believed, was due not only to unhappy relationships between the parents, but also to lack of opportunity for imaginative play. 'Children need space as well as time for play,' she said, 'if they are to grow into happy and creative beings!' I remember her first question on seeing the Higginsons' new small house in Waterloo Road: 'But where are the children to play?' When she heard that they would have to use the tiny kitchen she promptly replied: 'Well, then, you'll have to move the table – it takes up all the centre-space. Please *do* get a drop-side table and keep it against the wall, then they'll be able to romp about in the middle of the room.' In anticipation of her next visit Mrs Higginson felt obliged to follow this advice and with happy results.

Such was her manner, it never occurred to me to disobey her, and I wonder, had she been my mother, how she would have dealt with my rebellion against governesses. I remember, for example, one icy afternoon being taken for a walk in the park by one of these long-suffering women. When I was ordered to put my gloves on I threw them in the Ribble (we happened to be walking along the chestnut avenue on its right bank). Gloves seemed synonymous with all the formalities I was growing more and more to dislike. After this and other incidents connected with my desire to live in the country, the last governess left; my aunt having suggested that the high school would suit me better.

I loved every minute at school, a Georgian building at the top end of Winckley Square. Here, for the first time, I felt independent; one of my joys was to walk out in the afternoons to have tea with Aunt Edith on her rare returns to town (occasionally she came in to make sure that Uncle Charlie was being properly looked after).

She encouraged me to give full accounts of lessons and teachers, and this habit of relating to her has impressed those brightly-coloured days on my mind. After my learning to count and do addition and subtraction with haricot beans, our time was largely spent among sand and plasticine. Ardent six-year-olds, I remember with what eager hands we staged the Battle of Hastings, intently moulding the hill upon which Harold of England was to stand gazing improvidently upward into a hail of arrows. Joyfully we planted the fatal tree over whose root the horse of William Rufus was destined to stumble. We were the creators and life was on our side.

This sort of learning – the translating of abstract stories and ideas into concrete materials – was appreciated by Aunt Edith, who was then in the first glow of her 'Steiner' phase. Indeed, many of Steiner's ideas on education have been absorbed by our own primary schools.

But I also found my window-corner desk a happy retreat into an abstract world. Here, about thirty years earlier, my two aunts had themselves looked out on to the trees and gardens of Winckley Square.

While Aunt Alice, the practical one, never retreated into the abstract, Aunt Edith combined a capacity for action with a habit of reflection. At any rate, her sort of thinking, slow and deep, led to a rare diversity of doing. About this time she decided that she must learn to drive a car: pony-traps served for short distances, but now she wanted to be more mobile. Accordingly, a few months before Charles, the chauffeur, was due to be called up, she suggested that whenever he could be spared he should give her a lesson.

He used to call for her at 'Marigold' and take her out on the Southport road. 'She was that determined to learn quickly,' he recalled, 'she'd say: "Am I doing all right? Do I need another lesson?" She took in everything an' forgot nothing.'

During these lessons she spoke only of the matter in hand and was soon able to manage by herself. When that day came Charles was half-regretful; he had enjoyed teaching her – especially as the lessons had profited him as much as his pupil. The five shillings she gave him every run out was worth something in 1916.

When I questioned him further he recalled her strange clothes, slow speech and unusual activities: 'One day when I went to "Marigold" I found her on the roof mending t'thatch!' But when I asked for details of conversation he was silent a moment before replying: 'I can't rightly remember what she *said*, but I can tell you one thing – she was a very *heavy* thinker!'

Charles, an unconscious humorist, had a poet's faculty for expressing truth with economy.

As one would expect, my aunt always managed to find time for reading. Not only was she well informed; her mind was richly stored and cultivated, the result of reading slowly and pondering on what she read. Where books were concerned she was neither a plodder nor a skimmer. I have seen her, after reading a page or two, lean back in her chair considering whatever ideas had been newly presented to her before turning on. But apart from acquired knowledge she was gifted with wisdom; you felt there were deep wells within her, life-giving and inexhaustible. She was the sort of person you never came to an end of.

As a family we regarded her later reading in realms of mysticism and religion as distinctly queer, so that the present of a book from Aunt Edith was unwrapped with some misgiving. From her I certainly received unusual selections, even in my early years. No one would have expected her to buy the gaily-coloured annuals and story-books given by ordinary people at Christmas and for birthdays. Even so, her choices were odd, and generally beyond my grasp. I must confess that my heart, so eager to love all books, sank a little as I undid the familiar parcel from her.

Yet in those days she nearly always sent me a book about animals. Not the comfortable cats with blue bows, or friendly dogs and horses in picture-postcard surroundings which I had grown used to. Often they were foreign, and usually wild, creatures: Russian wolves, German boars, and wild asses from the Lebanon. But there were milder interludes of Brer Rabbit and Brer Fox. One of my happiest memories is of her delighted expression as she read aloud of their mischievous doings: 'Do what you like with me, Brer Fox, but *don't* throw me into the middle of that big thorn-bush!' Sometimes, flinging the book aside, she would continue with more thrilling adventures than any pressed into pages of print. Amid much laughter, head-shaking and wagging of an admonitory forefinger, I was led, enthralled, from episode to episode.

It was a new world, infinitely colourful, strange and moving, into which she took me. Although I spent so much more time with Mother, who often read to us, I can only remember my aunt's stories.

On my twelfth birthday she gave me *Lives of the Hunted* by the American naturalist, Ernest Thompson Seton. From this she read aloud extracts concerning Johnny Bear, Tito, the coyote, and her favourite Randy 'the roustabout sparrow with the pride of his white cravat and white collar-points'. But I was too young to appreciate the quality of these stories revealing our kinship with the animals. As I have suggested, this was one of my aunt's pet themes, so that the animals in the stories she chose for me generally displayed human characteristics.

As I grew older I learned to suspect meanings wrapped inside her gifts. In this instance it was her endorsement of Thompson Seton's purpose to encourage and preserve wild life, which he considered as important as the preservation of works of art. On our walks she would tell me about the animals in Yellowstone Park living in freedom compared with their unfortunate fellows in zoos and circuses. She even shook her head at our canary trilling in the caged yellow sunlight of a spring morning. I was assured that a robin redbreast (if not a canary) 'in a cage/Puts all Heaven in a rage'.

I believe it was largely owing to her that my mind didn't set too firmly in the nicely-shaped mould of Anglicanism and Conservatism into which I had been poured. In a class-conscious society, paved with the conventions of a prosperous provincial neighbourhood, Aunt Edith stood islanded, a source of release to those who wished to be free.

And during the war when the image of the Hun as a fat man in grey with a spiked helmet on his bullet-head was printed on my mind, I never heard anti-German talk from her. On the contrary, immersed by now in a study of the language and literature, she admired the German nation – if not its hierarchy. Shortly after the war she sent me, from Weimar and Eisenach, foxes and bears carved in wood, which were far more alive than the wooden translations of German poems and fairy-tales accompanying them in bulky parcels. I felt Mother's frown upon these presents; the war was too fresh in her mind for German parcels to be acceptable. And here I must point out that at that time she worked just as hard as Aunt Edith. I remember her setting out for all-night sessions at the station buffet, doing Red Cross work and knitting endless hideous garments of khaki.

Not surprisingly Aunt Edith held pacifist views which, as Mother acidly remarked, seemed to clash with her previous suffrage activities. But for all her German sympathies she did her full share of digging for England.

Our household was almost too peaceful now that Father's sharp-edged presence was reduced to an occasional postcard. From 1915 to 1919 he served with the R.A.M.C. in Mesopotamia, and when he came home on leave, looking very handsome in his uniform, he seemed almost like a stranger. We were awed by this aspect of him, commanding as ever, but more at ease, happier, indeed, than ever before or since. Encamped among the Arabs, with snipers continually around the tents, later acting-colonel in charge of a field-hospital, battling as much against typhus and cholera as against any other enemy, Father came into his own. Untroubled by fears of disease and death he thrived on danger. 'Had it not been for you two and your Mother,' he told me afterwards, 'I'd have never come back.'

He loved the heat and vastness of the desert. Loved its night skies and huge stars and the sense of freedom from human restrictions. Not all the flies of Arabia troubled him – nor a dead horse in the stream from which they drank. For his military services he received the OBE, and after the Armistice he remained on to continue research work on cholera, dysentery and malaria. Finally, he brought home a shipload of men stricken with Spanish 'flu without a single casualty.

In their pride of him Mother and Aunt Edith were at one for the first time in their lives.

My early war memories are of golden days ticking by and apples falling in the 'Marigold' orchard while distant guns rattled and thundered. But one spring, following a family attack of whooping-cough and measles, began a surprising interlude. Because we had all three been prostrated by these diseases, Mother decided to take a cottage in the country.

This revolutionary idea was fired in part by the example of 'Marigold' and in part by my constant pleading to go away from the town. Beneath Mother's conventional crust was a real love of the countryside and gardening. While half-deploring, I believe she half-envied Aunt Edith's way of life, though she tackled a spell in the country very differently from her sister-in-law.

Brock Cottage, except for its tall chimneys, was so thickly covered with ivy that you couldn't see the red brick underneath. Roses, clematis and honeysuckle twisted up the posts of a small verandah and clung to the ivy above. On the right of the path leading to the front-door stood a thick privet-hedge, clipped to the shape of turrets. Behind this fortress was the sort of cottage-garden one dreams about; a garden of low box-hedges and clipped yews where clumps of lavender and saxifrage, and cushions of moss settle themselves into corners of flower beds.

It was an old-fashioned garden where ancient 'lantern' poppies burned in the sun, and tough-leaved cornflowers flourished. Holly-hocks towered above a medley of columbines, lupins and peonies. And there were stocks and mignonette to fill the evenings with scent. Beyond a kitchen-garden buttoned with cabbages, bordered with runner-beans and peas, was an orchard of 'mossed cottage trees', otherwise known as Worcester Pearmains, with their sage-green crust of lichen. And, one better than 'Marigold', in the orchard there was a well, a Jack-and-Jill affair sheltered by a wooden roof from which hung a bucket and pulley. Actually we earned our drinking water by vigorous action at the pump in the backyard. But the well-water tasted better; moss-cool and with a tang of earth and iron.

Our education was continued by yet another governess whose Christian names were Anne Marie. She was genteel, several cuts above the gardener (we discovered to our surprise) and she taught us table-manners, French and *Little Arthur's England*. Nature, and a certain amount of human nature, we learned from Ernest, the farmer's boy. He also taught us to catch roach with a bent pin.

Mother deplored our relationship with Ernest. There was a regretted day when we crept out of the cottage at six in the morning to meet him for a glorious fishing expedition. It was spring and during the course of the morning he must have shown us dozens of birds' nests. Apart from this, we caught five fat, red-tipped roach and eventually, after devouring our hoard of biscuits and bananas, we arrived home bedraggled, hungry, elated, around tea-time. We were soundly spanked and sent to bed.

Most certainly this would not have been Aunt Edith's reaction. She, who always encouraged such encounters, would have welcomed its social implications. Though Mother, doubtless, was genuinely concerned by our long absence, she was even more concerned by our contact with Ernest, a rough, broad-spoken lad who could teach us more than we ought to know. I found such restrictions upon our country friendships irksome and couldn't understand her attitude. Why, Aunt Edith actually invited the neighbouring children to play with me at 'Marigold'!

Then there was our relationship with the gardener, Tom Rich, who had a strawberry-mark on his face and who also had a fund of knowledge to impart. From him we learned how to smoke out wasps' nests. We watched him kill the slugs which used the box-hedge as a harbour, and listened to his discourse on spiders – insects so much more desirable in a garden than butterflies. Though Mother discouraged our long conversations with him (because they interrupted his work) she obviously enjoyed talking to him herself, a great deal more than to Anne Marie who never deigned to speak to Tom.

One afternoon Aunt Edith drove up to Brock Cottage in her pony- trap. I think Mother was pleased to see her, but Anne Marie looked haughtily at this 'man-woman' (as she later referred to her) who 'took off her hat as she entered the house'. She pursed her lips when my aunt spoke to her across the tea-table, and lifting her cup she crooked her little finger more markedly than usual in defiance of leather and whipcord. Aunt Edith looked amused, and also half-baffled by this new type of person whose black velvet throat-band wobbled over her adam's apple.

After tea my aunt engaged Tom in a prolonged 'vegetable conference' while Anne Marie, silent and sniffing, cleared the table before putting on her hat and bicycling off to church.

In spite of the tedium of governess-instruction, the Brock Cottage idyll was as enchanting as that of 'Marigold'. We kept four hens, grew our own vegetables and spent hours gathering fruit. On wet days we used to watch Mother baking bread and preparing elderberries for wine. And here lay the biggest difference between my mother and my aunt. Whereas Mother excelled at housecraft and was able to turn her capable hands to anything, the idea of Aunt Edith cooking or sewing was unthinkable. There always had to be a Miss Tucker. And though 'Marigold' was attractive in its oak-and-folkweave fashion, Mother had a knack of making even a cottage look 'different' from anyone else's. Brock Cottage was as simply furnished as 'Marigold' but the curtains and chintzes were lighter and gayer. And in a corner-cupboard were arranged Dresden china shepherdesses. Aunt Edith never went in for such frivolities. Even her landscape pictures, compared with our pastel-coloured Birket Fosters, were heavy and strong with trees that might have taken root from Wagner's music. Indeed, while Mother herself resembled a Dresden shepherdess, my aunt was more like Brünhilde. And here in passing I must remark that though Mother was a real musician, it required the tenacity of Aunt Edith to sit through three performances of *The Ring* (at Bayreuth) with unswerving attention. I only hope she enjoyed them, but I suspect that, in line with her pursuit of the good, it might have been a feat of endurance. However, though she never professed to practise the arts, she always encouraged those who did.

In the intervals between sheer hard manual work at 'Marigold' she invited Patti and Amy Mayor to the cottage so that Amy might play for her guests. Sometimes Aunt Alice would come for the afternoon and play to us after tea. Though not a distinguished performer, her carol-playing added much to the 'Marigold' Christmas. Having no children of her own, Aunt Edith used to celebrate Christmas by inviting the neighbouring boys and girls to a party. She would decorate the huge tree with red and white candles and a star just touching the ceiling. while Miss Tucker spent hours concocting trifles and cakes in the kitchen.

Aunt Edith was imbued with the German idea of Christmas celebrated on Christmas Eve, with the tree and star at the heart of it. At home, in spite of my begging, we never had a tree – few people had in those days. But I longed for one because the Christmas tree, unlike our rounded English oaks and beeches, pointed up to the star, as though linking the earth with the sky. At least, this was the thought I was groping after though I couldn't then put it into words. Later I came to realize that my aunt regarded her Christmas tree and star as symbolic of the relationship between earth and heaven.

Relationships between people and our relationship with the universe – this theme constantly recurs. And work on the land and with animals, to her way of thinking, was fundamental to human well-being. She deplored any kind of life which cut people away from their roots. That is why, whenever possible, she took women and girls who worked in factories for a day out in the country where they might breathe their share of green and growing things.

With 'Marigold' came the opportunity to do just this for her 'Brook Street' girls. On fine summer Sundays she drove them to her cottage in her pony-trap. After a good lunch and a rest they were invited to help in the garden – invited rather than expected, as in the case of the suffragettes! Work in the garden was a delight to girls who for most of the week were shut up in factories. And not only a delight, but also an education. Maggie, for instance, was amazed to observe in the orchard a row of hen-coops from which ducklings emerged in quacking content. 'But 'ow d'you mak 'em cum out 'o th' ens' eggs?' she exclaimed incredulously. On inquiring into the feeding-apparatus of a mother-hen, she was equally astonished to learn that hens do not suckle their chickens.

For these girls the countryside began and ended with Moor Park, and in their eyes all birds were sparrows. Perhaps my aunt's object lessons in natural history were more vital to them than a taste of music and the arts. According to her, anyone who grew up ignorant of the worlds of nature stood little chance of maturing into an adult with a whole and balanced mind – an opinion not so widely recognized in those days.

To increase her own knowledge of the subject Aunt Edith approached Mr Harrison, botany lecturer at Preston's Harris Institute, and asked if she might attend classes and accompany students on their expeditions. These outings proved her to be not only an enthusiastic student, but also an unexpected teacher.

While Mr Harrison pointed out scientific aspects of leaf and flower, Mrs Rigby made observations on other levels. There was the afternoon when she watched the lecturer's careful dissection of a wild rose into its component parts: calyx, corolla and so on. After all had been counted, listed and entered into notebooks, Mr Harrison flicked the remains on to the grass. 'And now,' his new pupil commented, 'we've learned all about the rose, but in the discovery the rose itself has vanished!'

Answering the lecturer's expression of surprise she pursued her train of thought: 'We can't *know* a flower, or anything else, by analysis; we can only learn certain facts about it. But in the process the essence has gone. Dissect a rose, and where is the scent? Where is *it* ?' After this unusually long speech, observing the bewilderment of her listeners, she smiled apologetically. 'But I mustn't divert you with philosophy; that's another matter. Though somewhere I believe the two matters meet.'

What Mr Harrison made of these excursions in which the path to knowledge led through such byways, I don't know, except that he told Mrs Higginson he found her an unpredictable person.

IX

*Eurhythmy. More of anthroposophy. Dr Rittelmeyer
and the Christian community. Methods in agriculture.
Dr Heidenreich. Uncle Charlie in retirement.
Women's Institute.*

MR Harrison's conclusion was frequently echoed by Uncle
Charlie. I remember him shaking his head at my father and
remarking: 'Well, Arthur, your sister Edith certainly is a curio – I
never know what she'll be up to next!'

As for the rest of us, we had long ago come to expect the unexpected from
her. So that her new venture into the realm of eurhythmics was accepted
almost without comment, except for mother's 'Imagine Edith designing
dance-dresses!'

Eurhythmy was the new art of movement, devised by Steiner, to which
my aunt boldly introduced her followers in Preston. Years later I heard
about these classes from Mary Yeadon, daughter of the Albert who had
obliged over the matter of a keg of paraffin (and a bicycle). Mary had been
one of the first members of the eurhythmy group. 'We used to dance in
white sleeveless tunics' (which my aunt had indeed designed) she told me,
'they were very short and full to allow plenty of room for free, swinging
movements. As Mrs Rigby explained to her class: "Body and soul together
in rhythm of movement and song!" '

Mary described how they sang songs of Blake to the accompaniment of
wide, sweeping gestures. 'And we danced barefoot and with our hair loose.
Mrs Rigby encouraged us to spread our toes, relax our limbs, and imagine
we were waves or branches in the wind. I remember singing: "How sweet is
the shepherd's sweet lot!" And playing imaginary pipes, and running up
and down imaginary hills – it was all very energetic.'

This account fits perfectly with my own picture of Aunt Edith, whose
password at the time seemed contained in Blake's *Energy is Eternal Delight* –
even though (in *The Marriage of Heaven and Hell*) this phrase is ascribed to
the devil!

Sometimes she would lead her class to pad softly as though on moss
sinuously between invisible trees, while they sang together: 'Tyger, Tyger,
burning bright/In the forests of the night . . .' A moment later they would
become the wind – all flowing hair and arms and garments, soundless
before singing: 'Never seek to tell thy love . . .'

They 'did' *The Little Black Boy*, *The Lamb* and *The Sunflower* in which,
after lying stiff on the floor for a few lines, the dancers arose, following their
leader in graceful movement to stand on tiptoe with lifted arms and faces

aspiring to the sun.

In her conception of the unity and harmony of life, my aunt, rainbowed by Blake, was already standing, if not dancing, in the path of Rudolf Steiner whose definition of eurhythmy as 'visible speech and visible song' she had so faithfully carried out.

Eurhythmy also embodies Steiner's idea of 'the threefold being of man', body, soul and spirit, in harmony with himself and his environment, which expresses one aspect of anthroposophy. My aunt's interest in the whole subject deepened the more she read of its remarkable founder. And once she had actually met Dr Steiner and heard him speak, she was wholly won over. At last, it seemed, she realized the purpose for which she had been born. In the words of Arnold Freeman, author of *Rudolf Steiner's Message to Mankind*, who was to become one of her closest friends: 'Through Anthroposophy she found her complete fulfilment; it satisfied the mystic, as well as the practical, side of her nature'.

Steiner was more than merely ahead of his time; he seemed to speak out of another dimension. Yet his life had begun in very ordinary circumstances. The son of a stationmaster, he was born in 1861, in a small village near Vienna. Because of his father's occupation the family moved about from place to place so that the young Rudolf was late in learning to read. Even so, his school report invariably commented on his unusual intelligence and eventually he won a scholarship to the Vienna School of Technology.

Even as a young child Steiner was aware that he lived in two worlds: the transient world of colour and sound and touch, ephemeral as a dandelion-clock, and the real world, the continuing city beyond human destruction. Soon after learning to read he came upon a geometry book on his master's desk and asked if he might borrow it. For some time after this, he writes, 'my mind was full of triangles and squares and polygons. I tormented myself with asking where parallel lines meet'. In this way he came to an awareness of forms independent of the senses. In his autobiography, speaking of himself at the age of eight, he says:

That there is something one can lay hold of exclusively in the spirit – that gave me immense joy. It was in geometry that I first found such happiness.

Out of geometry there emerged for me a way of thinking which developed further and further. Already, even though more or less unconsciously, it lived in me during my childhood; when I was about twenty it became fully conscious and took explicit shape.

Geometry exemplified for me a kind of knowledge which while seeming to originate in man, has a significance all its own . . .

The reality of the spiritual world was to me as completely certain as that of the physical world. But I felt a need to justify this to my own thinking . . .

Recalling his ideas at the age of fourteen, he continues:

The spiritual world stood self-evident before me. But I felt I must enter it through the doorway of nature.[1]

From now on he resolved to prove that his experience of the spiritual life was as valid as that of life in the body. And, undoubtedly, to his own satisfaction and that of his followers he was to succeed in this undertaking.

We were baffled by my aunt's attempts to explain the processes of such a mind. And yet, though she couldn't transmit his message intellectually, I realized even then that she was groping towards a truth beyond our reach. As I grew older I was reassured by the thought of Steiner's logical and mathematical mind, and by his analytical approach (through matter) to the spiritual world.

While he was studying mathematics, chemistry and philosophy at the School of Technology in Vienna, he developed his imaginative gifts to pursue the inquiries begun in childhood. The next step was the practice of severe spiritual and mental disciplines which led him to a knowledge beyond the range of most of us ordinary people. He called himself a 'spiritual scientist' and no better name could be found, even if it appears contradictory to some schools of thought.

When Steiner lectured, his listeners were amazed at his learning and authority. A scholar in so many fields – for example, he edited all Goethe's scientific writings – he remained a man of vision. Throughout his more than six thousand lectures he spoke without notes, addressing the audience with the full power of his personality. Indeed all who heard him believed that while being fully conscious of the ground beneath his feet, he was speaking from the spirit. At any rate, this was the effect he had on my aunt and Arnold Freeman who were attending his lectures at about the same time, though they didn't meet each other for some years.

Aunt Edith spoke of Steiner as a prophet, but she never gave me a clear idea of him as a person, whereas Arnold Freeman described the man: 'I was drawn to him first of all by the warmth of his handshake – though he must have shaken hands with thousands of people, there was always a personal welcome for each newcomer. And faced as we were, with his vision and complete integrity, it was impossible to doubt.'

A similar tribute comes from Eduard Schuré, the French authority on the Ancient Mysteries. Referring to a lecture-cycle given in Paris he writes:

1 *Rudolf Steiner's Message to Mankind*, by Arnold Freeman.

When Rudolf Steiner was describing the events and realities of the spirit-world, he seemed to be absolutely at home with them. He was not merely describing, he was actually seeing objects and scenes from these unknown regions, and he made them so visible to others that cosmic phenomena appeared actual. Listening to him one could not doubt the reality of his spiritual vision, which appeared as clear as physical sight, but with a far more extended range. I would have crossed the Atlantic to hear him.[1]

In writing this book I have spoken to many of Steiner's followers who reveal a man of quite outstanding gifts in whom intellect and imagination are finely balanced. I only wish I had listened when my aunt spoke of his 'sense-independent, rational thinking' which led him to discover powers undreamed-of in daily life. But for me, as for most of us, the way through to this unexplored region is too hard. It requires daily meditation and spiritual disciplines. With Steiner meditation and action went hand-in-hand because he combined the wisdom of the East with the practical Christianity of the West. And so he attained levels of consciousness beyond the reach (and the desire) of most people. The main theme of his teaching is the spiritual evolution of man through life after life. To understand this is to begin to understand what we truly are, and why we are here among the struggles and conflicts of this earth.

Steiner's message came at a time when the life of the spirit was everywhere at a low ebb. As my aunt pointed out, while he was sowing good seed in one furrow, another was being prepared for Nazidom. And the tares, springing from the cracks of a divided Church, were, for a time, to overwhelm the wheat. Many thoughtful people in Germany were aware of these dangers until one day in 1921, a group of ministers appealed to Steiner for guidance. Could he not help them to renew the religious life of mankind?[2]

One of these ministers, Dr Friedrich Rittelmeyer, the well-known Lutheran, was at the time attracting larger congregations than any other preacher in Berlin. But the meeting with Steiner entirely changed his outlook. In his remarkable book: *Rudolf Steiner Enters My Life* he explains that Steiner 'had always emphasized that the Anthroposophical Society was not a religious organization and could not undertake to set up a Church'. Such a responsibility must come from outside. But with this understanding he agreed to give his help.

And help he gave, to the full extent of his power, so that when Rittelmeyer received Steiner's ritual for the Act of the Consecration of Man (which corresponds to the Eucharist), a great idea came to him. 'It

1 *Scientist of the Invisible*, by A.P. Shepherd.
2 *Rudolf Steiner's Message to Mankind*, by Arnold Freeman.

began to dawn on me,' he said 'that here a religious service might be created in which all true Christians could be at one; which could serve as the centre of a true Christian community life around which a new, many-sided, ever-growing religious life could unfold.'

So it happened that Rittelmeyer, inspired by Steiner, became in 1922 the first leader of the Christian Community. This movement he described as 'the birth of a new sacramentalism founded out of spiritual vision'.

Today there are about a hundred Christian Community churches in Germany and elsewhere, including this country. The Community offers the seven sacraments to Christians of any denomination – an expression of unity which greatly appealed to my aunt.

She was full of admiration for Rittelmeyer's sincerity and courage in an enterprise which meant breaking away from his enthusiastic following. I well remember her warm, soft voice as she pronounced his name and spoke of his wonderful book which, soon after meeting him, she began to translate.

About this time she made another 'Steiner' contact destined to lead her into really heavy seas of translation: Dr Hermann Poppelbaum, whose name, constantly on her lips during the years ahead, was to provide us plentifully with family-joke material. (Like everyone else, we were driven to laugh at what we couldn't understand.) Dr Poppelbaum, it seemed, had written a book, *Man and Animal*, expressing Steiner's views on spiritual, as well as physical, evolution, which I will discuss in a later chapter. Meanwhile, my aunt seized upon it for future tussles with the unknowable.

Besides meeting professors and leaders, she was introduced to many other members of the group which included an unusual medley of businessmen, artists, teachers, workmen and students. Freed from bars of class- and colour-prejudice, released from ties of religious dogma, at least they spoke a common language in their common search for truth.

Among this odd-coloured crowd Aunt Edith was in her element. On our breakfast table would appear ecstatic postcards, of angels, statues and churches, from Dornach, where she now spent much of her time. On a brief return visit to 'Marigold' she called to see us one afternoon and stayed for tea. She never made the usual obvious remarks about the weather, and after inquiring if we were all well, she began, hesitantly, to talk about the development of spiritual organs. This made me uncomfortable, thinking of celestial kidneys and liver, but Mother refused to be drawn into a discussion which seemed to her a contradiction in terms. Rather flatly we relapsed into the commonplaces of afternoon-tea conversation. With Mother and my aunt at the same table I felt constricted and uneasy, never quite knowing which side I was on. And here I must make it clear that though my aunt held such strong convictions, she never tried to force her ideas on other people. If she converted anyone it was achieved by her example, even by her silences rather than by what she said.

Obviously Aunt Edith never asked us, the uninitiates, to her 'Steiner' gatherings in Preston. All the same, I sometimes wondered what was said on these occasions, knowing that my father's derision was based on ignorance of the subject, and Mother's on prejudice. Perhaps she assured her group, composed mostly of women, that Steiner believed women to be less earthy, and therefore more ready for spiritual truth, than men. Whether or not this was true of her listeners, it was true of herself.

As I grew older I began to take an interest in some of her ideas, especially when she got on to the subject of etheric and astral bodies. According to Steiner the etheric body is the storehouse of memory. More than this, he described it as a system of soul-forces 'which have built up and maintained the life of the physical body from birth onwards . . . these forces are the same as those by which the brain functions in thinking'.[1]

If this sounds too difficult I believe Spenser said the same thing three hundred years earlier in the simpler language of poetry:

For of the soul the body form doth take
For soul is form and doth the body make.

At death, it seems, the etheric body with its memories is released to expand in the invisible world. The astral body, on the other hand, represents a higher level of consciousness when the mind, emptied of physical images, is ready to receive supersensible beings and events, and to cross the threshold of time. This may happen after intense practice in meditation; it also happens in those dreams which take us to places we actually visit in the so-called future.

Even though I have had such dreams, I was sceptical of my aunt's talk of 'astral travel', and when she assured me: 'You don't need to get on a train to visit people; you can visit them in the astral!' I wondered whether she was joking.

Everything which to my solid schoolgirl outlook seemed real and durable appeared to her as a reflection, while thoughts and ideas, she assured me, are *things*. She had an aesthetic sense of beauty, not only in people, art and the world of nature, but also, as I discovered to my surprise, in regard to clothes. Confident of her approval I had once tried to act up to her by remarking that to dress well was a waste of time. But she shook her head and reproached me: 'That's a mistake, you know. It's important to look your best.'

Nonplussed, I wondered if she had revised her opinions. Then I realized that although she dressed in the oddest fashion, her strange

1 *Scientist of the Invisible*, by A.P. Shepherd.

garments were always of good materials and in striking 'off-the-catalogue' colours.

'Don't misunderstand me,' she went on, gazing into infinities through her leaf-strewn orchard, 'though everything in the material world changes and dies, here and now these things *are* important!'

Another day, while looking round a country churchyard, she pointed out a Celtic cross and explained to me that the circle around the intersecting cross-beams represents the Eternal Sun, the Light of the World, behind the physical sun which burns away. 'And in this,' she said, tracing round the circle with her forefinger, 'pagan and Christian are brought together.'

I began to see why Herbert had had to spend that night before Midsummer in a hayfield. And looking back, I wonder if she finally chose north Wales to be her home in anticipation of archaeological delights. And also because in 1923, two years before his death, Steiner himself had stood on the summit of Penmaenmawr mountain. He had gone there to examine two intersecting stone circles which greatly intrigued him because, as he exclaimed to his companions, they were very similar to the ground-plan of his Goetheanum in Dornach.

And here I must digress to describe the Goetheanum, an impressive wooden structure consisting of two intersecting domes which Steiner had designed from his knowledge of circles and cromlechs. In 1920 the building had been completed as the Free University of Spiritual Science and the New Science of Man to serve as a centre for courses on education, medicine, agriculture and religion. Here also all the arts, including the old mystery plays and the newly-devised eurhythmy, were encouraged and developed.

Although membership of this society was increasing in every country in Europe, it faced a strong opposition from politicians, theologians and scientists who feared that Steiner's enlightened teaching might disturb their set ideas. In 1922 this opposition blazed out, literally, in the great Goetheanum fire. Steiner and his followers could only stand by and watch while the fruit of years of devotion and toil was utterly destroyed. After this disaster Steiner felt his creative genius overwhelmed by evil forces. But eventually, in an upsurge of energy and hope, he designed another Goetheanum, similar to the first, which was completed after his death.[1]

I have come across a postcard of this virtual temple to Goethe addressed to Nancy Watchurst by my aunt, who has written on the back: 'It has been too full of beauty and wisdom here for Michael.' Who the unfortunate Michael was I don't know, but *à propos* the post-card I have discovered that in 1928 Aunt Edith, with a party from England, attended

1   *Ibid.*

the opening of the new Goetheanum. It was built of concrete, and I can't help wondering if this fact recalled her own burning of Lord Leverhulme's bungalow, by now rebuilt in stone.

I should explain here that Steiner's reverence for Goethe had begun when he was a student attending the lectures of the famous scholar, Karl Julius Schrör. Later he became so absorbed in Goethe's life and works that he edited several philosophic papers as well as all the writings on natural science. Finally he went to live in Weimar and helped to produce the massive 150-volumes of the complete works.

It was through Steiner, of course, that my aunt developed her own interest in Goethe which led her, many times, to Weimar for meetings and lectures. It seemed to be part of her pattern that while she was living at 'Marigold' she came upon Goethe's idea of the Urpflanz (Ideal Plant) in which she tried to interest me. But this seed fell by the wayside of my understanding until she reverted to good, plain English and explained the relationship between plants and insects which depend upon one another, and spring from a similar archetypal plan:

Behold the blossom! It is a butterfly fettered to the earth.
Behold the butterfly! It is a blossom freed by the cosmos.

This was one of her favourite quotations, so that in her presence I began to imagine blue fritillaries as flying harebells; and a primrose became a yellow brimstone captured in a fist of leaves.

Aunt Edith had been more distressed than I realized when her bees had had to be destroyed on account of brood-disease. It was in searching for a reason for this calamity that she lighted on Steiner's nine lectures on bees. One of them she translated into English, along with several other papers on agricultural subjects.

Through her labours she discovered that bee-diseases had been almost unknown till the 'nineties, when bee-keepers began experimenting with their eyes on profit from honey rather than on the welfare of the hive. 'We lost our English Queen through love of honey-money rather than love of the honey-bee!' my aunt remarked with a pleased smile at so rare a witticism.

Care for their own prospects rather than for those of the bee-colony no doubt led keepers to mechanize functions which should be organic, to feed their bees with sugar in spring, and, in general, to interfere with the Law of the Bee until gradually our English species died out. Although Aunt Edith had bought a fresh lot of Dutch bees which, along with 'Italians', were then being imported, they too succumbed to the fatal brood-disease.

As always, Steiner warned against exploitation which ignored a true understanding of the creature. He believed that man must first of all love the animal, insect, even vegetable, from which he eventually hopes to profit. Through his teaching my aunt also learned that beet sugar, taken from the root, is less suitable food for bees than cane-sugar from the stem. Over the tea-table one afternoon we had quite a lecture on the subject. 'Winged creatures, after all,' she said, slyly dropping three lumps into Miss Tucker's cup, 'were never designed for underground food!'

Another day, as I watched her spraying fruit trees, she told me that Steiner was a poet as well as a scientist. 'Behold the tree!' she exclaimed, shooting her spray at a promising Worcester Pearmain, 'It is a bee-colony fettered to the earth!'[1]

This way of looking could see that an apple-pip set in the darkness of the earth corresponded to an egg; the leaves were larvae transformed; the bud represented the chrysalis; and the blossoms, with their lovely, not-useful petals, were the drones, to give delight but not to labour.

After hearing all this I felt pretty well grounded in the theory of correspondences, and when later, to my intense pleasure, I came upon the same idea in Swedenborg's writings, I realized that it must be as old as thought itself, expressing the view of poet, mystic, philosopher and of every scientist who has the vision of 'a world in a grain of sand'.

Coming upon Steiner fresh from 'Marigold', my aunt, to begin with, was naturally most interested in his argicultural lectures. One in particular, concerning the soil, gave her immense satisfaction because it showed that she had already embodied some of his ideas in her own work.

She had always eschewed chemical sprays and the constant use of artificial manures, believing that to upset the soil is to upset the balance of man. I won't beat again on that well-sounded drum except to point out that in Steiner's youth artifical fertilizers and manures had been greeted as God-sent. He saw them as what, in fact, they are: man-made products to be used with caution, and he taught that unless scientists are prepared to carry out experiments in accordance with the spiritual, as well as the natural, laws, disease and death must follow.

Having learned a lesson from the bee-disease, Aunt Edith explained to me that whenever we interfere with nature it must be with good intent and not just for profit and convenience. And then, getting into her stride, she impressed me with our responsibility as human beings, 'the only creatures who've been given a choice in the matter. If we ill-treat nature we ourselves suffer in the end. And most people blame God!' she admonished lightly, not wanting me just yet to feel too heavily involved. All the same, it seemed that one had to be religious in order to be a really good farmer.

As to the results of treating nature almost too well, I recently heard an amusing story concerning Jimmy Watchurst, whom she had coached in

1 *Understanding the Honey Bee*, by C.T.G. Barker.

Steiner methods. In accordance with this new teaching, Jimmy, who was a keen gardener, had prepared a patch of land to receive some brussel-sprouts seedlings. In due course the seedlings, planted under a waxing moon, grew up tall and strong and sprouted sprouts: compact buds that swelled almost visibly until they appeared to be half the size of cabbages. Amazed at the sight, Jimmy invited his friends one Sunday morning for a glass of sherry. But first of all they were led into the kitchen-garden to view his sprouts. 'They must be some new kind of vegetable!' a fellow-grower exclaimed incredulously. From that moment they became the joke of the neighbourhood, and were ever afterwards referred to as Jimmy's 'Rudolf-Steiner' sprouts. Not even Aunt Edith could rival him here.

In later years she deplored the new battery system of keeping hens, though it was Aunt Alice, thinking back to her beloved White Wyandottes, who shook her head at the sight of night-lighted hen-cabin windows. 'Those poor birds!' she exclaimed with grief in her voice. 'They make them work in factories now!'

But it was an article in a country magazine – on the artificial insemination of bees – which disturbed Aunt Edith most of all. While I was thinking what a tricky process this must be, she was pondering over future possibilities, from insects to animals to man. Such a method of profiting from frustrated instinct was anathema to her. She saw in it not merely a working against natural law, but an affront to life for the sake of material gain.

Such unspiritual science was more than upsetting to my aunt with her belief in archetypes: original patterns and forms of which the natural shape, whether plant, insect, or animal, was the temporary expression. She reverenced all forms of life and believed that plants and animals, like ourselves, have their place in the heavenly kingdom.

When she was talking on these lines I used to imagine furrier bees of black and gold coming to rest on the blue flowers of heaven. And in those pastures,whose every blade of grass is greener and sharper to the feet than our own, animals grazing in freedom . . .

I vividly remember one afternoon we got on to the subject of horses, and knowing that here she was sure of my interest, she let herself go: 'He has a *fine* etheric body, the horse!' she exclaimed enthusiastically as she demonstrated pricked ears with pointing forefingers.

People said Mrs Rigby's head was in the clouds because she spoke of cosmic forces affecting human actions and vice-versa. If she restrained me from killing spiders because they ate harmful insects, she wouldn't allow the destruction of butterflies which laid eggs on her cabbage leaves.

Even in the matter of killing such pests as wasps, magpies and mice she did her best to preserve the balance of nature. The cats, of course, were allowed their fill of mice because they were obeying their own laws. As to ourselves, she would have rejoiced in a law which forbade cruel methods of killing animals, such as trapping, hunting, and bleeding calves and pigs to make the flesh white. 'The very word "slaughter-house" is so barbarian,' she used to say.

She hated the sight and smell of a butcher's shop, and was amazed that their Easter placards of lambs gambolling among primroses could do anything but encourage vegetarianism. Later in life when she assured me that a lettuce has a sort of consciousness, and that a tree cries out when it's cut down, I wondered how she managed to eat anything at all.

Her talk of cosmic rays and their effect on plants and animals intrigued us, but when she went on to explain that the sun is connected with the metal gold, the moon with silver, and the planets Saturn, Jupiter, and Venus with lead, tin and copper respectively, we laughed, little realizing that a German scientist was soon to endorse these findings.

I liked best to hear her on the subject of sowing seeds according to the phases of the moon. This seemed to make sense. One afternoon she called to me from where she was working in the garden: 'Just look at these sweet-peas!' she exclaimed as she proudly surveyed a row of lusty seedlings which were at least two foot higher up the canes than our own. 'They were sown on the fifth day of the last quarter.' Invariably she planted her broad beans two days before the full moon; the best time, so I learned, for all liquid-loving plants. 'But the temperate potato,' she added with a smile at my unbelief, 'likes to be planted when the moon is on the wane.'

I was bound to admit there was reason in her madness. After many tangible proofs of her success I took heed of the care with which she arranged plants in groups and colours sympathetic to one another. But Mother, always practical, remarked that to harmonize colour-vibrations, as my aunt called it, was merely a matter of artistic sense. Anyway, both their flower-gardens flourished, though we never had her success with our strawberries!

Aunt Edith would insist that plants receive the greater part of their nourishment from the cosmic rays; and she certainly grew such outsize fruit and vegetables that we used to refer to her 'cosmic cabbages'. According to her, the influence of these rays upon the three natural kingdoms had been explained by Steiner half a century before scientists arrived at the same truth.

Through her slow translations of his writing she absorbed many of his ideas, some of which have now been accepted. For instance, the use of gold in the treatment of heart-disease and for the relief of arthritis is connected by followers of Steiner with his teaching that both cosmic- and sun-rays enter into the substance gold, so investing it with healing properties.

On one of her 'Steiner' trips my aunt sent me from Dornach a carved wooden plaque bearing Blake's words:

> It will be questioned, 'When the sun rises, do you see a disc of fire somewhat like a guinea?'
> 'Oh no, no I see an innumerable company of the heavenly host crying Holy, holy, holy is the Lord God Almighty!'

Words that express her own vision. The sun symbolism of the Celtic cross harmonizes with Steiner's teaching that the sun's spirit is Christ – Divine Love – to give strength, light and healing. When Steiner looked at life he saw it whole, all things related to all things. And he saw a world where religion, philosophy and science must ultimately meet.

These were among the ideas discussed at a 1929 Bradford conference on Steiner methods in agriculture, a meeting which introduced my aunt to Dr Heidenreich, who became the leader of the Christian Community in this country. She must have been impressed, as I was, by his fine, strong appearance, his friendly blue eyes and sympathetic manner. Although when I met him he was about to go to a meeting, he allowed me to chatter to him as he ate a hasty supper. Because it was cold in the room he thoughtfully laid a rug across my knees.

And the first thing he remembered about my aunt was that she had withstood the intense cold of March 1929, the date of the conference, better than anyone else. This was during a period of six weeks when lakes, canals, even rivers, were frozen throughout the country. Dr Heidenreich described the shivering members' tours of inspection to the nearby village of Huby where Maurice Woods was farming on Steiner lines.

My aunt's enthusiasm, apparently, kindled fires sufficient to quell the cold so that she enjoyed the demonstrations at the frozen farm even more that the lectures in heated rooms where again it was stressed that policies for getting quick returns from the land, without making ample returns, were policies which could only result in soil, animal and human starvation.

Warnings were sounded against soil erosion and inertia as well as against new and more virulent consequences: diseases and death. But above these warnings came a positive note: 'From where we have gathered in we must put back – life – in full measure'. And life, in this instance, meant good, rich, animal manure.

During the early 'twenties, in pursuit of anthroposophy, my aunt almost neglected 'Marigold' and established the Yeadons there to look after it and Uncle Charlie. He who refused to take this 'cottage craze' seriously described it as 'just another of Edith's expensive whims'. This remark was made with some feeling because by now her passion for antiques and ancient jewellery had made inroads into his capital, so that he began to hope she would soon grow tired of 'Marigold' and decide to sell it.

He would have been astonished could he have foreseen that he himself was to provide the reason for this very decision. My aunt's objective in persuading him to give up his practice and retire to 'Marigold', though soon achieved ('poor man, what chance had he?' as Mother shrewdly remarked), led to unexpected results.

Never in all his practising life had Uncle Charlie been so busy as in retirement. According to Aunt Edith: 'The Preston doctors exploited him shamelessly'. Always demanding Dr. Charles's assistance was someone on holiday or someone ill. Never before had there been so invaluable a stand-in. Old-fashioned though his methods might have been, his patients recovered miraculously, warmed back to health in his kindly hands. No wonder the Preston doctors lengthened their holidays and protracted convalescence!

The result was that Dr Rigby, having forsaken No. 28, spent far more time at other numbers in Winckley Square or Ribblesdale Place (the Harley Streets of Preston) than in digging the plot pegged out for him around Marigold Cottage.

Because he could never refuse a request for help there was no respite. Very soon he discovered in doing *locum tenens* for doctors a far more onerous task than merely attending to his own patients.

So it was the attempt to rescue Uncle Charlie from his own kind that drove my aunt to consider leaving 'Marigold'. After much thought she decided upon north Wales as a suitable place for their new home, and planned to build a house from the proceeds of the sale of No. 28. These had been considerable; past extravagance in the form of antiques had been transformed into very welcome present gains.

What she now wanted was a plot of land near the mountains and the sea yet within reach of the social and art circles of a town. Her search led eventually to a sloping field above Llanrhos, about two miles south of Llandudno. Here were a few green acres which might become available for building.

My aunt was never one for backward glances. As Beth has rather sadly summed up (after her abandonment of interest in the suffrage movement) 'she loved to tackle something difficult, and then when she'd mastered it she dropped it and took up with something else'.

At this point, charged by dynamic contacts and ideas from Dornach, she christened her future, as yet unbuilt, home in north Wales by giving it the name of Erdmut: Earth Courage.

Uncle Charlie, who had no desire to live in the country, let alone among the mountains, was much amused by her name for their home-to-be. Indeed, without his warm sense of humour, which attracted so many friends, I wonder what he would have made of the irregularities of his married life. As Mrs Higginson put it: 'Though she was the one for smiles and twinkles, all the laughs came from him. If he hadn't had a wonderful sense of fun he couldn't have put up with it!'

In a broad way he was more human than Aunt Edith, more widely loved – because everyone who knew him loved him – and certainly more readily understood. Her fellow-members at the Hutton and Howick Women's Institute, for instance, while respecting her, would have done anything for their beloved Dr Charles. Many a one came in to give him a hand in the garden when she was away.

How they reacted to Mrs Rigby's anthroposophy is not difficult to imagine. Yet to their credit they voted her onto their committee, and she served as secretary for more years than one. Not only this, she was shortly afterwards elected to the executive committee of the Lancashire Federation of Women's Institutes. One of her former colleagues told me that Mrs Rigby, whenever at home, would turn up for meetings. Invariably she arrived by bicycle, wearing trousers and sandals. This unconventional costume, combined with her bobbed hair (the new-styled 'American Crop') and no hat caused some comment among the ladies who came properly attired to such meetings. But Mrs. Rigby's unselfconsciousness and firm grasp of the matter to be discussed overcame any objections to her appearance. Soon she was accepted as being even more forward in ideas than in dress.

In writing this chapter I have turned up some notes from her local Institute which further illuminate this unexpected field of activity. Once again I see that for all her pursuit of the stars, she related personal vision to matters of fact.

No matter whether she attended Mrs Ramsbottom's money-raising committee meeting or the monthly meeting in the village-hall, she entered into the whole business of arranging talks, parties and visits to factories and farms. It was she who invigorated the Annual General Meeting with thoughts of fellowship and service, and encouraged Mrs Dobbin, a near neighbour, to be a diligent treasurer.

Indeed, with Mrs Dobbin on her right hand and Mrs Duckett on her left, my aunt was blessed with good neighbours. And when Uncle Charlie was later taken ill the Ducketts were to prove 'a very present help in trouble' in the full meaning of the phrase.

But I stray away from the subject of Women's Institutes, which my aunt regarded as pillars supporting the temple of National Enlightenment. More than this, she loved the countrywomen themselves for their broad humour and crisp common-sense. Mixing with them after exhausting days closed up with lectures and books must have seemed like breathing the air of an orchard.

And so, cheerfully and earnestly, she supported competitions for jam-making, dress-making and the growing of vegetable-marrows. Nor were entertainments lacking in this full programme. These ranged from talks on music and art and a performance of *The Cricket on the Hearth* to a demonstration in making fancy bows from tissue-paper. Nor was health forgotten. Mrs Rigby saw to it that Dr Sharpe, the Medical Officer of Health, addressed the group. Though she didn't lead them into eurhythmy, members were encouraged to form a country-dancing class, as an antidote, perhaps, to the too-tempting results of cookery competitions.

A further item from the notes states that nominations for the new committee were read out from headquarters by Mrs Rigby. So she was a power in the Institute! And she was, for all her high-flown ideas, ready when required to come down to earth. If she did indeed live in two worlds, she managed at the same time many lives in this one. From cosmic discussions in the Goetheanum at the feet of Rudolf Steiner to a village-hall judgment of hats made from newspaper was, after all, no mean leap!

During the February of her last year at 'Marigold' my aunt, after returning from Nottingham where she and Uncle Charlie had been staying with the Watchursts, wrote the following letter to Nancy. I quote it in full because, apart from comments on the Women's Institute and her way of entry into the I.L.P., it also reveals divergent paths in their friendship, something of her own problems, and much of her character:

Marigold Cottage,
February 20th 1926

Dearest Nancy,

How very lacking we are, sometimes, in the recognized decencies! Not to have written promptly on our return from Nottingham. Forgive please. We were both very tired and have had v. full days since. It had been a big week for us, only 1½ days poss. in the garden till 5.0 p.m. One whole day Lancs. Federation Women's Institutes in the County Hall, *quite* interesting (ours was the first in Lancs; now there are over 40 villages with a W.I.): and that same night I could not miss my friend's (a young mother with 1st child) paper on Anatole France, wh. she gave in really beautiful style with a serenity of judgment – such ironical insight of a life 'fundamentally bad' as A.F's. (How profoundly the teaching in which we see a great Light differs from that!)

I've just been potting honey this morn. Folk keep asking me for it and I have so many things on hand – *that* keeps getting left: also all the cleaning of the house cupboards and drawers wh. I like to do myself! – they've been left!! For if a housewife with a too big garden will insist on learning German energetically, and will act as secretary and organizer (involving near 200 letters last year; and the working up of occasional public meetings) of William Blake Group of A.S. [Anthroposophical Society] well, something has to go, and it can't be the stockings of the 2 in family, So!!!

I think you manage simply wonderfully with Dora's help – and must I not say, Percy's? – that large house and all the humans who go through it. You have a very busy week on, I remember well.

We both wish we could share more fundamentally each other's life-interests. You do, and surely I do. You have made your grand gift of music a real blessing to me (even) let alone all the others it has blessed, and you yourself.

Do you know, Gertrude Champness was one small link in the chain – thro' asking her to go with me to a Women's Trades and Labour Council Annual mtg. at M/c. Univ. Settlement in about 1903? That resulted in my heading into the I.L.P. in 1905 and helping in their first great electoral victory in 1906, *and* in the attack on that same I.L.P. soon afterwards – re Suffrage. Even if you'd been free you would not have taken that path, could not. Let alone the later developments. This should, ideally speaking, with the great toleration and Love, have made of our diversities a great riches to share. Can it but do now, if both can be more simply tolerant and open to light from wheresoever it comes.

You can't abear to hear about the study in spiritual science I am on: no word of interest in my journey to Dornach last Easter from you at Leicester, you remember. I *did* listen to your things, didn't I? But I know I am liable to be very snobbish and overbearing about all that unwittingly; and *must* learn to be meeker and less superior, – that is only dirt and grit of my own carelessness in its working. Then I realize fully you don't need this, at least intellectually; emotionally the criss-crossing of life as at present interpreted by accepted standards of knowledge tries you much. I see that well.

Well, we must each get on with the day's work, thankful it's such a grand one. It is fine to have *this* very 10 years of life between 50 and 60, when the fruits and experience of the 50 years are in hand.

It was very good to see you now being saved some of the money strain of all these last years; and with the children all unfolding their life and powers with your loving help and Percy's.

Now, it is a quiet Saturday aft. and I must go out 3.0 to 5.0 p.m. and prune apple trees – only 30 done yet out of 200 and odd, and wrist already slightly sprained with that.

Thank you both for so very much kindness to us both.

Always, your loving,
Edith.

X

BY the summer of 1926 the building of Erdmut was almost completed. Out of those few green acres of Llanrhos now sprang two short rows of semi-detached houses divided by a cul-de-sac which resembled a river bed.

One bright morning in July, for the first time, Aunt Edith walked into the shell of her new home. The best view was from the bedroom window facing south and east. For her it was an inspiration to look towards the giant mountains: the Glyders, Foel Fras and Carnedd Llewellyn. Today they stood clear, grape-blue in the distance. She believed that Charlie, freed at last from incessant demands, would be uplifted and renewed in this atmosphere. One of the sloping fields in front had been mown for the second time and a strong scent of hay came with the south wind through the window-frame not yet fitted with glass.

By October the house should be ready. And then the horse-chestnuts in the lower field would have turned to the colour of rust. She would plant two white poplars at the bottom of the unmade garden; their twinkling leaves reminded her of those old-fashioned, glass-pendant toys which also glittered in the sun. And Charlie liked poplars – because they flourished in the town – better than the larger forest trees.

As she stood there, happy in thoughts of a peaceful life after the battling years, a knock on the door resounded through the hollow house. Wondering who it could be, she went downstairs to find a telegraph boy standing outside. 'It was addressed to the post office,' he explained as he handed her the orange envelope, 'but they knew you were here.'

She hesitated a moment before opening it, watching the boy as he whistled his way, hands in pockets, down the road. The message told her that Charlie was gravely ill.

At the best of times the journey from Llanrhos to 'Marigold' was slow and tedious, halted by draughty waits at junctions, with taxis to be found at both ends. Not all the philosophy in the world could have smoothed the hours of that dragged-out day. When, about five o'clock, my aunt arrived at 'Marigold' and Mrs Duckett opened the door, she read the truth in her face. Uncle Charlie had died about an hour earlier. Sandy, who had been called home from work, was already there, silent and uneasy. 'It was a very sharp attack of pneumonia,' he told me later. 'The doctors didn't know how ill he

[128]

was till the morning of the twenty-third, the day of his death'. For the first time Sandy saw Aunt Edith shaken out of her composure. 'She was frightfully upset at not having even known he was ill, and then not getting to him in time.'

Such a sharp separation on the threshold of a fuller life must have felt like the slamming of a door. Yet in the midst of her grief she was immeasurably grateful to Mrs Duckett and Mrs Yeadon who had nursed him, and to the neighbours who had given their help. But she was not pleased to learn that the Preston doctors, once so demanding, had flocked to her husband's bedside, never leaving him for a moment's quiet, prescribing too many, and conflicting, treatments. She would have been less than human had she not, in a bad moment some days later, exclaimed to Mrs Higginson: 'He was killed by the Preston doctors! When he was alive they drove him to death, and when he was dying they gave him no peace'.

Left to herself she would have refreshed him with herb-tea and allowed him to sleep.

The funeral service in St James's Church (where she had taught the young wives) was taken by the Reverend Larry Spencer. Even at this hour, looking upward, she chose for her message: 'Say not Good-night, but in some brighter clime/Bid me Good-morning!'

'I'll never forget her face in church,' Mrs Yeadon recalled. 'She looked so serene and composed, almost happy.' Because of this natural composure some of her friends imagined she didn't suffer. But they were wrong. Her grief at the snapping of a thirty-three years' bond of loyalty and affection was intense. My aunt was a person of genuine feeling; though she said nothing she must have had regrets for their so often broken-into married life. By chance I came upon a revealing comment in their visitors' book. Opposite the page inscribed: 'C.R. and E.R. at 28 Winckley Square' she had copied two lines from Æ:

The joyful beauty of the heavenly wise
To see the beauty in each other's eyes.

This is dated 28th January 1915.

However much she had bewildered Uncle Charlie, he had admired and loved her through to the end.

Only the thought that he had attained to 'an inheritance incorruptible and undefiled' lit the dark days following his death. It was well for her that she believed, with the saints of old, that the day a man dies is his true birthday when he is received back into his real home. She also believed that we are given the choice of being born again, choosing our parents and the circumstances necessary for progress. And then at birth, she would tell me, the blind of memory is drawn down:

Our birth is but a sleep and a forgetting:
The Soul that rises with us, our life's Star,
     Hath had elsewhere its setting . . .

By no means all Christians go as far as Wordsworth (and Steiner and other mystics) in believing that before birth we already *are*. And yet it would seem an incomplete sort of immortality which only began at the end of a life. My aunt probed into such mysteries, choosing her words slowly and gazing upwards through her newly-acquired gold-rimmed spectacles. I remember how the light glinted on them as she spoke: 'For us, caught in the circle of life, no ending must surely imply no beginning!' Wrestling with infinities, she paused, worlds away, before earthing her glance in my direction.

One day I tackled my father on these imponderables. He was busy and evasive and brushed my question off with: 'If anyone comes knocking at *my* coffin I'll tell them to go away!' Mother accepted all that was written in the New Testament. Aunt Edith, with her 'third eye', had her own visions and was quietly certain.

But I was far from accepting these beliefs when I left school (a few days, as it happened, after Uncle Charlie's death) and came home to nurse Mother. She had developed an incurable cancer. Day by day I was to watch this vile thing slowly gripping her and strangling her to death. In less than two years its evil was accomplished. Just before her last Christmas Aunt Edith came over to see her and was deeply impressed by her bravery. On Boxing Day she wrote to her with a new warmth and understanding:

My dear Gertrude,

We are thinking of you these days, and even understanding that some joys are shining very bright for you in the warm love of your dear ones. Perhaps even the very shadow and darkness of this winter-long night makes their love, which will always surround you, better seen and known.

I know how your brave spirit will have encouraged and provided for the two girls to be as gay as sunbeams. This will surely shine back in your (and in Arthur's) eyes, as well as theirs. I saw that radiance around them both. 'A change from a dream of Beauty, to Beauty.'

                                    With loving thought from,
                                         Edith.

Like many another relationship, this one had to wait for death to reveal its deeper nature. Two days after Mother died Aunt Edith wrote to my father:

Erdmut,
Llanrhos,
April 25th, 1928.

Dear Arthur,

I hope you have someone near you to comfort you as you did me when Charlie left us: maybe your comfort is in shielding those two girls and helping them to see further on. There was – to ordinary daily thought – some mercy in it that the brave sufferer was not left longer to go down that terrible slow way. To that knowledge which is above and beyond ordinary daily thought – and which at rare times is seen in humans – is alone given some coherent vision of what you and that brave little wife have really been put through . . . and that it is not in vain and the dear soul is not alone, nor are you alone in that darkest place. That there is a road and a chart and a kingdom.

The only real words Gertrude said to me when I saw her last were: did I know that she had tried to get a house for you nearer town. Indeed, I did know, I told her. And I knew that was the one immediate sign she could give me of her love for you. Do you realize you can't *see* Love; no one can: only its signs. Yet one knows it. Does that help one recognize the soul living on, though we cannot see it with physical eyes?

I hold on to the thought of Gertrude's high quality of courage and will and thoroughness which she spent in the way she thought best. And as to what is the best way – that is something we are each one learning from birth to death, and to go on again, more wise for that last life, more loving. No waste there.

My best loving thought to you Arthur and the two girls,
from Edith.

My father, who always said he couldn't make 'moss or sand' of Edith's letters, must have found something to cling to in this – in spite of its typical oddness – because I discovered it in his desk after his own death. Meanwhile he wrote back almost immediately. And on April 30th she replied:

Dear Arthur,

Alice and I have read your letter with such heart-felt concern. I see the jewel shining in both your hands – which had cost so much pain to produce (from such fiery molten furnaces only are diamonds made). Strange: how differently we as ordinary mortals looking down the paths we shape (not fully conscious what we are doing) how differently we would make the jewel if we could, by what quite different processes; and those jewels we make and choose ourselves are often spurious. But not that one you have – of those happy, holy passages before she had to leave you . . . We are both so glad you and the two dear children were away afterwards even just for a few days.

Very much love,
from Edith.

After this ordeal I no longer wanted to ask questions about life and death. I wanted only to get on a horse and gallop for miles around in the clean and springing countryside. Unfortunately Aunt Edith was rarely able to stay with us, and my father, more than ever absorbed in his work, arrived home late every night, tired, irritable and unapproachable. Elaine was still at school. Because I was without an anchor, I reverted to utter philistinism and thought of nothing but pleasure – riding, dances, parties, which led speedily into marriage. But marriage led, so I imagined, into life rather than death.

During this period I hardly saw Aunt Edith. And when we visited her on our summer holidays her few words were a reproach to my way of life. And yet she always gave me the feeling that somewhere at the end of a blind tunnel there was hope.

Twenty years went by before I returned to her way of thinking. And here, for a moment, I must skip ahead to that point, because I can only explain her beliefs through the experience that led me to them.

If the horror of Mother's death had closed my mind against fundamental truths, twenty years later it was opened to the full when our twelve-year-old son was drowned during his first summer term at boarding school. We had just nursed him back to health through years of illness, and for his own good had sent him to school in the south. So that his death, the result of carelessness, seemed all the harder to accept.

I couldn't believe that life could be so unjust. And not merely unjust, but downright ironic. For the first time I was brought up against rock edges of thinking and, like a rebellious child sent down to the lowest form, was made to begin the search for truth by looking facts in the eyes. At first I was stricken by the thought of the boy's body so recently restored to health and beauty. The 'thing' fished up after three days' search was not he. Where, then, was he? And why did he have to go from us at this moment? Could this 'death by misadventure' have been avoided? Was the determining factor the carelessness of man or the will of God?

I groped towards ever-receding answers. Clutching at straws I fell back on the hard bed of reason only to remember Aunt Edith's 'Reason brings argument against brick walls'. My questions, I knew, could never be answered by reason alone, though reason accompanies the questioner to the full stretch of its power. One has to wait, after such a tragedy, in a suspension of doubt and disbelief, for the slow inward dawning of truth. And at such times one does not fool oneself.

Eventually, through a mist of metaphysics, I came upon one patch of firm ground which can be turned over with a spade: the soul is not the body which it forms and informs. Therefore it has a life independent of the body. This being so, the fact that a body can be killed by something so trivial as a bacillus, a splinter, or the skid of a car, doesn't necessarily mean that the soul, like a servant, is instantly dismissed. Surely, as my aunt believed, the soul is the master of the body rather than its servant?

After the gradual opening of one door I sometimes found myself, while asleep, in places and with people whom I came upon and vividly recognized later in time. These experiences again recalled Aunt Edith's talk of years ago. The idea of astral travel, which had once amused me, now seemed to have some foundation. And I wondered how, during my 'philistine' years, she had been able to slip any message under my closely-fitted doors.

But I must return to the time after Uncle Charlie's death when she had her own broken threads to tie together and new threads to spin. 'Marigold' remained to be disposed of, and Aunt Edith eventually handed it over to the Yeadons who for some time now had been living there.

By that phrase 'handed over' I mean, of course, that 'Marigold' was sold rather than given though, as Mrs Yeadon expressed it, 'Mrs Rigby always preferred to be at the giving end' – this in recalling the many presents and invitations to No. 28 in the old days. Already it had been arranged that Aunt Alice, who since their mother's death had been living in the Lakes, should take the other half of the semi-detached 'Erdmut'. The sisters knew well enough that the Establishment could never occupy the same house as Free Thought, though both might live comfortably under the same roof. But in the case of Aunt Alice 'comfortably' is hardly the word to express her dire financial struggles. She was left with a very much smaller income than her widowed sister, and seemed to us to exist almost on the brink of poverty, crouched over a small oil-stove, unable to afford even stewing steak more than once a week. Had Aunt Edith not been very generous in the matter of food, she must have very nearly starved to death. Indeed, we wondered how she was able to feed her cat, June, the one luxury (frowned upon by Aunt Edith who disliked cats) which she allowed herself. On the other hand she whole-heartedly disapproved of many of Aunt Edith's possessions, habits and ideas.

[133]

And we too (my father, sister and I) when we had first driven to see the aunts in their new villas up the pleasant hillside cul-de-sac, had been startled by Aunt Edith's brilliant orange porch and purple front-door. Even the wine-red gate bearing the name, 'Erdmut', was in strong contrast to the other gates in the road. (Those were the days before bright-coloured woodwork on houses and, in fact, all the neighbouring doors and gates were a decent dark brown.) And though we had lifted the bronze Shakespeare knocker with some misgivings, we were not prepared for what was to come.

Miss Tucker, almost blessed in her ordinariness, opened the purple door. Behind her Aunt Edith, looming large in embroidered sackcloth, welcomed us in. From a tiny passage into which the five of us (or six, including the life-size statue of Venus) were crowded, she indicated the sitting-room on the right. It was called 'Four Winds' – a card to this effect, written in her own hand, was pinned to the bright blue door. This was our first intimation that Erdmut was going to be peculiar in a big way.

When we walked into 'Four Winds' we were hit, not merely in the eyes but in the solar plexus by the pictures. This shock of awakening (to ordinary beings) was probably what the artist intended. Dominant chords of colour vibrated through the air: cobalt, scarlet and gold. It was like hearing the trumpets sounding from the *Book of Revelation*. And all the time adding to this effect were the cornflower-blue walls. Our timid sensibilities were given no respite; we tried to draw in the horns of feeling, like snails. And if our silence seemed to be the silence of extinction, it spoke worlds – physical and spiritual in one ball – for the artist's power.

Through her love of Blake's painting Aunt Edith had come to admire those of 'Steiner' artists. Aunt Alice found them both meaningless and fearful. As for my father, with his taste for Birket Foster and the Victorians, he spat at the new schools of art. But the ones we saw here, such as *The Spirit of the Corn* with its swirling, whirling strokes of gold, made us feel dizzy. We were sadly unconditioned to modern art and could only gaze bewildered at these highly-coloured expressions of what were described as the 'super-conscious'. I can never forget the impact of those dynamic, wave-spreading and disturbing pictures.

I was thankful when Aunt Edith ushered us gently into the south room, called 'The Bink', for tea. But even here the afternoon light illumined yet another strange painting. This showed a figure emerging from rainbowed cloud, a figure beaten with rain and crowned with sun against an azure background. At its feet roared flames of tiger-bright ferocity. I supposed the face of exalted suffering to be the face of Christ.

Somehow in that presence it seemed inappropriate to be eating scones and honey. But Miss Tucker, this afternoon addressed by my aunt as 'Carinthia', munched away unperturbed, so we overcame our scruples. Conversation struggled like a spent stream. It was an embarrassing meal with too many vibrations crossing over the table. My father dabbled honey on to wholemeal bread with medical precision. Elaine and I avoided each other's eyes.

In time we grew accustomed to this new version of Aunt Edith as someone initiated into celestial matters. And fortunately the 'matter' part still held good. She retained her humanity and reverenced the earth as much as the sky.

Nearly every day of our annual holiday in Llandudno we went to see the aunts. Sometimes Aunt Alice would come in to Erdmut for tea; sometimes we visited her alone in her next-door 'semi', Mount Grace. We thought this name for her 'modest abode', as she called it, rather ambitious in its opposition to Earth Courage. Compared with the German-stove warmth of Erdmut, Mount Grace was icy; mountain-top temperature combined with cold mauve curtains and covers. 'Lilac is such a beautiful colour!' Aunt Alice would exclaim as she tried vainly to coax a cushion of that shade into plumpness. And she herself, by the way, seemed to have become thinner every year we saw her, in spite of vests and jerseys redoubled. And no wonder, with so little in the larder, and the wick of the Junior Valor Perfection only half turned up!

On wet afternoons she played hymns for us on the Broadwood. And though she infected even that performance with her gaiety, we were thankful to go in to Aunt Edith's for tea. We never had a meal at Mount Grace – not for want of hospitality, but from sheer lack of pence. Though my father paid the coal bills the atmosphere of Mount Grace remained too ascetic for our taste. Aunt Edith's brand of spirituality, on the other hand, allowed for considerable latitude in this respect.

No housewife, like her sister, Aunt Alice was much more fun on the hills. She must have known every blade of grass within a twenty-mile radius, and was ever ready and eager with suggestions for walks – Tal-y-Cafn, the Conway mountain, the Gloddaeth and Bodysgallen woods, apart from more strenuous expeditions (accompanied by Aunt Edith) up Foel Fras, Moel Siabod, the Glyders and Carnedds.

She reminded me of a bird, bright-eyed, perky, hopping from stone to stone as lightly as from episode to episode. A Mother's Union tea-party to the steeps of Carnedd Llewellyn; for her it was all in a stride. Only in this respect were the sisters alike. For the rest, Aunt Alice was content not to probe the mysteries of existence or to ask unanswerable questions.

Aunt Edith always had to have a purpose. For instance, one afternoon when we arrived hoping for a mountain walk, we were greeted briskly at the gate by Aunt Alice ominous in hat and coat. 'Now my children,' she announced, 'Ede has decided we're to go by car to Roe Wen and walk up [she named some hill] in search of Roman remains.'

She laughed at my woeful expression because at that time I hated pottering about looking for stones among boggy wastes. I was ever eager for another mountain scalp. And we knew what an afternoon plodding in the wake of Aunt Edith's determined figure meant: no respite until the 'remains' were found and thoroughly examined.

All the same, I wish I could now remember her discourse on that particular Roman camp as clearly as rough ground, wet feet and herself with walking-stick, eagerly striding ahead. Because when eventually we reached a grey huddle of stones and a mossed-over road, her animation made up for a mountain unclimbed. She had a gift for peopling such ruins and that afternoon we could almost hear Roman chariots clattering over sunken cobbles.

By now a vigorous member of the Llandudno Field Club, Aunt Edith made many such excursions. The moment she heard of a 'new' cromlech or circle she would let us know, warning of a summons to visit. I have never discovered if she was among the party of anthroposophists who had accompanied Steiner up Penmaenmawr mountain, but knowing her I should think it most likely. At any rate, it is on record that she met him on his arrival at Llandudno Junction station. I should mention here that only a year after her own arrival in north Wales she started an Anthroposophical Circle with a weekly study-group at Erdmut, and occasional public lectures held in Llandudno.

Another time on another hill we came upon a satisfactory cromlech consisting of a large flat stone resting upon four standing stones. My aunt explained how these prehistoric structures, fairly common in Wales and Celtic regions, were used by the druids. It was after I'd objected that no one could worship the sun shut up inside what amounted to a draughty cell that she gave us quite a lecture on the subject.

Standing there on rocky ground, in her sandals and with her blue cloak lifted by the wind, she might have been a priestess. At least she seemed to be an intermediary between us and the days of druidic rites and rituals. Looking up, she began to speak slowly and quietly. But an occasional sparkle broke through her words so that we listened intently to what she had to say.

'The druids had a secret that we have lost,' she began, 'they were able to separate the vital forces of the sun from its physical and chemical effects.' She went on to describe how the druids sat and prayed in these cromlechs, breathing deeply, meditating and absorbing the cosmic rays. It was their belief that the roof-stone acted as a kind of filter to drain off the surface rays of the sun while they themselves received the vital, cosmic power which enabled them to cure certain diseases. This was the power, my aunt believed, which Christ used for healing the sick, restoring sight and giving back speech to the dumb. As for raising the dead, it was possible that Jairus's daughter, and even Lazarus, were restored to life, not from death but from a state of coma.

As she spoke she stooped down and picked a harebell from a cluster which scratched a living among the stones. 'Even this,' she said, holding out the tiny flower, 'receives its strength from the cosmic rays, the strength which enables a blade of grass to push its way up to the light!' Here she pointed a finger to the sky.

That picture of my aunt in her blue cloak, standing on rock and offering a harebell to the cosmos, should have been painted to her memory.

I was reminded of this day and those boggy expeditions by Dr Heidenreich who stayed with her after the Bradford conference on agriculture in 1929. 'It was the end of March,' he told me, 'and still bitterly cold. But every day we tramped those Welsh hills – great brown bears grizzled with snow.' He shivered at the memory. 'It was like Siberia!'

Even he, a quarter-century in hand and accustomed to the frosts of Germany, had been subdued by these near-Arctic expeditions. Comfort in the house never made Aunt Edith soft. Nor, in those days, did she ever seem to tire. 'Although she was beginning to stoop a little,' Dr Heidenreich went on, 'she was indefatigable – always in front on those frozen mountain tracks.'

Nor was her guest allowed any respite after icy days on the hills. In the evenings he was expected to give lectures. For one thing, my aunt insisted that he address the Llandudno Field Club on druidic remains. But the members had not as yet been sufficiently injected with anthroposophy. 'And I felt I put across Steiner and his theories a little too strongly for them,' Dr Heidenreich told me. 'When we got back to Erdmut, talking over coffee and sandwiches, I asked your aunt if she didn't think I'd overdone it. She was silent a moment, considering the point. "Well, and if you have," she said with a twinkle, "I think it's done the old fossils a certain amount of good!" '

Nevertheless, some of these 'old fossils' were to form the nucleus of the Anthroposophical Circle. Among the most enthusiastic of her followers in this new venture were the Griffiths who lived near Llandudno Junction. 'I remember them well,' Dr Heidenreich recollected, 'Mr Griffiths was a herb-grower . . .' Instantly, as he spoke, I could see my aunt rounding up all the Wordsworthian characters in the district. Indeed, anyone interested in botany, geology or archaeology was approached with promises of new lights and insights on each subject. In this way many seekers were gathered into her net.

Arnold Freeman, also ensnared, gave my aunt a great deal of his time and energy in the cause of anthroposophy. Their friendship began when she lent her house to him and his family during August, 1928. This typical gesture of generosity was to be repaid many times, because with Arnold's co-operation she arranged conferences and meetings in various parts of the country. Tuned in as they were to the same wavelength, they shared a vision in following Steiner, and led others in the same direction.

Another interest in common was a love of the theatre. Alongside his work for the Sheffield Educational Settlement, Arnold ran the small theatre which has produced more classic plays than almost any other of its kind in the country. With him my aunt was able to recall her earlier struggles – with less promising material – at the Brook Street Club. Philosophers both, along with economics and history he had read philosophy at Oxford, while she had graduated through experience. And both agreed that philosophy was more important to the world than economics. But their enlightened views on education as 'the bringing to expression of the inwardly limitless' (to use Goethe's words) brought them most closely together on Steiner's path.

I can't resist adding here that my aunt and her new friend also shared an addiction to cold water. For many years Arnold had begun his day with a cold bath at four a.m. And it was shortly after she met him that Aunt Edith took to bathing in the sea before breakfast, winter and summer alike. Whether he was really responsible for this new habit I don't know, but I remember Aunt Alice's dismay when her sister began taking a bus to the sea at such an early hour, wearing only a bathing suit under a thin mackintosh. What was worse, after the bathe she returned home in her wet suit, having neglected to change or even dry herself. 'I like to feel the salt soaking into my skin,' she explained as she walked dripping, impervious to protest, up to her front gate and into her house. This exercise, she insisted, cleared her brain and, like Arnold, she spent the following hour before breakfast in meditation.

She drove herself relentlessly in all directions. And, as both Arnold and Dr Heidenreich have testified, she drove others too. A holiday at Erdmut carried with it certain inescapable conditions. It was not easy to say 'No' to Aunt Edith.

When Arnold described her as 'a dynamic person', I felt this to be an understatement which also applied to himself. In a *Manchester Guardian* article he has been likened to 'the atom of radium which burns a hole in your palm'. No wonder they needed cold baths and early morning bathes in the sea!

Of course, there was more to it than that. My aunt believed this practice not only cleared her mind but also provided a physical discipline to balance mental exercises. Soon she was to begin the long labour, already referred to, of translating Hermánn Poppelbaum's *Man and Animal* – a theory of evolution comparing the descent of animals with that of man, and also considering the ascent of man into a creature with a soul. I shall return later to this struggle with Poppelbaum, whose name irresistibly appealed to our schoolgirl sense of humour.

As if this wasn't work enough, she tackled alongside it the translation of Bernard Shaw's *Man and Superman* into German. No one but a superwoman would have run these two in double harness. At any rate, she completed the job and presented her German edition of the Shaw play to Uncle Charlie's niece, Mabel Leigh. I imagine that Mabel looked on this as a purely exhibition piece of work for the unread portion of her bookcase. Nevertheless, she cherished it. By now her family-by-marriage were half-proud of their strange relation.

Happily my aunt's earnestness and zeal didn't prevent a capacity for an almost sublime descent from the cosmic to the commonplace. When, for example, Herbert, now seventeen and in training on H.M.S. *Erebus*, came on leave to Erdmut, she willingly broke off her communion with the stars. I believe she loved Herbert more than any other human being and we always felt her Great Love was reserved for the heavenly hierarchy; she was altogether too rarefied for animal passions. Even her love for Uncle Charlie took the form of deep affection and understanding. I never heard her talk about sex and I still think it extraordinary that she had consented ever to be married. But Joan Watchurst had it from her mother that Uncle Charlie, who could never say 'no' to a request for help, refused absolutely to take 'no' from Edith Rayner. Besides, she liked to experience everything possible in life.

Herbert, who was not an intellectual, expressed in his simplicity the very heart of her beliefs. His nature was clear; his eyes, typical of a sailor, seemed bluer for gazing at skies and the sea. Being with him must have made her wonder why her own approach to the spiritual world was so complicated and demanding.

Indeed, seeing them together, I have often asked myself how two such obviously 'good' people can be so different in their approach to reality. Reality for my aunt seemed to lie beyond a mountain climb of thinking, probing and speculation; all that following of Steiner, those travels, lectures and translations, seemed necessary to light her way in the search for truth. On the other hand, there was Herbert, hands in pockets, so to speak, standing easily on the shore of that sought-after country. He was already there without having had to search. But the difficult path leads to a further view. While those of us with a grasp of the here-and-now do what must be done without asking too many questions, the Aunt Ediths of this world see ahead and into the heart of things.

Herbert wisely made no attempt to understand anthroposophy. Instead he taught Aunt Edith to play rummy. She proved a good and interested pupil, so much so that Herbert's parting shot in the visitors' book records her remark: 'Rummy is a game of great possibilities!' – a tribute, perhaps, to her view of the 'inwardly limitless' in every aspect of life.

Always, in spite of flights into the cosmic, she was to remain the same very human Aunt Edith. More human, in fact, than we as yet realized, as certain events will show. If I were asked to choose two words most typical of her vocabulary I should reply 'human' and 'cosmic', and in that order.

XI

Concerning a cat. Parish interlude. Music circle.
The Hutchins. Mountain adventure.
Steiner methods in education.

FOR all my aunt's pursuit of the life of the spirit, she retained an impishness we delighted in. So far from being a prig, she could at times be downright naughty, even at times rejoicing in her naughtiness. As for her part in the regrettable affair of Aunt Alice's cat, it seems to be inconsistent with her real self, and I can only preface the following account with Whitman's: 'I contradict myself? Well then, I contradict myself. I contain multitudes'.

Aunt Edith, lover of animals, disliked cats. And of all the cats in the world she most disliked Aunt Alice's cat. Possibly her opposition to Aunt A.'s conventional outlook was projected onto this creature which became her scapegoat. To begin with, she disapproved of the cat's name, June; secondly, of her facility in producing kittens to be drowned; but most of all she disliked June herself. Aunt Edith's etheric bristles must have risen up to hear her sister prattling on of June's achievements.

In spite of this attitude Aunt Alice once dared, before going on a holiday, to ask Miss Tucker to look after June in her absence. Miss Tucker agreed and Aunt Edith, with her lofty ideas as to each animal's place in the hunting-grounds of heaven, could hardly object. (In heaven, we understood, animals might hunt though they might not kill: a provoking sort of paradise for them.)

June was an unlucky cat. During her mistress's absence, she not only produced kittens but also made a mess on the carpet at 'Four Winds', a less forgiveable sin. We never knew how it happened, but when Aunt Alice returned home, eager to reclaim her pet, June was no more. She never mentioned this sore subject to us, nor did she ever get another cat, which was a pity because, for all her neighbourliness and interest in parish work, her life was a little threadbare.

Thereafter our picture of Aunt Edith as a preserver and redeemer of animal-kind was dimmed. We wondered whether she had taken June and her kittens down to the sea in a sack. But none of us dared ask any questions.

We wondered also how the aunts who with the passing years grew more apart managed, on the whole, to remain good neighbours. Perhaps it was because at bottom they were both (with deviations) good Christians. And there were two bonds thicker, even, than blood to hold them together: a love of mountains and a love of music. While Aunt Edith was the initiator of climbing expeditions, Aunt Alice was the mainstay of the Music Circle, herself filling gaps in the programme with tinkling sonatas.

Aunt Edith, however, founded the Music Club in Llandudno and personally arranged the programme. Although she played no instrument, she paid full homage to music and musicians, and was determined to love good music. Her real regard for Bach is made plain on another postcard to Nancy Wathurst, written from Eisenach and dated September, 1928:

> Have just come out of the house in which J.S.B. was born and lived his first ten years. Four most deeply interesting things to me: Frederick the Great listening to J.S.B. playing. Second, J.S.B. and the Morning Remembrance (recollection: Andacht) the morning song he played while his big family, all sizes, joined in. Best of all was a cast of his face taken during life by an unknown artist. There it showed what far, high-reaching power lived in this man, dwelt in flesh. Last was a model of his brain, in their thorough German way: seeing what it meant for a human vessel to hold such sight, feeling, will, communion. One almost saw it coming into human form.

With this way of looking, so different from Aunt Alice's surface glances, it is not surprising they were estranged in the world of art. More unexpected was their divergence in the matter of underclothes. This was manifest on fine summer afternoons when there were to be seen, suspended from Aunt A.'s back window-sills thick woollen combinations and knickers of the type called 'equestrian', because of their design to grip the thighs. Whereas the Erdmut clothes-line flew diaphanous garments of silk and lace worthy of a ballet dancer.

'Those fripperies of Ede's!' her sister would exclaim, 'it's a wonder she doesn't get pneumonia – *and* after those early morning bathes!'

A fresh crop of shell-pink and lavender 'fripperies' blossomed from the line between the poplars after Aunt Edith's holiday in Paris during the early summer of 1928. This was the holiday, spent at a guest-house near the Sorbonne, when she had invited the Mayors to join her. From Patti I learned afterwards that my aunt had become friendly with the owner, Madame Baduel-Renaud (who had been governess to the children of the Czar until he and his household had been murdered by Bolsheviks). Shortly after the Revolution the resourceful Madame was engaged in running a pension for artists. And here it was, before one of her trips to Dornach (almost certainly for the opening of the Goetheanum) that Aunt Edith most happily landed.

The governess-refugee-artist set-up immediately appealed to her; she lengthened her stay and helped Madame by conversing with the guests and discovering new ones. Before long she was writing to the Mayors, urging them to take a holiday at her expense. For Patti it would be an opportunity to meet fellow-artists, and for her mother a chance to rest after an illness. My aunt felt the time had come for Patti to be recognised by the fashionable schools which practised the 'new art'.

The students laughed when Patti confessed she had been brought up on Leonardo, Della Robbia and Rembrandt, but Mrs Rigby insisted that they should examine her drawings. And suddenly Patti found herself being treated with new respect; they agreed that she could draw better than anyone in the house, better than many in the galleries. To show their appreciation they invited her and my aunt to supper at an artists' café, *La Brune et La Blonde*, near St Lazare.

'They were a mixed lot,' Patti told me, 'two flaxen-haired Norwegian girls – very *avant-garde* – a Hungarian pianist, a Hindu, a Pole, and a French officer – all artists. I remember how splendid your aunt looked,' she went on, 'arrayed for the occasion in a purple gown with a topaz necklace. I couldn't help thinking that Aphrodite was tranformed into Pallas Athene. It seemed strange to see her there, nodding wisely in a corner. It was such a *gay* café and so different from anything in Preston!'

A pencil portrait competition was arranged at the supper table. Aunt Edith must have been pleased when Patti's drawing – of the French officer – was easily voted the best. 'Although they painted freely in bold colours, they weren't very good at drawing,' Patti told me, adding modestly: 'but perhaps that night they'd had too much champagne!'

Although Aunt Alice thoroughly approved of her sister's friendship with the Mayors (they hadn't even been suffragettes) she was reserved in her opinions of the anthroposophists and their goings-on. Regarding the occasional services held at Erdmut, which were conducted by a priestess who wore robes and burned incense, she had nothing to say. For the first of these services, after much deliberation and in the name of Christian unity, Aunt Edith had invited Aunt Alice. But Aunt A. would have sooner attended a Black Mass than trust her soul to the ministrations of the anthroposophists.

I first received a hint of this prejudice one afternoon when out walking with her. After referring to a meeting which had prevented Aunt Edith from accompanying us I innocently enquired: 'Who are these people anyway?' To my amazement Aunt A. turned with an expression of truimph and relief. 'My child!' she exclaimed, delighted to be consulted at last, 'they're a miserable lot . . . a m-i-s-e-r-a-b-l-e lot!' And having got that off her mind, she strode on, sprightly and gay, through Bodysgallen woods.

Another friend acceptable to both sisters was the first visitor to

Erdmut, Marie Byvoets, the talented woman who had given Sandy piano-lessons and played marching songs for the W.S.P.U. Miss Byvoets, as housekeeper to Ramsay MacDonald, now lived at No. 10 Downing Street where my aunt, for many years a friend of the family, often stayed – at this period on the right side of the railings! She even used to boast that Miss Byvoets ran the show in admirable style with only six maids.

Commenting on an Erdmut holiday, the resilient Marie reports herself to be 'greatly refreshed after many short cuts and long laughs'. One wonders how these particular short cuts, up Snowdon and Carnedd Llewellyn – the two highest mountains in Wales – were achieved.

With Miss Byvoets next door Aunt Alice came into her own, trilling like a canary in happy expectation, practising the treble parts of sonatas by Haydn and Shubert. These two played well together and allowed Aunt Edith, for once, to play second fiddle which, in fairness, she was very happy to do. She had been delighted to comply with Aunt A.'s request for a music circle: 'Let us have a melody to leaven all those solemn discussions!'

No sooner, then, was the Anthroposophical Circle (with its weekly study-group at Erdmut) properly turning than the Music Circle was begun. Aunt Edith never lived in a square world; all her wheels seemed to revolve smoothly. In this instance with her usual initiative she prevailed on well-known artists to inspire the new group. Sybil Thorndike, for one, obliged by giving a play-reading as well as playing the piano and delighting everyone with the richness of her personality. Besides, Miss Thorndike, as she was then, was interested in the Steiner movement.

From now on my Aunt's visitors' book-cum-diary is studded with Steiner friends and activities. It appears that everyone enjoying an 'Erdmut' holiday was required also to do a certain amount of work – by giving a lecture, helping with a meeting or conference, or, at least, assisting in the house and garden. Long walks or climbs and short periods for reflection were included in the day's pattern.

Probably she herself worked harder than anyone. For instance, in one month, apart from many routine activities, she arranged a Mozart concert in Llandudno, a lecture on Goethe by Violet Plincke (one-time student at the Women's University, St Petersburg) at Bangor university, and a reading of Faust for the Colwyn Bay Literary Society. Lecturers and artists, always invited to stay at her house, invariably commented on the warmth of her welcome, only sometimes on the coldness of the hills they were required to climb.

It was at a meeting of the Colwyn Bay Literary Society that my aunt first met Eileen Hutchins, whose vivid recollections are worth recording. Eileen, then teaching English at Penrhos College, was engaged that evening to lecture on Galsworthy. Recognising a fish for her net, my aunt asked if she was related to Beatrice Hutchins, the well-known Fabian. In spite of a negative reply she invited her to Erdmut.

'My first impression of your aunt,' Eileen told me, 'was of a massive and imposing figure wearing a large hat, blue cloak and sandals. A few days later when I found myself hesitating in front of Erdmut's orange porch and purple door I began to wonder what I was in for.'

She wondered still further when confronted with the Venus coquettishly sporting a tweed hat, and the stolid Miss Tucker who led her upstairs to take off her coat in 'Mustardseed', the diminutive back bedroom. (It follows that the other two were 'Peaseblossom' and 'Cobweb'.) Finally, the cornflower blue walls of 'Four Winds' with its weird pictures revealed how far this Penrhos girl had travelled.

At the meeting that evening Aunt Edith wore a purple waistcoat edged with fur, and a heavy silver brooch loaded with mystic symbols. Below long, flowing skirts of midnight-blue her feet, far removed from those 'little mice' beneath the petticoats of Sir John Suckling's *Ballad*, were broadly expanded in the usual sandals (and she wore these even for weddings!).

'Her face was characterful,' Eileen said, 'and almost masculine, but her blue eyes behind thick spectacles looked wise and benevolent. And with her grey hair arranged in a sort of page-boy bob, she seemed to me like a medieval Pope or some high dignitary of the Church.'

The room where they talked struck chords of orange and blue against dark oak woodwork. Here were reproductions of Blake, and Dürer's *Praying Hands* alongside strange carvings and ornaments and even stranger pictures culminating in *The Last Supper of the World*.

Eileen was mildly surprised to hear that my aunt had met Rudolf Steiner, but was really impressed to learn of her friendship with Ramsay MacDonald, and eagerly asked for details of the suffrage days. Reluctantly Aunt Edith (as Eileen soon called her) admitted to Downing Street railings, to prison, hunger-strike and the rest. But she spoke of these things with regret rather than pride.

Before long Eileen had introduced her sister Shirley, also a teacher (of music) at Penrhos, to Erdmut and gradually these two who came there, to begin with, to meet famous and entertaining people, learned to appreciate my aunt for her own worth. She treated the girls most wisely, never pressing them, or even speaking of Steiner till they were ready to listen. Only then were they invited to join the weekly study-group and read some of his lectures. One evening when discussing some abstruse matter Eileen became argumentative and critical. Aunt Edith merely gazed at her with her far-seeing eyes and said calmly: 'It's good that you raise such problems. These thoughts are very profound. I cannot say after all these years I fully understand them'. And then, after a pause, 'I think now that we must ponder them deeply during the coming week and perhaps next time we shall see more light'.

At such times my aunt, aware of Miss Tucker on the other side of the door, suspicious of these meetings, scornful of many of the people involved, went out of her way to be kind and to include her on every possible occasion. 'Dear child,' she would say, 'leave your work and come and sit with us for a moment!'

Fortunately the 'dear child' accepted the Hutchins sisters as being forthright and sensible. Indeed, the three of them often shared a backstage laugh at the fantastic attire and conversation of many of the eccentrics who knocked on the purple door. In spite of this the contact with Aunt Edith proved to be a turning-point in the Hutchins' lives. And when Arthur Sheen, then teaching at the New School (later Michael Hall), at that time the only Steiner school in England, came over to speak about his work, they were wholly converted. Mr Sheen, so vigorous and practical, helped to dispel their fears that followers must be oddities.

Whenever my aunt had a distinguished visitor she would invite the Hutchins to Erdmut. In this way they met George Adams Kaufmann (which last name he dropped during the war) secretary of the Anthroposophical Society in Great Britain. Apart from his scholarship and power as a lecturer Mr Adams was also a formidable mountaineer. He was a wonderful friend to my aunt and proved to be the mainstay of many expeditions as well as conferences. But of all the people they met in this way perhaps Martha Heimeran, later a priestess in the Christian Community, chiefly influenced them towards involvement in the society.

The immediate result of this was that Eileen and Shirley agreed to join Aunt Edith for a weekend conference in Derbyshire. Here, once again, she was to display her unusual force of will. After a long coach drive, a memorable lecture from Dr Wachsmuth in Sheffield followed by intense discussion and a further drive to a guest-house in Hope, all members, by midnight were more than ready for bed. All, that is, except for Aunt Edith, who insisted that before going upstairs they should finish the day on a suitable note. Without more ado she announced that she was going to read them Goethe's fairytale, *The Green Snake and the Lovely Lily.*

'For all that she seemed so placid and tolerant,' Eileen told me, 'I had discovered by this time that once Aunt Edith had made up her mind on a course of action, nothing in heaven or earth could divert her from her purpose. So it was, we sat round in the entrance hall, our cases at our feet, half-listening, half-dozing. But something magical in that story came through and has remained with me ever since.'

A great deal more than magic was at work on the two sisters. In 1931 Shirley left her post as music teacher at Penrhos to become a helper in the Rudolf Steiner Curative Home, Sunfield, in Birmingham, and by Christmas Eileen was in charge of a group of normal children at the newly-formed school there. These changes came as a great blow to their parents. Although they had accepted Shirley's decision with sympathy, they were grieved and upset when Eileen also gave up a secure job. Unfortunately Aunt Edith's attempts to act as a mediator completely failed; indeed, she was regarded as the focus of their trouble, which, all unwittingly, she most certainly was.

All the same, though she had inspired the girls by her talks and discussions on Steiner's ideas for teaching normal, as well as backward, children, she had not suggested these moves. During the early days of their acquaintance she had, in fact, encouraged them chiefly in making expeditions, such as the one to the British camp on Conway mountain, an outing which gives another view on her extraordinariness.

For this excursion beginning from Erdmut the girls brought a friend who gazed incredulously at Aunt Edith's appearance in her blue cloak and sandals. But today she also carried a staff to aid her on the climb and on her head she wore a navy-blue beret adorned round the edges with multi-coloured rings flashing in the sun, so that it exactly resembled a halo.

'Oh!' gasped the newcomer aside to Eileen after Mrs Rigby had gone on ahead, 'she looks like Moses leading the children of Israel into the Promised Land!' Thereupon, helpless with laughter, she collapsed on the grass.

Throughout this expedition, as though acting a part, Aunt Edith maintained a prophetic mood and oracular way of speech. At one point half-way up the mountain the three of them were assailed by a flock of gulls whirling and screaming above their heads. Raising her right hand in an admonitory gesture, she solemnly announced: 'Birds of the air have cries; man alone has speech!' This sort of behaviour was altogether too much for their guest who was obliged to walk behind while Eileen and Shirley engaged my aunt in conversation.

It was shortly after this episode that Aunt Edith introduced the girls to George Adams, who was speaking at a conference in Llandudno, and persuaded him to take them up the Glyders. Although when staying at Erdmut he always seized an opportunity for climbing, George viewed this proposal – to lead two beginners over the rocky hazards of Glyder Fawr and Glyder Fach – with some misgivings. However, at her command, he was obliged to overcome his diffidence and extreme shyness. The expedition which began in silent constraint ended happily enough with the making of a fire for tea, after both peaks had been conquered in mist and cold.

On another occasion, after lecturing during a strenuous weekend, George spent the last evening climbing the Idwal Slabs where he pitched his tent and slept the night prior to a stiffer climb at dawn – and this in mid-November. Whatever we may have thought about my aunt's friends, they were a doughty lot!

She herself, in January 1930, accompanied Herbert (on leave with a telescope won for seamanship) over Foel Fras (3091 ft) and, to quote her remarks in the diary: 'descended in bad snow holes and rocks, four feet deep in snow, down to Aber. 30 miles'. Not bad for a woman of fifty-seven. I can only hope that Herbert carried the telescope and gave her rewarding views from the top before returning to H.M.S. *Revenge*.

Her climbing days were by no means over. In the summer of 1931 she took a leading part at a conference in Deganwy, and during this week asked Eileen to arrange afternoon expeditions. Once again George Adams was prevailed upon, this time to lead a small party, including Eileen and a few experienced climbers, over Crib Goch, the formidable rock ridge on Snowdon. At the last moment, greatly to Eileen's consternation, Aunt Edith insisted on joining the group herself. By now heavy and no longer supple, she was wholly unfit to tackle such a climb. But she did more than merely tackle it.

All went gaily until they came to the ridge, when everyone except my aunt became silent with apprehension. She, unperturbed, followed George step by step, proceeding with infinite slowness and undaunted determination along the razor-edge. To Eileen, watching from behind, every movement was sharp with peril. George turned back when possible to help her with a sort of old-world courtesy. Occasionally she dislodged a stone which to the watchers' eyes seemed to bounce down through eternity . . . But they needn't have worried. Though if she had fallen she would have fallen to her death, Aunt Edith was completely confident of her ability. She crossed the ridge at her own majestic pace and soon afterwards was smiling contentedly on the summit. Little did she guess the enormity of her companions' relief!

An even more hazardous journey occurred later in the year. Once again the indefatigable George Adams was staying at Erdmut where Eileen, having by now left home, was also a guest. On this occasion my aunt proposed that George should properly try Eileen's skills as a rock-climber on the frowning crags of Carnedd Dafydd. Her idea was to accompany the two of them as far as Llyn Ogwen, give them her blessing, and withdraw.

The day of the climb was the first of November, with All Saints trumpeting sunshine and blue skies, sounding a Last Post to summer. This was too much for my aunt who, standing by the sparkling waters of Ogwen, was tempted to climb a few hundred feet to a smaller lake hidden in the mountains. This lake, she knew, would be an ideal place for lunch. And here on a grassy ledge they camped down in the sun. Eileen began to have uneasy stirrings. Her foreboding was justified when my aunt, strengthened with coffee and sandwiches, announced that she felt beckoned to the summit. The sun and the blue mountain wind had banished all plans of retirement from her mind. By now both Eileen and George knew better than to try to dissuade her. Fitting their pace to hers, they plodded on up the steepening, sharpening track.

Suddenly, after about two hours of hot sun, the weather changed. The blue-and-gold Saints drew on black hoods and breathed out swirling vapour shrouding the summit in smoky wreaths. Eileen remembered the number of climbers who had been killed on the Carnedds. Inch by inch the three of them felt their way to the cairn. After adding three stones to its height, they crept into the hollow, hoping for the mist to lift. For some reason George was in a merry mood and entertained his companions with an American jingle:

> Two lads of noted power and pep
> Were Albert Ein. and Jacob Ep. . .

which went on for many verses but did nothing to dispel the mist which by now had settled upon them, sullen and thick as wool.

Time was passing; they decided to move from shelter and attempt to find a way down. Again the mountain changed its mood; short, sharp cuffs of wind hit them as they twisted among the rocks and before long the mist was beaten to a rolling smoke. Wildly the gale roared till even Aunt Edith was blown off her feet and they were all three compelled to crawl on hands and knees.

With sudden cliffs and precipices, the Carnedds are dangerous mountains. Many people have fallen from the rocks of Dafydd; some have died of exhaustion on its lonely ledges or been lost among desolate stretches of bog. George knew the risks of proceeding haphazard in these conditions. He ordered the two women to shelter under a rock while he went on to explore. Obediently they sat, icy-cold in their blankets of mist, for what to Eileen seemed aeons of time. As the moments went by and grew to be an hour and more, she became gravely anxious. Had George fallen or got lost? Should she try to assist Aunt Edith down without him? Or must they wait until darkness and death came hand-in-hand?

As for Aunt Edith, she sat in her niche unconcerned, seemingly oblivious of danger, and gave Eileen an interminable lecture on Rudolf Steiner's methods of education.

At long last George appeared through the thickening mist. He had found a possible route down the gully of a stream by which they could descend to the Bethesda road. Eileen went first, negotiating about ten feet at a time, then standing aside while George assisted Aunt Edith in her ponderous descent over steep drops. Progress was hindered by her considerable weight; every few feet she loosed a scatter of stones which hurtled threateningly into the echoing depths. But not once did she show the slightest sign of anxiety or apprehension. On the contrary, she kept her course like a battleship assured of victory.

Eventually the three of them reached the stream and were reconciled, in this comparative safety, to being soaked to the waist. At least they were off the rocks. But now they were obliged to negotiate slopes treacherous as glass, for here, out of the wind, the mist had become racing sheets of rain. Water poured in at their necks, out at their boots; the running grass was slippery as seaweed. After a weary descent they came to a wall, and on the other side, miraculously, was the road. 'I feel like the princess commanded to climb the glass mountain!' said my aunt putting her head on one side – this time to allow the water to course off the brim of her hat.

The rain swept down in curtains; through this lay three trudging miles to Bethesda. When they finally arrived, wet beyond caring, there was more than an hour to wait for the next bus. But my aunt led them to a café and asked for a pile of old newspapers. With these they proceeded to pad themselves under their clothes. Thus attired, the three of them sat and steamed in front of a fire coaxed up by the proprietress who brought them a pot of tea and a pile of hot toast, and made no complaint at their lamentable condition.

This epic condensed in my aunt's diary reads thus: 'From Llyn Ogwen by Fynnan Lawr went up Carnedd Dafydd. On top into mist and fierce winds. Descended by a wild gully too far south-east of Bethesda'. Which masterpiece of understatement illustrates her way of minimising difficulty and danger.

After this adventure Eileen saw little of Aunt Edith; her time and energy were absorbed by her work at the Sunfield Children's Home to which my aunt's enthusiasm had led her.

And here, in connection with Steiner's work on education, I must mention the Llandudno Conference of 1931 arranged by my aunt and Miss D.V. Barber, secretary to Arnold Freeman at the Sheffield Educational Settlement. Staying at Erdmut at the same time was A. Cecil Harwood, author of the well-known book on child education, *The Way of a Child*. Mr Harwood, who became been president of the Anthroposophical Society in Great Britain in 1937, was once offered the Chair of English Literature at Oxford University. This offer he refused in order to take on the new Steiner school in Streatham where, as mentioned earlier, Arthur Sheen was teaching.

Aunt Edith believed that Mr Harwood could let in some new light at her old school, Penrhos College. And undoubtedly, during the course of the conference, he injected this orthodox girls' boarding school with some of Steiner's ideas. These ideas, which I can only briefly touch on here, must have come as a shock to staff and pupils alike.

To begin with, Steiner believed in co-education, because in a mixed class the children learn from each other's virtues while helping to overcome corresponding vices. Apart from this, he found that segregation tends to a morbid, rather than natural, interest in the opposite sex. Boys and girls growing up together must obviously have a more balanced outlook. And because girls are more 'spiritual, artistic, intuitive and, in the early years, quicker to learn', they should be educated alongside the boys whose slower, more solid and logical intelligence develops later. All teachers in mixed schools know that in a class of ten- and eleven-year-olds the girls are usually in advance of the boys; four years later the positions, as often as not, are reversed.

Mr Harwood expresses Steiner's view in the following words:

> In an external way co-education is something like a marriage between art and science. And the two sexes can not only impart some of their natural virtues to each other; they can help to cure each other's vices. For while boys – by themselves – indulge more in physical brutality, girls are equally guilty of such spiritual cruelty as spitefulness. But this can only satisfactorily be done in an artistic education . . . where the artistic sense penetrates the domain of science.
>
> . . . co-education of the children will lead naturally to co-operation of men and women as their teachers. There is something terribly arid and unreal in a staff of women teachers only, or exclusively of men with some wives in a dubious position in the background.[1]

In a Steiner school no homework is given before the age of twelve in accordance with the teaching that the threefold faculties of willing, feeling and thinking are developed in seven-year cycles. Up till the age of seven a child is developing his will, making plain his needs and wants, then learning to walk and talk. At this stage he learns in colour and rhythm and sound, picking out a red bead, perhaps, from a string of other colours, beating a tattoo on his tray with a spoon, learning so much of the strange new world that Steiner would not compel him to learn to read.

And then, with the stirrings of adolescence, between the ages of seven and fourteen, children explore the world of the senses and emotion. 'Play is more important than study at this stage, 'the Penrhos girls were told. Indeed, by the end of the lecture they must have wished themselves at a Steiner school: no hard intellectual work until the age of fourteen!

I remember how my aunt reproached me for encouraging our seven-year-old with his arithmetic: 'You must understand that his real creative energy is released in play!' She became lyrical on the subject: children whipping tops or playing hop-scotch according to the craze of the moment, children swinging, skipping, roller-skating, bowling hoops and jumping puddles. 'A young child has a wonderfully strong sense of rhythm and pattern and colour – all to be encouraged,' she said beating time to her words. 'It's a sad, bad thing to harness that happy boy to book

---

1 *The Way of a Child*, by A.C. Harwood.

work too early, and turn him into a book-worm instead of a creator!'

She went on to tell me how the various impressions absorbed by children are registered and 'learned' during sleep – that vital part of their education. And because homework interferes with sleep Steiner discouraged it, at least before the age of twelve. Again to quote A.C. Harwood: 'All that has been learned throughout the day is passed down during sleep to deeper levels of the mind where it is transformed and worked upon and changed into capacity'.[1]

In other words, learning becomes useful to us when it has become unconscious; when we are able to write, spell and solve problems, as it were, by 'second nature'.

In a Steiner school there are no set time-tables. The morning starts with an intellectual subject such as maths, which may continue for two hours while the children are fresh. This will be followed by some strongly rhythmic exercise such as eurhythmy, games or music; then back again to intellectual work. Lessons continue for as long as the children remain interested, which is longer than the forty-minute periods in an orthodox school, because a rhythmic programme is not tiring, nor is teaching which applies to the emotions as well as to the intellect.

I was amazed to hear of a maths lesson which occupied a whole morning and was spent in a field where the children enjoyed themselves hugely measuring its area, calculating how many bricks would be required for a shed, what length of piping for drainage and so on. These 'Steiner' ideas have by now penetrated into many modern schools; then they seemed revolutionary.

And the practice of the teacher moving up each year with the class instead of the children moving up to a new teacher seems revolutionary still. In every Steiner school the seven-year-old meets the teacher who will accompany him through the next seven years of his school life and who in this way learns to know each pupil individually. Only a truly dedicated person with a deep understanding of children is chosen for this most impressionable group. And then, at the age of fourteen, the children are taught by specialist teachers.

The reason for all this is that young children accept learning as a unity and not as a set of subjects sealed into different coloured boxes. So that if, say, Miss Green reads with her class Wordsworth's *Daffodils* or Tennyson's *The Brook*, she may aptly refer to something said in the last nature lesson. And she might remark that the French for daffodil is 'amarylis', because in these schools the children learn languages from the first year.

In the same way a myth or legend is woven into the fabric of a scripture, history or geography lesson. And because Miss Green teaches

1 *Ibid.*

all subjects in relationship the children are led to the crossroads where maths and science meet other kinds of learning. From this awareness springs the desire to model or paint or write a poem because art, created out of experience, can never be separated from living knowledge.

Such ideas as these my aunt had tried to explain to Eileen in the mists of Carnedd Dafydd. And some years later she sent me A.C. Harwood's book which clearly sets them forth. But when I first tried to read it I put it aside as one of her eccentric choices. In those days we wouldn't have considered a school where children were not chiselled into shape, inlaid with good manners and forced with facts sufficient to pass examinations. As to the rhythmic process of growth, release of creative power, and spiritual unfolding, these had no conscious part in our pattern of life.

Aunt Edith merely chided me for being too preoccupied with the boys' physical welfare. 'It's a fine thing,' she said, 'that you take such care of them in matters of food and clothing, but there *are* other, more important, things. Children thrive on love as much as on vitamins.' But those were the days when bread, to me, meant bread alone.

I remember her head-shaking over Martin, our eldest, when at the age of seven he would run home after school, not to play hop-scotch or the glockenspiel, but to sit in a corner avidly reading the *Daily Mail*. To restore the balance she sent me a book of Steiner's prayers for children.

One thing about Rudolf Steiner had really impressed me – even in those unenlightened days – and that was how he had been able to transform the life of a backward child. It happened that after finishing his degree course (when he was twenty-three) he had been obliged to take a post as tutor in order to pay for further studies. He was engaged to teach a family of four boys, the youngest of whom, at the age of ten, could hardly read or write, and was unable to concentrate on anything.

Before long Steiner found himself entirely responsible for this boy's mental and spiritual welfare. He soon realized that although ordinary methods of teaching would be useless the boy could be reached in other ways. Accordingly, he shifted the lines of communications from the 'top half' of the brain to the deeper level of the soul. And thus, seeing into the child's real self, he made vital contact. Gradually he roused the boy from a sort of inner sleep and beckoned him forth into the light of the world outside. To quote Canon Shepherd on Steiner's remarkable achievement: 'He established an intimate soul-relationship with his young pupil and thereby gradually changed his defective soul-outlook'.[1] After two years the boy was able to go to a public school and, guided all the time by Steiner in the background, eventually qualified as a doctor. This significant experience led Steiner towards new methods in education and his unique treatment – now widely recognized – of subnormal children.

1 *Scientist of the Invisible*, by A.P. Shepherd.

XII

Man and animal. In hospital.
Alice Crompton and Lilian Winter.
Trouble with Miss Tucker.
Holiday in Greece. The Bleasdale Circle.

WHILE these ideas were being loosed in educational circles in north Wales my aunt and Miss Barber called on the headmaster of the Woodlands Boys' Preparatory School in Deganwy asking permission for a further conference to be held there the following August. Miss Barber's one memory of this visit was the preoccupation of the headmaster's wife, who was concerned lest these strange anthroposophists damage the fresh white paint. However, the conference was duly arranged and took place without mishap. This time the chief speaker was Dr Hermann Poppelbaum whose *Man and Animal* my aunt had recently translated.

And here I must break off to mention her mountainous work in connection with the book which had occupied all her 'between-times' for the past year and more. Immersed in this giant task, she had enlisted the help of all her German-speaking visitors, persuading them to spend many an hour reading through and correcting the manuscript. Finally she appealed to the well-known writer on 'Steiner' subjects, Owen Barfield, solicitor and German scholar. According to Arnold Freeman, she so harried Mr Barfield with letters and queries that he was driven to exclaim: 'It would have been far less trouble to have translated the whole book myself!' In fact, part four is entirely his work.

Dr Heidenreich was also involved in her wrestlings over a highly controversial theme. I dare hardly touch the fringes of this research which sets out to explain how in the processes of nature material is constantly evolving out of spirit.

Dr Poppelbaum belonged to the younger schools of European biologists. As a pupil of Weissman he had been well grounded in the theory of evolution according to Darwin and Huxley, which saw man as the final product in an ascending line of animals. In later years he came to accept Rudolf Steiner's view, and described man as 'the central fact of creation from which the manifold aspects of animal life are, in a sense, off-shoots . . . The older ideas,' he said, 'have led to an attempt to understand man through the animal kingdom, whereas the new suggests that we can only understand the animal through man'.

During the conference Dr Poppelbaum pointed out that before the nineteenth century 'the various forms of life were each regarded as being separately created. But it was in England that Charles Darwin . . . collected and classified the evidence for his theory of evolution which presented the manifold life of the animal world as an organic whole, and where Thomas Huxley framed his daring ideas about man's place in nature . . . their picture made it increasingly difficult to retain the older religious idea of man as a spiritual being'.

Steiner, who saw man as the apex of creation, could never accept a theory which degraded him to little more than a higher animal. Later when we came to read in my aunt's translation that man's physical evolution lags behind that of the animals, we challenged her on what seemed to be an absurdity. But we had to agree that the human body has become less physically effective through losing contact with its natural environment. Animals, on the other hand, she pointed out, have evolved so successfully that they have actually become captive in their surroundings. So much so that they cannot expand into a mental life. Whereas the whole purpose of man is the evolution of consciousness towards self-conscious freedom. According to Dr Pop. (as we privately called him): 'the evolution of the earth begins amid quite other conditions from those which natural science can describe. Everything that comes into being rises from a spiritual source . . . the germ of the visible world arises out of the invisible'.

Here we felt ourselves on the firm ground trodden by all founders of religions. This seemed not very different from saying: 'The Word was made flesh and dwelt among us'.

We found the subject too teasing for holiday excursions, and my father, glad to be free of scientific discussions, took care not to be involved. As Aunt Alice said to me *sotto voce*: 'Ede made religion so complicated. I'm sure we weren't meant to worry our brains to *this* extent!'

But Aunt Edith had her own row to hoe; she never let herself off lightly from any self-imposed task. Her manuscript was handed by Dr Heidenreich to biology and archaeology lecturers at the University of Aberystwyth but, alas, it was not received with sympathy.

Undaunted, she proceeded with her plans, and in 1931 the translation of *Man and Animal* was published in London by the Anthroposophical Society. The following year, after the Deganwy conference, Dr Poppelbaum came a second time to stay at Erdmut and spoke to the study-group. It was a happy visit without the strain of public lectures. At all events, his departure note in the visitors' book runs: 'With very many thanks for those days which I never shall forget'. For the loan of this lively and colourful book I am indebted to Miss Barber. Its pages make it abundantly clear that my aunt could indeed persuade people to enjoy doing what they didn't want to do. So that even Miss Barber, after a hard-working visit, finds herself writing: 'Now I feel I've really had a holiday!'

Perhaps Aunt Edith sometimes persuaded herself that she enjoyed doing things she didn't really want to do – as, for instance, when the diary shows her sitting on the floor playing Noah's Ark with Sandy's two boys (while his delicate wife rested in 'Peaseblossom'), and then paddling and sailing boats with them on the West Shore. One day, we read on, she took Sandy for such an epic mountain walk that he was obliged to return home by bus. 'No ordinary person could keep up with her!' was his rueful comment.

Whether her powers of endurance came from wearing sandals or making friends with gravity, I don't know. But I remember one occasion out walking with her – on pavements – when we came to a downhill stretch and she suddenly broke into a trot. 'Let's make use of the force of gravity!' she exclaimed as we panted behind. 'To walk downhill is to pull away from a given power!' And so we continued – walk, trot, walk, trot, all the way home.

At any rate, such co-operation with natural laws kept her in remarkably good health; so that we were surprised when (sometime in 1933) she went as a patient to the Preston Royal Infirmary. It was impossible to imagine Aunt Edith a victim of hospital routine. And, indeed, so far from allowing a spell in hospital to prevent more important business, she took with her a pile of 'Steiner' literature.

Three days later her god-daughter, Edith May Higginson, then a pupil at Preston High School, went to visit her. Expecting to find a patient resting after an operation, she was astonished to see her godmother surrounded by German books and papers, sitting up and writing in bed, oblivious of visiting-hour chatter. Not until May was actually beside her, proffering a bunch of marigolds, did she look up. Then, smiling happily, she pushed the books on one side and made May feel really welcome. 'The nurses keep asking me to tidy my books away,' she said with the familiar sly smile that meant 'nothing doing'.

Afterwards I learned that the matter of Mrs Rigby's books had caused a rare stir in the ward. Insisting that her work was more important than a tidy bed, she had refused to obey the staff nurse's orders. Whereupon the ward sister descended upon her like a lioness. 'If everyone's bed was littered with books,' she began angrily, 'the ward would be a disgrace!'

Without replying Mrs Rigby looked at her for a long moment. Then, putting her head on one side, she gently repeated what she had said to the staff nurse. When Sister objected that this would lead to trouble Mrs Rigby offered to speak to Matron. Accustomed to dealing with prison-wardresses and matrons, she felt herself more than equal to this occasion. (And here she was secure in the knowledge that her brother's hospital services were being fully exploited.) The books continued on her bed.

Although May visited Aunt Edith every day when she came out of school, read to her, and brushed her hair, even that was not enough. A week before she was due to leave my aunt decided that she must have a shampoo and set. How she slipped the noose of hospital regulations by getting dressed and departing in a taxi to the hairdresser's I cannot imagine. Nor can I imagine anyone else having the nerve to confront the much-tried staff after such an excursion. I have it from Mrs Higginson, who also visited her once or twice, that everyone in the hospital (except for the maids) was truly thankful to see her go.

This episode makes me realize why her friends felt constrained to do her bidding and, after their various love-labours, write glowing letters of thanks. Hers was the habit of command; she rejoiced in disciples. One of the most faithful of these was Alice Crompton, an ex-suffragette, who latterly became deaf, and wrote to my aunt after a visit:

> My disabilities must have been very trying for you, but you never let me feel it for a moment. You are a wonderful friend indeed, and your earnestness and loftiness of mind and aspiration is an example and stimulus to us all . . .

Had my aunt destroyed this letter she would have been less than human! In fact, she kept many such letters: if she enjoyed giving people pleasure she considered their tributes her just reward, and took a very poor view of visitors who failed in this respect.

Another intimate friend of the Erdmut years, whose name came up so often in conversation that I longed to meet her, but never did, was Lilian Winter. I only knew that Lilian, teacher of elocution in Llandudno, loved poetry, drama, music and above all the countryside. My aunt, who met her at a verse-reading, invited her to an evening discussion at Erdmut. Fortunately Aunt Alice took an instant liking to her – sure sign of anyone's not being peculiar!

Lilian was young enough to be a daughter, and my aunt looked on her in this light, guiding her into paths leading away from the social life of Llandudno. 'My child,' she said to her one day, 'you enjoy your life, which is good; you enjoy lessons, and that is good too, but still I feel you're not doing *quite* enough for your fellow-men!'

Then came a suggestion that together they might form yet another circle to give Lilian an outlet in providing interest and pleasure for others. So began the New Circle lecture-group which, with Lilian as secretary and my aunt – to begin with – as treasurer, was to continue for twenty-five years. Aunt Edith persuaded celebrities such as Lady Violet Bonham-Carter and Christina Foyle to address the group, whose success formed a real bond between her and Lilian. Together they went for long walks discussing topics of mutual interest, but when, inevitably, Aunt Edith touched on anthroposophy, Lilian could no longer follow.

The relationship was not easy for two reasons. In the first place Lilian's family considered my aunt too eccentric and too old a companion; and the 'Steiner' ideas, even though Lilian was not responsive, further antagonized them. So that her departures to Erdmut were regarded with the same sort of misgivings felt by the Hutchins' parents.

The second obstacle, I was amazed to hear, was Miss Tucker's jealousy. Though I had often felt the 'dear child's' presence to be cloudy, even ominous, I never dreamed of a worm within her adoration. But this relationship which had begun spontaneously as guest and voluntary slave on the one hand and accepting, though grateful, hostess on the other, gradually changed until the slave, though still willing, became possessive, watchful and suspicious.

In the early idyllic days at 'Marigold' my aunt had taken in Miss Tucker as a life-partner; she had always treated her as an equal socially, if not intellectually, so that there had never been any question of employer-employee. Because Mrs Rigby had money and Miss Tucker had none, payment passed naturally from one to the other. Thus the question of an insurance card had never arisen; besides I don't believe Aunt Edith ever gave it a thought.

With the passing years my aunt, devoted to outside causes, became ever more dependent on Miss Tucker who, justly, was more amply rewarded. Sometimes, even, it seemed as though Miss Tucker were the more solvent of the two. Frequently my aunt was obliged to borrow from her in order to pay the grocery bill or a train fare. 'Carinthia,' she would say in her most beguiling manner, 'do you think you could *possibly* lend me two pounds?'

The two pounds was always forthcoming and without fail paid back. It seemed that a wholly agreeable sliding scale of payment had been arrived at. And not only in regard to money. My aunt fully appreciated Miss Tucker's capability. For instance, during one of Beryl Watchurst's visits when many household irregularities occurred, a note in her hand runs: '*À cause de . . .* it was a mosquito bite on Miss Ford-Tucker's leg which felled our oak'. When most aware of her services she would refer to her thus; and Herbert, primed by my aunt, never omitted the 'Ford' in his letters of thanks.

With Herbert and the Watchursts, who had almost grown up at 'Marigold' and in Miss Tucker's sight, there was no awkwardness. In those green-apple days they had many times been bound together in happy conspiracy against 'the Missus', as Miss Tucker, half-amused at her goings-on, had then called my aunt. But as the children grew up and were more able to enter Aunt Edith's world invaded by constant newcomers, Miss Tucker found herself increasingly alone outside the fence, and increasingly resentful of guests admitted to the inner pasture.

My aunt, of course, made extra efforts to include her in mealtime conversations and the fringes of 'group-talks'. People like ourselves, outsiders, counted little in Miss Tucker's eyes. But when Lilian Winter, who lived near at hand and could come often, became a real friend with common interests – anthroposophy apart – it was altogether more than the 'dear child' could take. Lilian suffered, first of all, from the 'Tucker silences'. Then it was made plain to my aunt that she must be sparing of invitations. She dared not ask Lilian too often for fear of Miss Tucker's disapproval. Slowly the players in this game were changing places until, finally, it seemed that Aunt Edith was almost afraid of her one-time slave.

And by now the unmentionable matter of the insurance card festered between them. Miss Tucker, in her 'fifties and prompted, no doubt, by low voices at her elbow, seemed suddenly aware that no stamps meant no pension. I can only suppose that my aunt's inconsistency with her ideals sprang from a feeling that it was now too late to make amends. And had she come into the open she might even have found herself, this time ingloriously, in gaol!

The matter was never directly alluded to, but Miss Tucker's overt remarks regarding pensions must have sorely troubled my aunt's conscience.

However, 'Carinthia' was eventually assured that she would never be in need, would be treated as a sister – an assurance she seems to have accepted. At any rate, soon after this smoothing of the way my aunt, having borrowed a few pounds for immediate necessities, was happily writing to Arnold Freeman, asking him to go to Greece with her, all expenses paid.

Perhaps it was fortunate for her finances that he was unable to accept this offer. As far as I know Aunt Edith, armed with books and field-glasses, went on her own. This was in 1932 when she was away for six weeks 'doing' Greece in her thorough fashion – archaeologically and geographically.

A minor hitch in her programme is described on yet another post-card to Nancy Watchurst – this one from Athens:

> A lovely day and I am to stay in with a hurt foot which late in its history turns out to be a very slight fracture. No man or woman should or *could*(!) get things just as they plan (what a fruitless world it would be!).

which sheds as much light on her philosophy as on her foot.

In spite of this she was soon limping eagerly among the temples and ruins, leaving no turnable stone unturned. When we next visited her it was Hymettus honey for tea while we listened to an account of her ascent to Mount Parnassus, on a mule because of her injured foot.

The visit to Greece had been partly inspired by her involvement in one of the most exciting archaeological discoveries in Great Britain: the wooden circle at Bleasdale, only about three miles from our own home, Sullom Holt. It appeared that even the hill, Sullom, on which we lived, was originally Sollom, a shrine of sun-worshippers. The circle, which had been first discovered about thirty years earlier, was by now completely hidden under bushes and trees. My aunt determined that the site should be cleared and excavated, a plan requiring a considerable sum of money.

Investigations into this new venture brought her often to the district and sometimes to our house. One summer evening she called to see us on her way home. Still wearing her blue cloak and a beret, she sat down to supper hardly noticing what we passed her. She was set on getting my father's co-operation in launching a preservation fund. As always she spoke softly, but her eyes, alight with enthusiasm, seemed bluer than ever. 'You don't know how privileged you are,' she said, 'to live near such a place!'

Indeed, I was amazed to learn of a circle, older than Woodhenge, hidden among the reeds of our familiar country. Having walked or ridden almost daily for years over the heathery fells of Bleasdale, I imagined that every fir wood, stream, stone wall and acre of bent grass was known to me.

The whole business of the Bleasdale Circle began with my aunt's visit to Higher Fairsnape Farm to see Thomas Kelsall, who in 1898 (before his son Edward took over the farm) had actually discovered the circle. Answering her many questions, he eventually told her the whole story which I relate here.

One day, while digging on the lower land, it happened that his spade drove into an upright post of timber. Wondering what it could be, he filled up the hole and left it alone. Some weeks later, on a frosty-bright May morning, looking down across his land, he saw with surprise a green circle stamped plainly among the sparkling grasses. And again he wondered. But the gods were at his elbow. Not long afterwards a fire started in a spinney of birches and racing over the rough grass burned an unmistakable circle on his land. It seemed like an act of Providence; one might have said that the hand of God was in the spade and the frost and the fire.

By now alight with curiosity, Mr. Kelsall confided in a neighbour, Shadrack Jackson, who was an amateur archaeologist. Mr Jackson agreed that the circle should be dug over, and offered to pay a share in the expenses. So began the dig that was to bear such fruit, though not for some time yet. Several men were engaged to uncover the outer rim which was found to consist of sunken oak posts about thirteen feet apart. Fortunately these timbers were left in the ground. Within this outer circle (150 ft in diameter) was a circular ditch line with poles of bog-oak well preserved in the peaty soil. Contained again within this area was a concealed horseshoe circle (34 ft in diameter) composed of eleven oak posts, the 'nails', as it were, of the horseshoe whose gap opened towards the Midsummer sunrise.

With mounting excitement the men lifted the 'nails' to the surface and dug over the centre of the horseshoe until they came upon a bed of ashes containing two urns, each about eight inches high. These were greeted with a mixture of awe and delight, lifted from the ground and, as though lamps of Aladdin, rubbed clean of grit and proudly carried into the farmhouse. Mr Kelsall placed them upon the kitchen dresser, where they stood, constant reminders of mortality, until 1901 when the curator of the Harris Museum came to claim them for Preston and the nation.

Naturally the Kelsalls had looked inside the urns, to discover the remains of what proved to be human bones and in the larger of the two an incense-cup which was taken out and set alongside its companions.

Meanwhile, distinguished archaeologists were on the scent. Under the aegis of Professor Boyd Dawkins, who came in June and again in August, 1900, a number of students visited the circle upon which, literally, the professor delivered a lecture. Edward Kelsall, among his audience, heard him describe the circle as a Bronze Age burial-ground. But in the light of future events, its uniqueness was not yet realized.

So far from the timbers being removed and treasured, they were lifted a foot and a half above ground and left to the weather. Worse was to come. In a misguided attempt at preservation the Circle was planted with trees and shrubs. And so, in wind and rain, a quarter of a century went by while the young trees grew stronger and the ancient timbers rotted. When, in 1925, the Bleasdale Circle was listed as an Ancient Monument, it was in danger of being lost for ever.

And still the seasons turned on in that wild, unvisited moorland until one day Mrs Rigby pushed her way through the undergrowth that hid the forsaken Circle and learned its romantic history from Thomas Kelsall. So began another story which opened with the following to the editor of the *Lancashire Daily Post*:

Dear Sir,
In a review of a book just now published on Woodhenge, by Mr and Mrs Cunnington, there is something of great interest to all Lancashire folk . . . who know Bleasdale.

In this book there is first an account of the findings of Woodhenge in December 1925 by Squadron-Leader Inscall, V.C. He detected from the air finds of human workmanship, previously unknown. Then follows the account of the Cunningtons' most thorough excavation of the site in 1926-28. Six concentric circles (or ovals) were found, into which columns of oak and pine were inserted, hence its name, Woodhenge.

Around the grave of a child (central) the long axis of the circles was aligned so as to mark the track of the Midsummer sunrise. This lies two miles to the south-west of Stonehenge, which it resembles in its orientation to the sun.

A few Prestonians will remember, about 1900, the finding of two similar circles in wood columns on a rounded hill, in the upper valley of Bleasdale. It was observed first by Mr Thomas Kelsall standing at the door of his farm above it. Professor Boyd Dawkins was brought to see it, and he prepared a drawing and plan of the lie of the oak columns.

Will Preston people be vexed or pleased to be reminded that in the show-case of the Free Library, which purports to represent this [circle] there is no copy of this plan; there is no statement of the actual orientation of the sun – whether true east or to the Midsummer sunrise? With the cinerary urns there is only a painting which is not accurate in its indication of the real position of the circles. It only shows the plantation of young trees planted then and which, in almost twenty years, has almost obliterated the [circle itself] . . .

I have just written to Professor Newstead, F.R.S., who described the recent finds of similar urns in Cheshire, to ask if there are any other wooden circles orientated to the sun (as the Bleasdale Circle) known in England. Surely there are some people who will not let this wonderful heritage found by us . . . be lost, through neglect and lack of interest, to the generations of men who are to follow us?

Yours etc.,
Edith Rigby.

Llanrhos
January 29th, 1930

No sooner was this letter printed than my aunt appealed to Colonel Hines, headmaster of Hutton Grammar School, to help her to form a Bleasdale Preservation Committee. Whereupon he wrote immediately to Herbert J. Fleure, Professor of Geology, and the archaeologist, Professor Myres. Before long these three were standing on the circle discussing possibilities. The professors were agreed that although systematic excavation was desirable it might well lead to nothing.

When Aunt Edith heard this she was more than ever determined that the scheme must go ahead. She herself felt certain they were on the brink of unique discovery. At any rate, she continued prodding Colonel Hines until he decided to risk raising a fund. From under his mortar-board he brought forth names of influential Lancastrians and wrote to them all: Lord Derby, the Earl of Crawford and Balcarres, the Bishops of Manchester, Liverpool, and Blackburn, besides industrial magnates such as Sir Meyrick Hollins, Sir James Openshaw and many more. Facing them with the alternatives – unique discovery and total failure – he begged from them five pounds apiece. 'They all responded gamely, prepared to lose their stakes,' he told me. In fact, many of them gave considerably more than asked so that with the opening of a public fund enough money was collected to begin work.

The archaeologist who answered the challenge to take entire charge of the excavation was a young man, John Varley, who has since won fame for his work on the Bickerton Hill Fort in Cheshire. Mr Varley came first of all to examine the site with his wife (also an archaeologist) and a few students. He went to work at once, removing all the soil from the horseshoe circle. When the eleven timbers disturbed more than thirty years earlier were lifted it was Edward Kelsall who dragged them to one side. And my aunt, who had brought Sandy to stay at the farm, eagerly followed every move: for her, the initiator of the work, much was at stake. Many a morning she would turn up complete with picnic-basket and camp there for the day. She watched Mr Varley carefully setting the eleven concrete blocks in place of the original timbers, and later uncovering the poles of bog-oak which lined the surrounding ditch. Some of these, the oldest existing timbers in Britain, were sent to the British Museum while others went to Preston and elsewhere.

Indeed, no timber was left unturned before the Bleasdale Circle was found to be unique in three ways: it is the first timber circle to be discovered in Britain; secondly, it is the only circle of its kind; thirdly, and above all, it is the only circle whose timbers still remain. My aunt, already preoccupied with the whole subject of circles, their use, meaning and symbolism, was alight with excitement at these findings, which led Professor V. Gordon Childe, in his *Prehistoric Communities of the British Isles*, to write: 'At Bleasdale, on the edge of the Pennines in Lancashire, one of the most remarkable monuments in England had been built round an Urn Chief . . .'

As for Mr Varley's own conclusions, these were published in the Antiquaries' Journal (vol. 18) in 1938.

Looking back, it seems incredible that I was unaware, at the time, of this amazing discovery on a piece of land I knew a great deal better than our own garden. But in 1931, when work on the Circle was seriously begun, I married and left the district. While history was being recovered on our doorstep, I was occupied with such flimsy matters as bridesmaids' dresses, curtains, carpets and catering arrangements. I have even forgotten how I came to hear of the results of the excavation. By then I was totally engrossed in having a baby which made everything else seem unimportant. So that the way in which I came to visit the circle for the first time – twenty-seven years later when I'd almost forgotten its existence – strikes me as very strange.

It happened one morning, some time in the autumn of 1958, while occupied in household tasks, that I suddenly said to my German Fraulein: 'Come on, let's leave the work and go to the Bleasdale Circle!'

In the car on the way there I began to wonder what I was doing. I hadn't thought of the circle once in nearly thirty years; I didn't even know its exact whereabouts, and was obliged to make inquiries at a nearby farm. Only with great difficulty, scrambling over fences and streams, we eventually reached the clump of trees surrounding the circle itself.

Crossing the plank over the horseshoe ditch I felt strangely excited. There in front of me were the eleven concrete blocks replacing the original timbers; as I stood in the gap of the horseshoe looking east to a gap in the fells where the sun rises on Midsummer morning, I was overwhelmed with a sense of wonder. To think I had walked so often over this land, yet had never until now stood exactly here!

The few rowans growing on the horseshoe had probably been seeded at the time of the clearance. We stripped off some branches beaded with flame-coloured berries – 'to keep the witches away' as I explained to my companion. And while we were gathering them together before leaving I found a compass in the grass.

Half an hour later, having tea in the nearby Brock Mill Cottage, I asked the owner many questions. She told us that for years past, every Midsummer's Eve a man on a bicycle had come here for high tea. After fortifying himself with bacon and eggs he would walk up to the circle, where he spent the night, to watch the sunrise. 'He won't tell me his name,' the woman said, 'but he's never missed a year since I've been here.' Very likely, I thought, he was the owner of the compass.

Some time later I heard that my aunt had herself spent at least one Midsummer's Eve in the circle. I wondered if that was at the time of the young man's (he must have been very young then) visitations. And if so what these two ardent sun-worshippers had found to say to one another.

When I got home that evening I sat by the fire thinking about the circle, and wondering what had prompted me to visit it, when the telephone rang. It was my father. 'I hope you were listening to that most interesting broadcast,' he said, 'I found it quite enthralling. Stewart Piggott has just been talking about the Bleasdale Circle.'

'The Bleasdale Circle!' I echoed, stupid with amazement, 'why I've just been there – for the first time – it must have been on the air all day!'

XIII

Thoughts on destiny and meditation.
Herbert's girl-friend. Introducing Æ.
Family weddings. Sisters-in-law.
Visit to America.

T O TURN back to 1932, I find an entry in my aunt's visitor's book, shortly after her return from Greece, which reads: 'Mr and Mrs W. J. Varley here and 'Robin' re the wonderful meetings at Bleasdale Circle to date. Three taken by W.J.V.' Unquestionably the Varleys would be presented with Steiner's views as she escorted them to a Druids' Circle and a Roman camp in the Welsh hills.

Through living too far away, my aunt missed some of the later work at Bleasdale, but she believed that in initiating the enterprise she had fulfilled part of her destiny by interweaving it with the destiny of the circle. 'To become human,' she wrote in *Man and Animal*, 'is to bear the destiny of the earth onwards to future stages of its existence.'

And to leave the circle at this point is to touch on one of her main preoccupations: the origin and destiny of man. Heading her translation of the final section (of *Man and Animal*), Destiny, are Steiner's words: 'The biography of one man corresponds to the whole history of the animal kingdom'.

This part of the book deals with man's developing ego and self-awareness. I quote one passage:

> The individuality passes through a series of incarnations in the different epochs of human history; in each life it appears as another personality . . . with new surroundings and new tasks which it has chosen for itself . . . always with new means and against new hindrances [it] wrestles . . . through to consciousness of its own true being. From life to life the relations to other men are woven; what has been left behind it once more taken up; what was broken off is united; what was failing can be made good. Each time the scene is chosen anew; the surroundings, the period, the place . . . Experiences are sought out [and] moulded into capacities; activities are undertaken which are an expression of the living being concerned; and they continue working so that later – like changing constellations – he is to meet them again having meanwhile changed himself.
>
> Thus destiny, *human* destiny, becomes not an overpowering fate and oppression, but a freely sought task, an opportunity to make good . . . Human destiny is individual destiny; it is the outcome of

decisions made before birth and continually grasped anew. The way in which, of his own impulse, the individual descends again and again to earth life and inserts himself into the path of human evolution, marks the particular mission apportioned to man in contrast to other creatures.

We have here no chain of blind chance, nor of fate; but a recurring plunge, each time more resolute, into the light of the freedom allotted to man.

If this is true, our responsibility is heightened to Henley's words:

> I am the master of my fate:
> I am the captain of my soul.

Every decision becomes significant with every achievement, every failure sending out ripples in a boundless pool and endlessly affecting the lives of others. So that knowledge of what we truly are and why we are here becomes a first purpose.

Steiner saw no limitations to knowledge and the power of the human mind. He maintained that although our physical senses must limit us to an understanding of the natural world, we can, if we will, apprehend something of reality and our true selves by penetrating into our real being and by expanding consciousness. Sense-perception by itself limits the entire view of ourselves and the world. As Martin Armstrong, the poet, puts it:

> Man, afraid to be alive,
> Shuts his soul in senses five.

Aunt Edith, never afraid to be alive, followed Steiner's suggestions for meditation, which, he taught, leads on to these discoveries. That is why, every morning early she practised his special exercises; and sometimes she would sit by the window gazing fixedly at one of the poplar trees. Observing how the leaves twinkled in sun and wind, she would hold some text in mind, or a fragment of poetry such as Wordsworth's 'soft eye-music of slow-moving leaves'.

Then she would close her eyes and see the tree inwardly. After much practice she told me that the image of the tree became far more vivid that the actual poplar out there in the garden. According to A.P. Shepherd this power of sense-independent thinking distinguishes Spiritual Science 'from any other form of occult knowledge' and justifies Steiner's claim to 'describe his knowledge of spirit reality as a science'.

Through the example and experiences of his followers I have come to believe that in this way the soul (or mind) can be set free from sense-impressions. And then, gradually, the 'soul-organs', of which my aunt used to speak, are awakened to a higher activity until, in Canon

Shepherd's words:

> . . . there arises within us the whole of our inner life of thought, feeling and will, from the beginning of our earthly existence. These events are present to higher consciousness as actual experiences, as though they were being experienced again. In this respect we find ourselves in a new relation to Time. Although these events happened in our physical experience separately and in succession, they now seem present to us as one unified whole.[1]

This kind of experience is described by people who have been on the point of drowning. After being rescued and brought back to consciousness they have related how the successive events of their lives were flashed simultaneously before them.

When Aunt Edith used to talk to me about 'stepping over the threshold of time into a dimension beyond time barriers', I remained unconvinced, imprisoned in three cages: past, present and future. And then one day I had a dream or, rather, I *forgot* a dream, on waking in the morning. A few hours later I was taken by the friends with whom I was staying to a place quite new to me – Brittas Bay in County Wicklow. During the afternoon I went off for a walk and returned to the bay about an hour later. My host and his two children were standing to the left of a sharp rock formation, intently gazing out to sea. As I drew near he shouted over his left shoulder: 'What d'you think? We've just seen a seal!'

I stood still and speechless because here was the dream, exact in every detail (but forgotten until now) I had woken up with that very morning. I recount this experience because it came to me in a flash that everything *is*, here and now and all the time. The future is already happening. In this instance, while my body had been in bed at seven o'clock that morning, 'I' had been with my friends in Brittas Bay. Aunt Edith's theories of astral travel began to seem not so impossible.

At any rate, after this experience I didn't laugh when she told me how she used to contact Herbert 'in the astral' during his sea voyages, especially on his birthday and at Christmas time. Which reminds me of one year when this sort of meeting was unnecessary because just before Christmas, 1935, a joyful telegram announced his arrival at Erdmut with the eighteen-year-old Betty Snook whom he was soon to marry. For my aunt it was a big thing to 'hand over' her beloved nephew into another's keeping. She decided to test Betty for qualities of courage and endurance. To this end she was required to climb into the Devil's Kitchen on Y Tryfan – a tough enough breaking-in for any potential housewife.

This feat accomplished, two stiffer climbs – the second up Snowdon by Crib Goch – were proposed by Aunt Edith in her role of fairy godmother,

---

1 *Scientist of the Invisible*, by A. P. Shepherd.

to ensure Herbert's happiness and protection. Betty, a champion tennis-player, had never climbed a mountain. However, she bravely attempted the ice-coated rock of the first pinnacle; thereafter the handholds became impossible so that the idea had to be abandoned. But by now her willing eager spirit was evident as much among mountains as at the sink. Aunt Edith accepted her as 'the right girl' for Herbert.

And Betty, for her part, accepted Herbert's strange aunt undeterred by eccentricities. For instance, the night before the Crib Goch climb, while trying on a pair of mountaineering boots, she happened to remark that she must cut her toe-nails. 'Not *before* the climb, dear,' Aunt Edith said gently. Much surprised, Betty inquired why not. 'Because,' replied my aunt, 'when you cut your toe-nails, some of the vitality goes out of you – unless it's done at the full moon.'

Such theories as these were included among the more lofty ideas discussed by her weekly study-group, to which I had no ambition to belong. All the same, I was interested to hear about some of its discussions, such as the one concerning the Irish poet, Æ. This was the name George Russell had given himself because, as my aunt told me, he believed he was an Aeon, and was able to see into the past, so discovering that the earth itself has a memory, stored up like the reel of a film. For example, he described how, on one occasion, while waiting for a friend inside a ruined chapel, he saw a crowd, which included a woman in a red cloak, kneeling before the altar. Facing the people on that altar step was an abbot, crozier in one hand, the other uplifted in blessing.[1]

This kind of seeing into the past was quite common with Æ. Visits to ancient houses and castles, sometimes even the reading of history, would produce similar imprints from the earth-memory. And, like Blake, he saw being from the spiritual world as well as spirits of the earth, to be transposed into poetry and colour. In fact, Blake and Æ, both mystics as well as artists, have much in common. Aunt Edith rejoiced in their link with Steiner, explaining how all three saw with the 'third eye' of perception into a rarer atmosphere, a world of spirit-beings. 'While we ordinary mortals,' she went on, 'are tuned-in to lower vibrations we can't expect to see what we're not in tune with.'

Though I could well believe this, I couldn't imagine Steiner seeing Æ's 'little folk' – fairies, elves and leprechauns – which he painted from life. My aunt found nothing strange in crossing boundaries of time and space into Æ's 'many-coloured land', an exercise which never interfered with her practical abilities. In fact, she made me realize how practical a genuine mystic must be. And here is a link between herself and Æ who, apart from writing and painting, started the co-operative movement in Ireland, and encouraged the people to be agriculturally self-supporting. If

1 See *The Candle of Vision*, by Æ.

he saw fairies at the bottom of his garden, he also helped men to plough productive furrows.

Alongside his creative work he edited *The Irish Homestead* and afterwards *The Irish Statesman*, which enabled him to launch many young poets into print. At the same time he held regular gatherings at his house in Dublin where young and old alike were encouraged to join in long discussions on every subject from philosophy to folk-lore – not so very different from the Erdmut pattern. Æ has been called the Socrates of Dublin; and if he couldn't distinguish between turbot and halibut, he had a flair for recognizing genuine poets.

Regarding intimate personal relationships, he writes: 'I think I would break any woman's heart, whoever loved me. She would find me elusive as the spirit itself:

> I sometimes think a mighty lover
> Takes every burning kiss we give . . .'[1]

And so thought my aunt who was never, as a young girl, interested in earthly love-affairs – at least for herself. It was all the more surprising, therefore, that she was so keenly interested in the love-affairs of her nephews and nieces, and made a point of attending family weddings. I look back with amusement on one of these which must have seemed foreign to her own ideas.

In an atmosphere of champagne, silver and white linen, I found myself sitting opposite her for the wedding-breakfast. A muted orchestra, hidden among palms, was playing tuneful back-numbers when suddenly a solo violin swelled into the Wedding March, and the bride, dark-haired and glittering, appeared on the bridegroom's arm. We all stood up while this lovely creature floated, rather than walked, down red-carpeted steps. Breathless we waited until her spray of lilies-of-the-valley was laid eloquently on the table. In silence we all sat down. Aunt Edith unfolded her pyramid napkin: 'I feel as though I'm in Hollywood!' she said.

Though I don't remember details of the following conversation, I do remember that she was dressed exactly as I would have expected. Her strong sense of occasion was not accompanied by a sense of fashion. If the majority of guests looked upon this wedding as an affair of mink and orchids, in her eyes it was a religious ceremony. Her long, loose garment of rich purple velvet I can only describe as a robe. Somewhere in the middle it was gathered by a girdle. She wore a heavy antique brooch, and around her neck was the familiar amber-beaded silver chain. On the wide brim of her hat reposed a large clematis – otherwise known as virgin's bower – in her favourite shade of deep purple.

She must have worn something like this – minus the hat – at the supper

---

1 *Collected Letters of Æ* (edited by Alan Denson).

party in Paris and I reflected that at least her clothes never went out of date. All her dresses were shaped like sacks, an unlovely fashion which, in the 'nineties, she had set herself in protest against tight-lacing and whalebone stays. The equally unlovely sandals were also worn, as she explained, 'to allow air to the foot and room for it to grow in nature's design'. She believed that women of fashion, cramped in corsets until they could scarcely breathe, and with feet pinched into narrow high-heeled shoes, could never live the 'three-fold life' of body, mind, and spirit. And so she went her own way, shod alike for all occasions.

The 'thirties proved to be a romantic decade for our family. Shortly after this wedding came my own, and then Herbert's, which took place on a brilliant July day in the church of St Nicholas at Great Kimble, where John Hampden had once stood up and defied the orders of Charles I by refusing to pay ship-money. My aunt believed that the vibrations set in motion by this act created the right atmosphere for her beloved Herbert's new venture. And indeed, if ever the sun blessed a marriage it blessed that one.

On the heels of this wedding came Elaine's engagement, and, last but unexpected as snow at midsummer, the announcement that my father was to marry a young girl who had recently been his patient, and who before that had waited upon him when he took his lonely meals in a restaurant. The wedding took place in May, 1939, when the bride, herself named May, on her twenty-third birthday linked her life with his.

It cannot have been easy for her to take on a widower with two daughters older than herself, and to face the running of a country house with its maids, gardeners and callers from the surrounding 'country gentry' arriving unexpectedly in the afternoons. Here again Aunt Edith showed her colours. Before news of the forthcoming marriage became known, she came over expressly to welcome May into the family and to silence the growing speculations of neighbours.

In spite of the gap in years my aunt welcomed her brother's engagement. She understood that the romantic side of him could only be fulfilled by someone with a love of poetry and the countryside. Such loves May shared with him; her responsive nature was eager to learn from this man, so clever and wise, who had restored her to health after a serious accident.

I might remark here that my father had several 'suitable' lady-friends (from a baronet's widow to a hospital matron) each one eager to make him a capable wife and hostess. But he knew well that that way led into the social round which he detested and which hindered his first love – his work. With May he would be blessedly free of social handicaps, a point applauded by his elder sister.

Anyhow, the 'Pygmalion' relationship held on many levels; and above all, perhaps, my father's strong sense of chivalry was aroused to feel this young girl in need of protection and himself acting knight to her fair lady.

Sensing all this, Aunt Edith took an immediate liking to May. Moreover, she was in sympathy with her background and upbringing in a simple home of working people. And although she could never approve the world of Sullom Holt with its pheasant-coverts and shooting-parties, she did her best to help May over the threshold into such a bewildering life. On the morning after her arrival she introduced her to the head-gardener: 'Good-morning, Watson! This is the young lady my brother is going to marry. I want you to meet her'.

It was a happy start to the life of the garden. Fortunately plants and flowers flourished at the touch of May's green fingers; and more important, she had a strong feeling for the life of the spirit and its relationship with the world of nature – a quality which doubly endeared her to my aunt. Though two more disparate sisters-in-law could hardly be imagined we had to admit that they shared the most important things. And if the truth were known the social life around Sullom Holt was as alien to my father as to May. Before long they left the district and went to live in a small, square villa near Preston. The removal was completed with my aunt's blessing and they were to be far happier living in what Aunt Alice described as their 'modest abode' and we nicknamed 'the Box'. Here they lived a secluded life, seldom going away except for a summer fortnight in Llandudno in order to visit the aunts.

May was received with the greatest kindness by them both. In fact, they were a great deal nicer to her than they had been to my mother, fully understanding her difficulties and her dislike for entertaining. On her part, May grew very fond of them, and was full of admiration for the way Aunt Edith ran Erdmut, almost as a non-paying guest-house. Here there was always someone staying, or a tea-party or a group-meeting arranged. And this gives me an opportunity to remark on my aunt's astonishing generosity. Apart from giving holidays and presents to individual people, she supported dozens of charities, not only by writing cheques but also by personal service. She lived according to these words, discovered in her diary after her death: 'the less a person lays claim to the fruits of his work, the more he is enriched; and whoever works only for himself becomes an egotist'.

Her friends were sometimes embarrassed by her gifts. For instance, after offering to take Arnold Freeman to Greece, she tried to make Miss Barber a present of a trip to America. And towards the end of her life she made her accept a treasured moonstone ring and zodiac napkin-ring. After one visit to Erdmut Miss Barber recalls: 'Edith insisted, at the last moment as I was leaving, that I should pack her prized red Moorecraft bowl into my week-end case'. And this at a time when she was feeling particularly hard-up.

That same weekend my aunt had entertained Miss Barber with an account of a visit to an antique shop. In the window she had observed two beautiful Paisley shawls and longed to buy one of them, but wondered if she could afford either, and if so, which to choose. After hesitating for some time she went inside the shop and lingered over the shawls, holding out first one and then the other. At this point in her story she glanced up with a twinkle in her eye and confessed: 'In the end I bought them both!'

No doubt she was again obliged to ask Miss Tucker for a loan. It was fortunate that her extravagance *was* matched by generosity, with time and endeavour as well as with money. I cannot think of a better exponent of the phrase: 'She put herself out'. If she was eccentric, self was not her centre; and with a flair for turning every occasion to good, she regarded personal inconvenience in the light of opportunity. Even when her hand so trembled with the Parkinson's disease that finally overcame her, the diary continues with exuberant jottings in almost illegible pencil-scrawl.

At the onset of this disease and before it was too late, she decided to go to America. First of all she wanted to visit the Rudolf Steiner Center in New York, and also the settlement in the country, about twenty miles out. During this same trip she planned to stay with Herbert and Betty (now expecting her second baby) and their two-year-old son David. At this time it happened that Elaine was suffering a reaction from her recently-broken engagement, whereupon Aunt Edith suggested this trip as an antidote and restorative. (The remedy, in fact, was to prove more effective than she bargained for.)

So it was, on a brilliant May morning in 1939, they sailed together from Liverpool in the *Laconia*. At first Elaine was too unhappy to heed the threat of war which clouded even Aunt Edith's buoyant spirit. (At this moment Germany, having swallowed Czechoslovakia and occupied the Saar, was threatening to annex Poland.)

All my aunt's German friends were anti-Nazi; many of them were Jewish.

No sooner had the gentle outline of western Ireland faded into an amethyst horizon than Elaine fell in with two Americans, Franz and Archie, who were returning home from Liberia. In Franz she recognized an affinity. He was tall, dark, handsome, rich and single. Providence could hardly have offered a better remedy for injured heart and pride. After the first drink together he suggested that the two men join Elaine and her aunt at table. Somewhat diffidently, while dressing for dinner in the cabin they shared, Elaine put this idea to Aunt Edith. Much to her surprise it was gracefully, even happily, accepted.

And so for Elaine began the voyage of restoration. Franz was gifted with sympathy and wisdom, as well as charm – qualities to which Aunt Edith was by no means impervious. She liked him immensely. She liked Archie too and remarked that meals on board were 'a deal pleasanter' for the young men's companionship.

As the blue days slipped by Elaine spent more and more time in Franz's company. They lingered over drinks in the bar, sat for hours talking together on deck, and, out-staying the moon, leaned over the ship's rail until sunrise.

'Whatever did Aunt Edith think of you creeping into your cabin at four in the morning?' I asked incredulously. 'I don't know what she thought, but she never remarked about it,' Elaine replied. 'In any case at that hour she was completely absorbed in her 'Steiner' meditations – I doubt if she even noticed me. But she did most strongly protest that Franz was spending too much money on me and that we were both drinking too much.'

Deeper than spoken protest, Elaine realized that her aunt was saddened rather than shocked by such deliberate and superficial pursuit of pleasure.

On the quayside at New York Aunt Edith was greeted by a tall, gentle-mannered and considerate man who turned out to be Mr Courtney, foreign correspondent to the *New York Herald-Tribune* and an ardent follower of Steiner. He had a car waiting and drove the two of them, as arranged, to the Rudolf Steiner settlement about twenty miles west of New York. Although Elaine had not wanted to go, imagining this to be nothing more than a colony of cranks, she soon had to revise her ideas.

Outwardly the settlement consisted of several blocks of attractive wooden houses, each in its own garden and surrounded by trees. Inside, for the first time, she was able to observe 'Steiner' ideals in practice. Before very long she came to realize how individual expression can flourish more strongly for its roots in community life. Though meals, household tasks and social activities were shared, there was always time and place for withdrawal from the community. Aunt Edith, already disciplined in the practice of meditation and the rhythm of work, reflection, and exercise, found herself completely at home.

There was no feeling either of compulsion or restraint: every activity, whether gardening, cooking, painting or playing the violin, was seen as equally important to the completed pattern. As to cooking, this was undertaken by members in turn who managed to produce delicious and imaginative vegetarian dishes.

All community members studied Steiner's lectures and followed, step by step, his suggestions for meditation. Such self-discipline seemed to generate an atmosphere of serenity and repose. So much so that several refugees, broken in health and spirit by Hitler's regime, came to the community for healing and peace of mind.

My aunt entered fully into the programme, taking her cold baths, attending lectures and helping in the garden. She even persuaded a musician to give her some lessons on the flute, Steiner's favourite instrument. But here Elaine, herself a violinist, outdid her by taking part in impromptu concerts.

After a fortnight's stay the two of them departed, very reluctantly, with Mr Courtney to the Rudolf Steiner Center in New York. Islanded amid the whirl of city life, this place was in strange contrast to the settlement. Yet in spite of traffic such as they'd never before experienced, the overhead railway and the ceaseless night-wailing of police-sirens, there was peace, if not quiet, in the building itself. In that inferno of heat and din Elaine was obliged to take sleeping-pills, but Aunt Edith found the habit of meditation more effective than tranquillizers.

Mr Courtney, always obliging, took them the rounds of the city: the Lexington, West Point Military Academy and Central Park. They drove up and down Broadway by daylight and by the nightlights of glittering advertisement signs, jerking, flashing, racing around every building like electric mice. Above all, the midsummer moon, cold and still, hung aloof from feverish a world.

They visited the New York World Fair and dined on Long Island. Aunt Edith, in spite of lack of sleep, general racket and the increasing tremble in her hand, enjoyed everything and was eager for more. When she begged Mr Courtney to take them to Harlem he agreed, on condition that they went on a Monday, teetotal night.

So to Harlem they went for dinner and afterwards, at my aunt's suggestion, to a dance-hall. Here she lost no time in getting into conversation with the Negroes whose gentle voices and good manners persuaded her that they were angels.

She was reassured to begin with, by the apparent absence of colour-bar in New York, though every time she stopped for a 'sandal-shine' it was a Negro who ministered to her. And it soon became obvious that the Negroes occupied inferior jobs such as door-keepers, attendants, fetchers-and-carriers in general for the whites. Preoccupied with this problem, she chose for their one visit to the theatre to see Tallulah Bankhead in *The Little Foxes*, the play so vividly depicting life in the deep South.

Meanwhile, on another scene Franz had reappeared, paying court to Elaine and respects to her aunt who willingly accepted their occasional divergences from her own plans. She might have been less pleased to learn that once more he was over-spending on his new-found 'Dresden china doll', taking her to theatres and restaurants and buying her anything she fancied, from a 'highball' to a new hat.

Aunt Edith, however, had her own unexpected fancies, such as a passion for ice-cream which Elaine found so trying. They seemed to be forever in search of a drug-store where my aunt would sit on a high stool intently studying the various kinds of ices available. Elaine fretted with impatience while she deliberated over the choice between Neapolitan and a banana-split. And then she was obliged to watch her turning the ice over and over with her spoon till it became creamy. She would skim it and savour it, with long, reflective pauses, until every particle had disappeared. She would linger lovingly over the automats supplying cooked breakfasts, but as a vegetarian her choice here, to Elaine's relief, was confined to waffles and maple syrup.

And there was her unexpected habit of dashing off in a taxi for a shampoo and set at least twice a week. By now her straggly grey hair required trimming. But first she consulted her Astronomers' Diary. 'I must wait until the moon is full before having it cut,' she said as she carefully marked the day with a cross.

Elaine, pressing on to keep dates with Franz, and impatient of these quirks, was thankful when her aunt departed to Halifax, Nova Scotia, to stay with Herbert and Betty. This left her free for a brief but romantic interlude with Franz at the country house in Pennsylvania where he lived with his sister. In this quiet green space they were blessedly able to come to themselves and see each other against a background of reality. The question of marriage arose and hung between them like a fruit not quite ripe for the picking. Elaine, made cautious by home-ties and memories, wavered on the brink and drew back. Thus criss-crossed by delight and doubt, she moved on to stay with Uncle Harold and his wife May, in Ontario.

Harold, the irresponsible practical-joker, was changed into an entirely different person. Uncertain years of hard work and quick decisions had transformed the sparkling youth into a somewhat irascible middle age. All the same, there was a good, kind side to him; he willingly put himself out to entertain his niece, whisking her away in his big Buick through hundreds of miles of grassland, woodland and fields thick with maize. St Catherine's, where the Rayners lived, is a fruit-growing country; here at last Elaine had hopes of a day's walk across the green miles of unfenced land. True to family instincts, she longed for hours of freedom from the buzz and cramp of motoring. When her uncle wouldn't hear of even a short walk (there were no footpaths as in England) she almost wept with disappointment. Nor, on rejoining Aunt Edith at Herbert's and Betty's home in Halifax, was she consoled by the opportunity for sea-bathing. 'All I can say,' she wrote to me, 'is that bathing in Nova Scotia – even in summer – is a miserable experience!'

The stinging cold, however, never daunted her aunt, who seemed prepared to swim among icebergs. Every morning, as was her custom at home, she ventured into the sea with a relish that amazed the others. Indeed, in Herbert's house she *was* at home. After her meditations she would turn to household affairs, helping to dry dishes – as best she could – and entering into David's world of bricks and plasticine. And she sat beside Betty putting forth Steiner's views on the significance of birth. After explaining that hospitals, so clean, clinical and impersonal, cannot provide the right atmosphere to receive the incoming life, she persuaded Betty to have her baby at home. 'After all,' she said, 'this young person has chosen *you*, and will expect his parents to welcome him where he belongs!'

In the midst of her stay she suddenly decided to visit a Red Indian encampment. 'I guess I'm becoming soft,' she said one evening, 'after so much of this New-World comfort.' At any rate, she had an urge to talk with people who lived close to nature and by their own endeavour. Elaine, out of curiosity, agreed to go with her. If they were expecting to find a tribe hardened by weather and unspoiled by civilization, they were disappointed. A few shabby wigwams, obviously put up for show, were inhabited by tired and dusty 'Reds' whose traditional feathered headdress drooped to their drooping shoulders. Birds of the forest caged for exhibitions – and moulting birds at that – confronted them, rather than the gleaming creatures of axe and tomahawk they had hoped to see.

Other expeditions made up for this one failure. Herbert, anxious to impress his aunt and cousin with the beauty and vitality of Canada, drove them to the home of a friend who lived up the St Lawrence river. After the bleakness of Halifax they felt exhilarated by this sweeping countryside of tremendous woodlands, green spaces, and powerful rivers. It is a land where the conflicting forces of nature seem echoed in the lives of the inhabitants; the rivalry between French and English has strong roots which strike deep into the earth and the past.

One day while they were out driving Aunt Edith asked Herbert to stop so that she might stand on a hill and get the feel of the place. Gazing into the distance, she remarked that here was a forceful example of the land absorbing the history of its people. 'The earth is a living being!' she exclaimed joyfully. 'Every stone and tree and blade of grass receives an imprint from the passing generations!'

All too soon the time came to say good-bye to the 'beloved nephew' and his family, so that the journey on the night-train to Montreal seemed more than ordinarily exhausting. Before sailing, the two of them spent a few days in Quebec where they lingered long in the churches – mostly Roman Catholic. In one of these Aunt Edith paused in front of a shrine and gazed at the ornate marble figure surrounded by candles and discarded crutches. 'Dear me,' she said softly, 'there's something spurious in all this – too much outward show'.

None the less, they were enchanted by this city on the cliffs overlooking the Heights of Abraham, by its white houses and cobbled streets where monks and nuns, silent and dark as shadows, hurried by. And by the alleyways that twisted behind the houses to disappear down sudden flights of steps. From a horse-drawn cab Aunt Edith surveyed this scene. And looking out she most thoroughly took everything in. Most of all she delighted in the incessant chimes from church and chapel which ring down every street and across each square till Quebec might almost be called a city of bells.

After such adventures the journey home in the *Athenia* (on its next voyage to be torpedoed by the Germans) seemed an anti-climax. Rather sadly the two of them looked their last on the grey drear of Newfoundland, whose vast area, bleak, sparse and desolate, betrays its romantic name. Not even the icebergs and monstrous spouting whales could dramatize such a melancholy waste.

The returning travellers were strangely subdued. A few days later when the pearly outline of Ireland glimmered on the horizon they hoped it might be a symbol of peace under threatening clouds. That was almost exactly a month before the outbreak of war.

XIV

War. Poems of Christian Morgenstern.
Pursuit of the stars. Reflections on suffering.
Wheel-chair adventures. Gradual decline. Last days.

TOWARDS the end of August Aubrey (my husband) and I joined
Elaine, May and Father for a holiday at Llandudno. On the calm
golden afternoon of Saturday, the second of September, we drove
together to Llanrhos to visit the aunts. As I slammed the car door Aunt
Alice came tearing through the gate of Mount Grace. 'It's war, my children,
war!' she cried in a frenzy of excitement, 'the Germans are in Poland!' At
that moment Aunt Edith appeared at her front-door. 'Yes, Ali, I know,' she
said gently. We were reduced to the banalities which accompany extreme
emotion until Aubrey, who was attached to the Duke of Lancaster's Own
Yeomanry, said he must return home at once to report. For the rest, there
seemed nothing, at the moment, that we could do. Aunt Edith suggested
that first of all we should go for a bathe, along with May Higginson and her
brother Basil who happened to be staying with her.
Whereupon the nine of us drove to the bay under the cliffs of the Little
Orme. Here the mellow air and sparkling water did something to restore
our balance, though I remember cutting myself badly against a barnacled
rock and emerging from the sea with blood pouring from my thigh. Aunt
Edith, unnoticing and seemingly lost in reflection, had come out first, and
was by now dressed and sitting on a rock, gazing out at the horizon.
  Her presence that afternoon shed calming, healing rays upon our
disquietude. The note in her diary for that day briefly records: *War. In the
Little Orme Bay. Two swims* – followed by our names.
  Aubrey and I, barely dry, bundled ourselves, towels and suitcases into the
car, and sped back home. Everyone and everything was in a state of
suspension. After all our hurry there was nothing to do but wait. Next
morning in the little country church at Barnacre (which we attended from
Sullom Holt) war was formally declared. The bare, dramatic
announcement made by the vicar from the chancel steps had an
extraordinary effect on me. To my extreme embarrassment tears streamed
down my face throughout the service. No-one else was similarly affected.
  Because Aubrey held a key position in the cotton trade he was retained
from work on the home front which, coupled with his services in command
of our local Home Guard, was to prove a great deal more arduous than any
army campaigning.
  Though at home we lived in comparative comfort and safety (nothing

[177]

more than a land-mine and a handful of bombs were dropped within a few fields of us) the hard labour and monotony of the war years were crushing. Apart from W.V.S. work, serving in a British Restaurant, and the black-out, there was the continual cycling and, during those iron winters, sledge-pulling to the shops more than two miles away.

Visits to Llandudno were rare, though we spent one summer holiday near the aunts and saw a good deal of them. Again Aunt Edith chided me for my excessive physical care of the boys, and reminded me that fear and anxiety could reap nothing but ill-health and lack of confidence. Perhaps, had I lived on a 'higher' level, Richard's recurrent ear-trouble might have been averted. He was a sensitive, intelligent child who had by now erected a fence against all attempts to educate him. It was at this point that she gave me A.C. Harwood's *The Way of a Child*, and suggested that a 'Steiner' school, by stirring his imagination and appealing to deeper mind-forces, would suit him 'a deal sight better' than the orthodox school we had chosen.

About this time she was immersed in a new love-labour: the translation of Christian Morgenstern's poems. Her knowledge of German, however, was insufficient to tackle this task alone. In any case, in order to translate poetry one has to be a poet. And even then poetry cannot properly be translated, but rather transposed, like music, into another key. Difficulties arise because of the different rhyme-schemes in any two languages; and in the varying number of stresses contained in words of the same, or similar, meaning. Even more teasing for a translator who is not bilingual are the subtly differing shades of meaning implied in 'dictionary-equivalent' words.

Problems such as these brought her to a standstill. Whereupon she approached Mabel Cotterell, an anthroposophist who had published more than one translation, including the poems of Novalis, and asked her if she would undertake some of Morgenstern's verse. Eventually Miss Cotterell did most of the work, translating about forty of the sixty poems included in the collection.

On this particular holiday, when we were out walking together Aunt Edith would halt suddenly and with a radiant look on her face, begin to recite a poem, first in German, and then hesitantly in English. One day while my father was out of hearing she repeated a saying of Christian Morning-Star, as she called him, which seemed to fascinate her: 'Parallel lines meet only in Infinity. There and then they are no longer parallel but Cherubim and Seraphim!'; a quotation which she carefully copied into her diary.

During one slow plod home (by now she walked with much difficulty) she talked about our very dim ideas of Christ's significance in the world today. 'Very little of His mission has yet been realized,' she said as she opened a gate with unseeing eyes. 'And now the war. But His purpose *will* be worked out beyond the destruction.'

She took comfort and courage also from the poems of Steiner. One of her favourites, translated by George Adams, began:

> I look into the darkness,
> In it there arises light, living light.
> Who is this light in the darkness?
> It is I myself in my reality . . .
> I shall find it again
> When with goodwill for the Spirit
> I shall have passed through the gate of Death.

One evening after reading some 'Steiner' verse and sensing my lack of full response, she half-reproached me for being too much in thrall to Pan. 'Your poems are full of nature's barbaric beauty,' she said kindly, 'but I miss a deeper spiritual content.' And then, after a moment's thought, 'Why don't you write a poem about your father? Now *there's* a challenge!'

It was a challenge that remained unanswered for twenty years. Meanwhile, her efforts over the Morgenstern translations continued. In 1945 she sent the manuscript to Dr Heidenreich who spent much of his summer holiday in reading and correcting it. And for another two years after this she worked on the poems; each day the hours between morning coffee and lunch-time were spent in making notes, copying and endless revising. Finally the typescript found its way into the Rudolf Steiner Library, but it was never published.

By now the tremble in her right hand had extended up her arm. Struggling to decipher the hieroglyphics in her diary, I have often wondered how she found the strength and the courage to go on. And not only with this work. Throughout the 'forties she continued to hold the weekly study-group meeting at Erdmut and arranged many public lectures in Llandudno. In March, 1941, she invited Adam Bittleston, a priest of the Christian Community, to speak at one of her 'Four Freedoms' meetings (to bring anthroposophy before the public). During the discussion after his address, *What Hope for Europe?* an angry, elderly man shouted abuse at the platform before stamping out of the hall. Aunt Edith was quite unruffled by such incidents, nor was she concerned when lectures seemed to be above the heads of the audience; she believed that at least some of the message was received by some of the people.

Mr. Bittleston appreciated her command of awkward situations. 'She gave no impression of illness,' he told me, 'but, on the contrary, of quiet and confident purpose, with a great capacity for gratitude towards life in general and towards other people.'

I have it from Elizabeth Davies, one of the earliest and most loyal members of her study-group, that during the war years my aunt was particularly interested in helping refugees, and entertained many a one at Erdmut. Elizabeth recalls that she preferred members of her group to address her as Junkerlein (little knight) rather than the formal 'Mrs Rigby'. She was always 'a one' for nicknames, and Miss Tucker, by the way, had now taken to calling her 'Princess' or 'Ladybird', according to mood. We were amused by that quality in her which drew forth such exalted titles from her followers, especially as she was a confirmed socialist.

By the end of 1945 she was finding it difficult to negotiate the stairs, and could only walk as far as the garden, and that with the aid of two sticks. Fortunately she had a way of not noticing physical disabilities and, while fully realizing its needs, seemed to live only half in her body. In this connection I'm reminded of an amusing story told against her by Uncle Bertie.

Some years previously he had taken her into his Manchester nursing home with a severe appendicitis. Before the operation, while she was lying in readiness on the operating-table, the doctors became deeply engaged in political discussion. As they scrubbed up and donned rubber gloves a capitalist flag was suddenly hoisted. Instantly Aunt Edith sat up and took a very lively part in the discussion. More than that, she refused to lie down until she had made her point and driven it home like a nail.

Only three months after this operation, and shortly before her sixty-fifth birthday, she actually climbed to the top of Snowdon; not by the easy Pyg track but over the ridge of Crib Goch. On hearing of this feat we all agreed that she had now wholly proved her theory of 'mind in control of bodily decisions'. Indeed, until she was completely crippled she continued to live the 'three-fold life' by conserving, as well as spending, energy. Apart from mental disciplines she ordered her day according to physical cycles. As always, 4 a.m. meditation was followed by exercise – bathing until she was past seventy – and this in turn by breakfast and an interval for reflection. Her morning was always busy with answering letters and making plans. After lunch she would retire to her chair in 'the Bink' and gaze at the hills or, in summer, to her hammock between the poplars where she delighted to watch the movement of leaves and clouds.

One afternoon I surprised her kneeling in front of a row of muddy shoes. She looked up with a sly smile. 'At this time of day,' she said, 'my mind and brain are not very clear. And so I clean shoes.' It happened that Sandy and the two boys were staying with her so she had plenty of scope in that direction. And here I must pause to explain that since Sandy's wife had recently become an invalid, my aunt was especially kind to them, never forgetting birthdays, and making sure they all enjoyed a good Christmas dinner. One year just before Christmas, when she herself was bed-ridden, she conspired with a neighbour to take them a large cake, a pudding and a bulky parcel of toys. In a dictated letter to Sandy she insists that she doesn't want a present from him, but would be delighted with a poem. His reply in the form of verses written in Iceland is a touching reminder of how she had awoken in him (at 'Marigold') his own first love for the stars.

As to herself, she never ceased her pursuit of the stars, in all ways. Gwen Newman, an anthroposophist whom she had met at the 1931 conference, came to look after her in September, 1945, and describes how my aunt would hobble into the garden at night and name the various constellations. In the centre of her bedroom she had arranged a mirror to catch the sun so that she might mark its reflection with a pencil on the sky-blue walls. This daily practice became a ritual, and before long the wall was closely patterned with pencil-rays.

Not all the trials of advancing age and illness could cripple her spirit; we never heard her grumble or complain – for one thing she was too occupied: 'Cosmic thoughts are very absorbing!' she once smiled at a friend's consternation for her plight. Helen Haynes, one of Arnold's students who came to help her for a short time after Gwen's departure, also remarked on her cheerfulness and activity in dictating endless letters to favourite charities. Helen, too, during her stay at Erdmut, learned much about the 'heavenly bodies'. And also about bodies not so heavenly. She was impressed by the excellent and plentiful meals with full respect paid to vitamins, which led her to think that Earth Courage had been well named. In view of this she was rather startled to discover one morning, while making her bed, a revolver hidden under the mattress.

Revolver or no, the end of the war found Aunt Edith a stauncher pacifist than ever. Regularly she attended meetings of the Pacifist Service Union to which the redoubtable Gwen was required to push her the two miles into Llandudno (and back) in her wheel-chair. In fact, a true memorial to her is written on the stone of the Howick Cross War Memorial (1914-1918) which stands at the entrace of the lane leading to Marigold Cottage. The unusual inscription, *To Commemorate Peace*, was her idea.

Gwen had only been in the house a few days when, as she was collecting the breakfast tray one morning, my aunt said to her, 'Please help Carinthia to wash up; she doesn't like doing it at all!' Indeed, Carinthia, now also in her seventies, was becoming rather peculiar, besides slowing down in an alarming way. Meals might be anything up to two hours late so that when Aunt Alice came in, as she usually did, for Sunday midday dinner (her one good meal of the week) she often had to wait until half-past two, by which time she was nearly fainting from hunger.

After her departure Miss Tucker would draw Gwen portentously to one side to inquire: 'Well, and have you noticed anything this time?'

In answer to Gwen's surprise she would declare that a handful of potatoes or carrots had disappeared, or perhaps a tin of peas. She was convinced that Miss Rayner helped herself in secret before returning to her own 'Mother Hubbard' larder.

Even Aunt Alice's most well-intentioned visits to help were regarded with suspicion. More than that, Miss Tucker believed this blameless maiden lady actually stole into the house and regaled herself with trifles such as shoe-polish and soap. This in spite of the fact that Erdmut was locked, barred and chained against any possible intruder. And on the morning before the trustworthy Miss Jones came in for the weekly clean-up Miss Tucker would lock every cupboard and drawer and hide away each valuable ornament. Aunt Edith, aware of these delusions, thought it wiser to keep silent. Fortunately the sweeter side of Carinthia was never lost, and at this time she put herself out to be kind to 'Ladybird'. Besides, she was an excellent cook.

Almost every fine day Gwen pushed my aunt, no light weight, in her chair to the Gloddaeth or Bodysgallen woods, or along the sea-front at Deganwy. She also pushed her to many other pacifist and philanthropic meetings in Llandudno. Now, more than ever, Aunt Edith appreciated lectures and recitals. Her diary records that she heard such speakers as Vera Brittain, Eric Newton, and Richard St Barbe Baker (of the Men of the Trees Society). Gwen always placed her chair in the aisle near the platform, and after the meeting the speaker invariably came down and conversed with her at length.

Because she could no longer climb mountains she learned to play chess. Lilian Winter, herself a good player, used often to come in for a game and, not surprisingly, she nearly always won. My aunt, however, didn't take kindly to being beaten, though afterwards she tried to make amends for her chagrin. One evening when Lilian had left her in an unusually silent mood she overcame her disappointment and said to Gwen: 'I'd like you two to be friends. Why don't you go out together some time?'

Because Gwen took her at her word an unexpected situation arose. While Carinthia glowered at her 'Ladybird's' enjoyment of Lilian's company, my aunt became half-resentful of the few occasions when Gwen arranged to meet Lilian in a cafe for a cup of coffee.

Inevitable pinpricks were soon forgotten in larger matters. Aware that she was slowly dying, my aunt accepted the fact with equanimity. If she needed compensations she found them in a hundred ways: watching the changing light on the hills, observing the birds from her window and the stars from the porch before going upstairs to bed. Such delights were intensified. And she was overwhelmed with gratitude for the kindness of her helpers. Nor did she ever lose interest in the world outside herself. As late as 1946 her indomitable pencil records meetings concerned with problem familes, housing and education. Most of all in her friends she found continuing joy.

Shaky entries for the 'forties mark return visits from all those I have mentioned, and many more. A note for January, 1947, in Gwen's hand, makes me realize yet again what a wonderful woman she was. This is an account of a party she gave for ten children of the neighbourhood. Even now, so near the end of her life, she refused to be let off!

Every day, as for years past, she resorted to the little black book of meditation which Steiner himself had given her. And each morning she repeated the prayer which begins: 'If I look into the sun I think God's Spirit ...' These prayers brought light to her darkest days and enabled her to practise the principle of action in inaction. There was nothing static in her outward helplessness, nothing pitiable in her suffering. In any case, she never regarded suffering as an evil but, on the contrary, as a means whereby evil might be overcome. So that when, in 1948, our son Richard was drowned, she helped me (as I have already described) towards a positive outlook. And this outlook helped me through not only a personal grief but also those expressions of horror from well-meaning friends, which make acceptance almost impossible. But above all I learned, though not for many years, that suffering, wholly accepted, can be a creative experience.

And because death is a condition of life, my aunt couldn't regard even the accidental death of a child as a tragedy. This appears to be a tragedy, she said, only to those people who think of themselves a nothing more than physical beings. Seen in the light of the real world, face to face, death comes as a release, and as a special kind of release for a child who has not yet rubbed shoulders with evil.

Continuing squiggles in her diary report 'real help given' by D.V. Barber and 'radiant talk' with Arnold Freeman. My father and May, Uncle Bertie, Herbert, Sandy and the Higginsons often went to see her. After one visit the names of Arnold and Marie Byvoets are coupled together with the inscription: 'Joyous Events' – words made strangely moving by reason of the trembling pencil. Indeed, judging by the many names entered during the last ten years of her life, she must surely have had much to give back to her friends. If they brought her comfort and love, she responded with love and courage.

An entry in her diary runs:

> The comfort which poor human beings want in such a world as this is not the comfort of ease but the comfort of strength.
> Charles Kingsley.

By her example she still gave this sort of comfort to her friends. And in return she also received unfailing support from Gwen, who for two years helped her to dress, helped her up and down stairs, in and out of the house, and who, by the end of her stay, must have pushed that wheel-chair more than a thousand miles. These services were given for love and certainly not the pin-money (all my aunt could afford) which she received.

In September, 1947, alas, Gwen was obliged to leave. And just at this very moment when my aunt most needed support Miss Tucker had a stroke and was taken into a nursing home. My father, summoned to the scene by Aunt Alice, could only exclaim: 'Well, it's a beggar!' And then after a moment's silence, jerking an eloquent thumb towards the ceiling: 'You'd think He'd done it on purpose!'

Aunt Alice, gravely concerned (for much of the burden fell upon her frail shoulders), blamed her sister's condition on those early morning bathes. 'I knew they'd bring her to no good!' she almost wept. Aunt Edith, however, accepted misfortune as a necessary part of the pattern. 'One must be thankful for obstacles,' she would say, 'because in overcoming them we have a chance to reach up to a better life. Why, as we are now, we couldn't *bear* perfection!'

Indeed, this obvious truth has often troubled me with visions of heaven as an intolerably dull 'place' in which nothing further remains to be done.

Meanwhile, 'helps' and nurses came and went. Mr Webber, a kindly neighbour, occasionally pushed my aunt out in her chair, and the weekly meetings continued. Gradually, day by day, she was growing weaker until it was hardly possible to help her into a taxi for one of her last remaining pleasures – a joy-ride among the Welsh mountains and passes.

When I went to see her the year after Gwen's departure she was lying in her bed, now removed downstairs to 'the Bink', where she could gaze at the hills through the window. She was wearing a speedwell-blue bed-jacket, and I remember thinking that her eyes were as blue as ever, if a trifle misted over. It never occurred to me to feel sorry for her because she was never sorry for herself. This was soon after Richard's death and, concerned with my own sorrow, I sought comfort from her, oblivious of her greater suffering. She spoke softly yet clearly and, as always, a smile lit her face so that you felt all must be well.

One of my deepest regrets is that when we were in Llandudno the next, and her last, year, I didn't go to see her. A picture that continues to haunt me is of herself, wrapped in blue cloak and rug, and wearing a wide-brimmed hat, being pushed in her chair along the windy sea-front. I just saw her as we sped by in our car on the way home. Of course we were in a hurry and I only glimpsed her by chance as we flashed past, but why, why, didn't we stop and say goodbye?

The following February, after our daughter was born, she sent her last message to me through Aunt Alice: 'Call her Mercia – saved from the sea'.

Absorbed by the needs of the baby, I had no idea how ill Aunt Edith was and when, a few months later, her nurse let her fall so that she broke her thigh, I didn't even then realize that the end was very near.

Early in July Mrs Higginson and Beth made a special journey from Sussex 'to see our beloved Mrs Rigby', as Beth wrote to me. 'She was very, very ill, and it was most distressing to see her suffer,' the letter continues, 'and as we were leaving we stood up with our eyes on her. I felt it was for the last time. She just said: "You may kiss me." '

Many another loyal friend came to say goodbye. And later in the month Miss Barber took the night-train from Euston to see my aunt about various important matters. Lilian Winter met her at the station, and when she arrived at Erdmut she was greeted by a nurse who was doubtful about letting her in, especially as my father was due later in the day, until she heard how far she had travelled and on what particular mission.

Edith was lying in her bed looking towards the hills. She was unable to move a limb under her favourite rainbow-coloured quilt, and Miss Barber, realizing that she was far too ill to answer any questions, sat in silence at her bedside. 'I was very touched,' she told me later, 'when Edith turned her head to give me the ghost of a smile, and roused herself sufficiently to ask if I was wearing a new hat.'

On her way out of the house Miss Barber paused for a few words with Miss Tucker, now recovered and actually making a sponge-pudding for lunch. Lilian drove her back to the station, and a few days later, on July 23rd, telephoned to say that Edith was dead.

I don't believe that anyone who knew Aunt Edith really well could ever be quite the same again. So many people have paid tribute to her influence on their lives: mill-girls, teachers, lecturers, doctors, scientists and ordinary housewives. Through them, if in no other way, she lives on. To quote her god-daughter May: 'She was so far-seeing, way ahead of her day and age.'

And in spite of illness and the passing years she never lost her love of life. The spirit of the twelve-year-old girl who had arisen early on Christmas morning to give presents to passers-by was buoyant as ever in the half-paralysed woman of seventy-seven giving a party for neighbouring children.

If, in this book, I have used the word 'giving' too often in connection with my aunt, it is because she so freely gave of herself. This quality, allied with tolerance and determination, enabled her to achieve much towards improving the conditions of working women and raising the status of women everywhere.

And here I pause to wonder what she and all those who fought for us would think of the way we are spending the fruits of their victory. Perhaps the time has come for another band of women to fight a still older battle in the name of chastity, which includes faithfulness, loyalty and emotional sincerity. Without these qualities those hard-won equal rights are diminished, in some respects anyway, to little more than equal wrongs.

This is all the sadder because, as my aunt and her comrades realized, women are more ready than men to follow an ideal and to obey a spiritual leader. Inasmuch as the women waited at the foot of the Cross while the men fled away, women still form the main body of the Church, which makes one wonder at the prejudice against their ordination.

Her own spiritual leader, on the contrary, welcomed the idea of women in the Church: Rudolf Steiner believed women to be less deeply rooted in the earth than men. Maybe now is our chance to prove his belief in us. We could, if we would, uplift the fallen standard of values and morals, and help towards making a better world.

Without doubt it was in following Steiner and passing on his teaching to others that Aunt Edith found her most complete fulfilment. The young radical and militant suffragette discovered that her search for truth led towards the quieter, yet far more difficult, ascents of the human spirit. She had to be different and live differently from the rest of us. And yet we never thought of her as a crank. She was a person who made her presence felt, a dropper of stones into pools whose ripples still have the power to disturb.

In attempting this portrait I have mentioned many colours according to the various phases of her life. Although I used to laugh at her talk of colour-vibrations, if I were an artist I would paint her picture in tones of blue: the colour of her eyes, of her favourite flower, the harebell, and her unusual choice of clothes. Blue merging into purple because the good red blood was mingled with skiey visions, and she loved, on state occasions, to put on her purple velvet.

Few women can have so harmoniously combined the qualities of eagle and dove. But more than an eagle, for she gazed over mountain-tops into infinities. And more than a dove, for I have heard her challenged and taunted without answering back. Her love for people was of the quality that 'is not easily provoked'.